W E R N ⬚ R   ⬚ ⬚ E D E R

REGGAE
From Mento to Dancehall

Music • History • Artistes • Producers • Discography

ERRATUM

Page 14
(COLUMN 2)
    – Stan "The Great" Sebastian should read Tom "The Great" Sebastian.
    – Sir Coxsone was a sound system owner, not a disc jockey as stated.

Page 15
(COLUMN 2)
    – Grandfurt Road should read "Brentford Road"

Page 32
(COLUMN 1)
    – Sir Coxsone was the founder of the Coxsone Dodd Recording Organization, not Alton Ellis as stated.

Page 56
(COLUMN 1)
    – The Rastafari colours are red, gold, green, and black.

Page 111
(COLUMN 2)
    – "Sly and Ronnie" should read "Sly and Robbie"

Page 114
(COLUMN 1)
    – "Son" should read "Soon"

LMH Publishing Limited

WERNER TROEDER

REGGAE
From Mento to Dancehall

Music • History • Artistes • Producers • Discography

LMH PUBLISHING LIMITED

First printed in German: 1993
by HEEL AG Schindellegi, Switzerland
Lithos: Ultragraphic Ltd., Dublin, Ireland

© 2010 Werner Troeder
First Edition
10 9 8 7 6 5 4 3 2 1

Responsible for the content: Werner Troeder
E-mail: troeder@pcwelt-premium.de

Editor: Tyrone S. Reid
Cover Design: Lee Quee Designs
Book Design, Layout & Typesetting: Sanya Dockery

Published by LMH Publishing Limited
Suite 10-11
Sagicor Industrial Complex
7 Norman Road
Kingston C.S.O., Jamaica
Tel.: (876) 938-0005; 938-0712
Fax: (876) 759-8752
Email: lmhbookpublishing@cwjamaica.com
Website: www.lmhpublishing.com

Printed in China   ISBN: 978-976-8184-66-5

NATIONAL LIBRARY OF JAMAICA CATALOGUING-IN-PUBLICATION DATA

Troeder, Werner
    Reggae : from mento to dancehall / Werner Troeder
        p. : ill. ; cm.
Includes bibliographical references
ISBN 978-976-8184-66-5 (pbk)

1.   Reggae music – Jamaica - History and criticism   2. Reggae music –
Jamaica – Discography   3. Reggae musicians – Jamaica
I   Title
781.646   - dc 22

CONTENTS

JAM

AICA

ACKNOWLEDGEMENTS

I would like to thank everyone who assited us by providing information for this book.

Special thanks to Mr. Bob Clarke of Irie FM (who has an extensive record collection, much bigger than ours), who assisted us by arranging some of the interviews, most notably with Freddie McGregor and Carlton Coffie, backstage at the White River Reggae Bash; Mr. Trevor "Boots" Harris, who writes for the *X News*, a weekly newspaper published in Jamaica. Harris provided valuable information on the Jamaican music business.

Thanks also to Jamaica's Minister of Culture, Olivia Grange, for her additional review, suggestions and editorial work on the English manuscript.

Finally, but by no means least, special thanks to LMH Publishing, who published the English version of this book.

PREFACE

A Caribbean dream – relaxing with an exotic drink by a palm tree under the tropical sun on a beautiful white sand beach. This is the introduction one could expect in a travel magazine about Jamaica, the island that is popularly known for its rum and reggae music.

In the summer of 1977, we visited Jamaica for the first time. We spent our three-week vacation in Ocho Rios, located on Jamaica's north coast. On arrival in Jamaica, our expectations far exceeded what we'd gleaned from numerous travel magazines. In reality, Jamaica was far more beautiful than any picture could capture.

The trees, rivers, the friendly people we met on the streets, and especially the music, with its pulsating and electrifying rhythm to which one must dance, all made for a memorable vacation.

This book, *Reggae: From Mento to Dancehall,* is the result of our love for Jamaica, which we visited several times from 1977 to 1994, and where we currently reside. Not only have we made lasting friendships, but we have also become involved with the Deutsch-Jamaikanische Gesellschaft in Germany and The Jamaican-German Society, located in Kingston, which both support and develop social and cultural projects in Jamaica and Germany.

It is also the result of our love of Jamaican music. The first reggae LP we bought, *Survival,* by Bob Marley and the Wailers, on which is displayed the national flags of many countries, formed the base of our collection.

We later became interested in and began questioning the origins of the

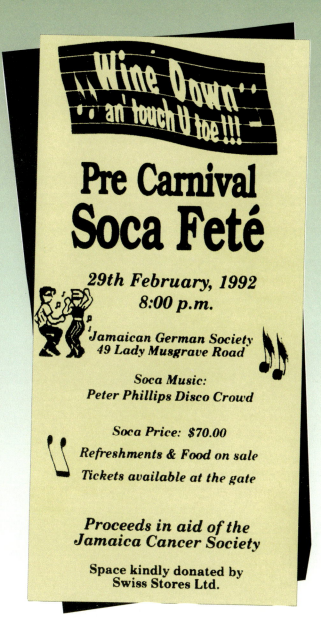

"Wine Down" an' touch U toe !!!

Pre Carnival Soca Feté

29th February, 1992
8:00 p.m.

Jamaican German Society
49 Lady Musgrave Road

Soca Music:
Peter Phillips Disco Crowd

Soca Price: $70.00
Refreshments & Food on sale
Tickets available at the gate

Proceeds in aid of the Jamaica Cancer Society

Space kindly donated by
Swiss Stores Ltd.

different types of music, such as ska, calypso and soca. *What or where is the root of reggae? What was the social and cultural background from which the music emerged?* This book is therefore our attempt at answering these questions and satisfying our quest for knowledge about Jamaica.

Reggae: From Mento to Dancehall, first published in Germany, documents the history of Jamaican music, starting with the origins of the music, and its emergence into the various genres – as well as the artistes and the music producers.

It is divided into several chapters, which provide information on Jamaican

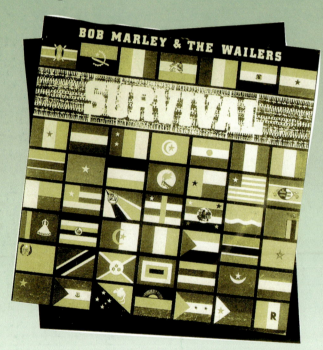

music and dance. For example, the chapter entitled Sources and Literature has a comprehensive list of guidebooks, which inform the reader about these two aspects of Jamaican culture. It also contains a list of magazines and publications about new records/recordings, artistes and poets.

The chapter on rocksteady, reggae bands/groups, artistes, studios and producers offers useful insights on the developmental stages of Jamaican music.

A comprehensive list of the recordings by artistes/performers, who have made significant contributions to the development and progress of Jamaican music and a biography on each is included at the end of the book.

Starting in the 1990s, new tracks/records and remixed versions of oldies became available on CD. The release year of the albums, when known, is also identified.

It is important to note that many of these records were released in Jamaica, as well as in the United States of America (on American labels) and in Europe (on Trojan or Island labels). As a result, the records that were produced specifically for the international market were somewhat different in sound when compared with those that were produced for the local market. This strategy was adopted by the marketing companies to attract a wider international audience, with the result that a more 'refined' approach was utilised by the recording studios when it came to the final mixing of the music, whereby the volume and power of the bass was substantially reduced.

We hope you enjoy reading this book, as much as we enjoyed writing it!

THE ARAWAKS

The Arawaks were a gentle and peaceful tribe of Amerindians who once inhabited the entire Caribbean. History has taught us that the Arawaks played a lot of music. During special festivals of thanksgiving or petition, they danced in the village court and sang the village epic. They sang and danced and beat drums in the public during their healing ceremonies. It was reported that when the Spaniards arrived in May 1494, and sang loudly their Christian songs, the Arawaks hid, as they thought that they were war songs. However, they began to like these songs so much that they formed musical bands and began playing music to these songs.

The bands consisted of four musicians who played wooden trumpets and a small drum. The trumpets were possibly made from the stem of the local trumpet tree or from the trunk of the papaya tree, as these stems or trunks were divided into sections like bamboo.

The smaller stems were cut and gutted to resemble the German flute. The Arawaks also made a big flute from a bone. It is not yet clear the specie of animal from which this bone originated, as during that time there were not many large, indigenous animals that could have produced this type of bone.

The drums, which could be heard from afar, were long and deep, and were possibly made from the trunk of the same tree or from another hardwood tree. The interior of the trunk was gutted with either firestones, stone chisels, hatches or an axe. The skin of the drum was made from a sea cow or manatee.

Some drums were made from stone dishes. The Arawaks hung fire stones perforated with holes in the wind, which made a whistling sound when the wind passed through.

Another instrument, the Aeolian harp, was made from the Aeto palm tree or from silk grass *(furcraera tuberosa)*. In addition, they played the timbrel, a kind of tambourine made from the trumpet tree and covered with different shells.

These instruments, the tabor or small drum, trumpet, timbrel or tambourine,

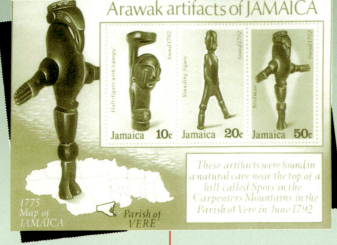

Arawak artifacts of JAMAICA

Jamaica 10c Jamaica 20c Jamaica 50c

Half-figure with canopy   found 1792
Standing figure   found 1792
Bird-man   found 1792

These artifacts were found in a natural cave near the top of a hill called Spots in the Carpenters Mountains in the Parish of Vere in June 1792

1775 Map of JAMAICA   Parish of VERE

flute and Aeolian harp were played when they sang songs at festivals for their sovereign to show their gratitude and to protect themselves from their enemies, the Caribs. These songs were also sung when the sovereigns won a battle or when they died. A call and answer technique was utilised, during which the women led the singing and the men answered.

Unfortunately, the Spaniards eradicated the Arawaks in the end.

CULT & RELIGIOUS MUSIC

Music and dance were very important to African slaves and were two forms of cultural expression that survived slavery. The African slaves utilised both as a means of cultural expression in their resistance against oppression. In fact, apart from sleeping and working, they were only allowed to sing and dance. They also communicated with their drums despite the unrelenting efforts of their masters and missionaries to stop them from playing their drums.

The Burru music was one of the few forms of African music that the slaves were allowed to perform. In fact, the slave masters often used this form of music, played by the Burru drums, to motivate the slaves to work. After emancipation, the Burru drummers settled in the slums of Kingston and Spanish Town.

The Rastafarians, it is believed, adopted the drums and the dance of the Burru tribe. Members of the Burru tribe reportedly began to practise Rastafarianism. It is interesting to note that it was the music played by the Burru tribe that Count Ossie used to develop the well-known Rastafari rhythm.

Music also played an important role in cult practices in Jamaica. It is widely used as a form of religious expression by the many cults and religions, including Kumina, Revival, the churches of Revival Zion and Pocomania, as well as the Myal/Gumbay sects, the Rastafarians and Jonkonnu.

KUMINA

Kumina is a traditional activity that forms part of African (Congo) religious foundation brought to Jamaica in the nineteenth century. It is widely practised in the parishes of St. Thomas and St. Mary.

The dance is performed for marriages, deaths, burial, engagements, political and social success.

The ritual language originated from the Kikongo language, one of the languages of the Bakongo people and their neighbours, who still reside in Zaire and Angola today. The drummers play an important role in the ceremony. The deeper bandu drum is similar to the fundeh drum played by Rastafarians, whereas the playing cas' is similar to the repeater drum.

The drumming in Kumina and Nyabinghi are based on the same beat and rhythm. In Kumina, two different groups play the drum in different tunes, while in Nyabinghi, the rhythm is constant, and the offbeat, which evolved from the reggae beat, is played from time to time. This drumming style is also very similar to that of the Congo tribe.

The development and spread of Kumina was influenced by the black Creoles, whom they referred to as their ancestors. The old songs were sung in the Congo language and the new ones in Jamaican

Creole, and were also known as Bailo songs.

"Wake Up, Mama Zellah" is a popular song in eastern Jamaica, which is dedicated to Zellah Beckford, also known as Gully Queen, who was one of the religious leaders (African Bongo) from Middleton.

The Baila and Kbandu drums are used to play the "Kyas" music. These drums are made from excavated tree trunks and covered with goat skins. The drummers sit on the drum and beat it with their hands, while changing the range of the tune with their heels.

The ghosts, characterised by frenzied movements, resulting from the rapid beating of the drum and dancing, should enter the participants. This continues today in some cult practices in Jamaica, and even in some traditional Christian practices.

Food is eaten for the participants to remain awake, and animals are also sacrificed during the practice. After every two to three hours, the participants take a break from the festivities. The Kumina songs are an invitation to cooperate, entertain, and communicate with the dead.

REVIVAL

Revival is considered an Afro-Christian religion which incorporates pocomania and zion dances. The foundation of the Revival cult in Jamaica was laid in the late eighteenth century, when the first missionaries, including two former North American slaves, George Lisle and George Lewis, started to teach Protestantism to the slaves in some parts of the island.

Long before the parishes became independent, the movements separated and adopted Christian principles and forms to suit their own situations and experiences. They also included some African-based practices, which were known as myal ceremonies, a kind of secret organisation for the slaves.

When compared with Kumina, there was very little Christian influence, and if present, it was merely superficial. The revival sects, however, are not only influenced by Christian principles from which most religions emerged in Jamaica, but it also spread throughout the island.

The word *revival* refers to the large number of local religious organisations, which exist with a certain degree of autonomy. That is, they have their own doctrinal principles. Some of these organisations are called Revival Zion (Zionists), while others are called Pocomania/Pukkumina. However, most are referred to as Revival 60 or Revival 61 (also known as Convince or Convince Flenke, respectively). These groups formed the basis of the Great Revival, which swept through the island during 1860-1861.

The Revival ceremonies consist of much dancing and the singing of melodious songs, which include marching songs and anthems. The singing is loud and cheerful, and together with the clapping of hands and the stomping of feet, the faithful participants often leave these ceremonies in high spirits.

The voice is used as a musical instrument, which takes on a percussion-like sound. The same goes for the stomping of feet and the clapping of hands.

The maroons, who settled in the mountains, retained and practised these aspects of the Revivalist cult. When they congregate, the singing and clapping of hands and the singing of melodious Ashanti-like songs and polyrhythmic clapping and complex drumming are important components of this West African-based music tradition.

The intensity of the movements prepares the participants and often takes them to such a level that important lifestyle changes are the result. In other words, music played an important role in liberating the maroons.

The most important musical instruments that were played included the flat, one head Gumbay drum and the abeng – a cow horn blown through a hole located at one end. They sang three main types of songs. These were:

* war songs
* The jawbone-songs, about real local events
* The Coromantee songs (by the Maroons), based on old African stories of Anancy the Spider

These stories and songs are still popular today.

THE ZIONISTS

The main musical styles of the Zionists, primarily a Christian group, also include the stomping of feet and hand clapping.

They punctuate each worship and praise session with shouts of "Amen", and other exclamations. The Zionists have ghosts, prophets, saints and angels, to whom they refer in their music.

POCOMANIA
(PUKKUMINA)

The Pocomania ceremony consists mainly of the singing of songs, praising and the reading of the Bible. It has antecedents in the myal cult.

The songs, which vary in melody, speed and pitch, are accompanied by the playing of drums. The base rhythm is a four-fourth rhythmic beat, with three similar beats, and on the smaller drums, there is a variation, with the shorter beat repeated on the first beat, and the rest in three beats at the last two cycles. The songs are accompanied by the blowing of trumpets and the beating of cymbals. At the height of the ceremony, the tone of the music changes, and is characterised by sharp, rhythmic breathing and short trumpet sounds. In 2007, Max Romeo released an album called *Pocomania Songs* on the Ariwa label.

MYAL/GUMBAY

Myal is banned in Jamaica. The myal dance is one of Jamaica's oldest, found mostly in St.Elizabeth. Myal involves using evil powers, while obeah is using devil powers. A myalist tries to use the ghost of the dead for healing. A myal ceremony is done in an open field or under a cotton tree. The dance uses a wide range of body movements and a lot of acrobatics during the ceremony.

The **Gumbay** cult, a derivative of Myal, utilised music in their healing ceremonies, combined with quick, strong drum beats and singing. The music impels one to dance, and at some of the many festivals, the participants do a chain of long-step sideway movements, backward

Inside a Baptist Church in St. Ann's Bay.

turns and forward tilts bending, even rolling somersaults, and claim trees as their own. The main musical instrument is a stool-like drum, which is beaten in a complex, speedy rhythm.

JOHNKONNU
(JOHN CANOE)

Johnkonnu is considered harmless Christmas entertainment. The name may have originated in East Ghana, where *"dzono"* means a magician and *"kunu"* means terrible or deadly.

According to African sources, this dance and march, which occurs during the Christmas season, took place on the only day off for the slaves. It was later mixed with European and Creole influences.

The main characters are the Devil, the Cowhead, the Horsehead, "Pitchy Patchy", and the Queen, which were possibly borne from the way slaves viewed their masters. Later, a false police officer, an Indian, and a pregnant woman were added to the characters.

The songs were accompanied by the beating of drums, the blowing of flutes and conch shells and the shaking of rattles. The Christian church eventually banned the Johnkonnu practice, arguing that it negatively affected the teaching of Christian principles.

RASTAFARIANISM

The Rastafarian movement was started in Jamaica around 1930 among poor ghetto people. Life was hard and jobs were not easy to come by. These people wanted to live their own way of life, not the culture of the British colonies. The Rastafarian movement was mostly inspired by the words of Marcus Garvey, who wanted equality for black people. He also encouraged black people to return to Africa.

Heaven and Earth. Haile Selassie visited Jamaica on April 21, 1966.

Howell, called "Father of the Rastas", introduced these principles for Rastafarians:
- Hate the white man
- Revenge the white for his wickedness
- Neglect, persecute and humiliate the government and legal bodies
- Acknowledge Haile Selassie as supreme and only ruler
- Repatriate to Africa

Today, however, much of this thinking has changed. Rastas are renowned for

COMMITMENT
KNOWLEDGE
FREEDOM
MESSENGER
STRENGTH

THE MIND BONDAGE

Cliff's garage

He also prophesied that a black man would be appointed prince regent of Ethiopia. Ras Tafari Makouner was crowned Emperor Haile Selassie I. The Rastas believed that Haile Selassie was the black Christ. Leonard Howell made this belief stronger when he said Haile Selassie "Rastafari" was the creator of

dreadlocks and ital foods.

The lion (Haile Selassie as Conquering lion of Judah) is seen on their houses and on their red, black, green and gold flags.

Their ritual, the Holy Nyabinghi, comprises songs, dance, beating of drums

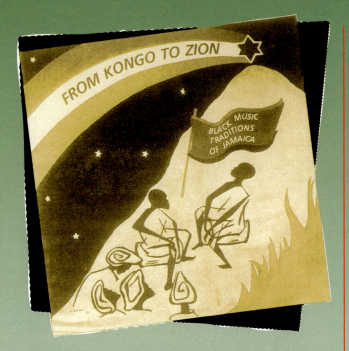

and the smoking of marijuana (ganja). Central to the theme of Rastafarianism is the struggle with evil oppressors, often referred to as Babylon.

Despite the differences in performances, Kumina, Revival and Rastafarianism share a common cultural and historical foundation and a common theme of African liberation.

The musical tradition of these three types of religions can be heard on the LP *From Kongo To Zion* (1983) on the Heartbeat label. It also demonstrates the influence of African traditions on Jamaican popular music.

The Rastafarian sect uses three types of drums in their ceremonies – the bass, fundeh, and repeater, which are beaten in a very slow rhythm. These drums are at the heart of Rasta music. (For description and pictures of the drums, see sub-section entitled *Count Ossie.)* The Nyabinghi style of drumming is more similar to the Burru style than Kumina.

The beats are based on doctrinal values in the Rasta culture.

It is believed that the music cures headaches, the common cold, and other ailments. The Rastafarians also worship and thank Jah Rastafari through their music.

There is a Trojan three-CD set of 50 tracks called *Nyahinghi,* issued in 2003, which is a very good selection of this music and drumming style, performed by Count Ossie and his band; Ras Michael and the Sons of Negus; Bongo Hermann, Dadawah, Max Romeo and even Jimmy Cliff with his song "Bongo Man A Come".

Jamaican musician Ras Michael, born George Michael Henry, in Kingston, but now lives in South Los Angeles, popularized Nyabingi by blending it with reggae during the 1970s and 80s.

In the early 1960's, he formed the Sons of Negus, a Rastafarian group of drummers and singers. He was also the first Rastafarian to have a reggae radio programme in Jamaica. "The Lion of Judah Radio" first aired in 1967.

Considered the heir apparent to Count Ossie, he built on the foundation

of Ossie's Rastafarian drumming, at times taking it to groundbreaking, breath-taking levels by incorporating reggae instruments like guitars, keyboards, bass, and horns. As a Nyabinghi "burru" drum specialist, whose style is roots, rock reggae, he is a true patriarch of reggae, among the purest of its sources, a constant conscience and keeper of the culture. "Love Thy Neighbour" of 1984 takes it a step further by adding dub-like effects courtesy of producer Lee "Scratch" Perry. The last three songs in particular offer little more than Rasta drumming and are likely to make many snooze. The sombre "Don't Sell Daddy No Whiskey" is the best track and one of Ras Michael's all-time most evocative.

Ras Michael changed his style on his later albums, but he still left some of the drummings on a couple of the tracks. Most of the songs are very melodic, some even similar to Irish ballads. He is a lifetime member of the Reggae Ambassadors Worldwide.

In addition to acting as an evangelist, ambassador and diplomat for the Ethiopian Orthodox Tawahido Church internationally, Ras Michael is one of the founders and president of the Rastafarian International/Marcus Garvey Culture Centre in Los Angeles, and the Fly Away Culture Centre in Kingston. He is a speaker, lecturer and presenter.

FOLK MUSIC: MENTO & CALYPSO

The rhythm of the "talking drums" in Africa came to be associated with the "riddim drums" in Jamaica. The calypso of the 1950s has its roots in Trinidad, and Harry Belafonte, with the "Banana Boat Song" and "Island In The Sun" (from the 1957 movie of the same name) on the label of the American record company, RCA, made this music so popular that it seemed to be the music of the Caribbean.

Every hotel and bar on Jamaica's north coast had their own calypso band.

There is close body contact between the two dancers below the hip. (See section entitled *Forms Of Reggae: Dub And DJ*).

The dance seems simple, direct, and almost pornographic. As a result, there was censuring of some of this music due to pressures from the church. Some of the records had to be sold "under the counter", and in addition, they could not be played on the radio.

During the 1930s and 1940s, mento was the music of the Jamaican people, and was most popular in the country areas. The musical instruments of the country bands (often home-made), included a rhumba box, bongos, guitar and shakers.

Mento, on the other hand, was the dominant folk music in Jamaica from its first appearance in the late nineteenth century up to 1940. The original mento was a form of dance, where the hips moved slowly and dipped occasionally.

The singers included Lord Debby, Lord Power, Lord Fly, Lord Flea, Lord Count Sticky, The Ticklers and The Pork Chops Rhumba Box Band from Montego Bay, who achieved much popularity through their music.

The folk music of Jamaica, particularly mento, is generally acknowledged as having the greatest impact on the evolution of modern Jamaican popular music.

An example of a mento recording can be heard on the album by the Jolly Boys (1990). This mento band consisted of four musicians from Port Antonio. They played songs inherited from their African and English ancestors, and also from French folk music, with Afro-Caribbean rhythms.

None of the tracks on this album are supported by electronic musical instruments. In 1991, the same band recorded an album entitled *Beer Joint & Tailoring*, which was a live album without "overdubs"; that is, without echo or other electronic sound effects. In fact, it consisted only of banjo, rhumba box, guitar and singing. The album, which is second to none, comprised fourteen songs, including mento to ska. One of the most widely-known songs is "Big Bamboo." This group has played with Paul Whiteman and J.P. Morgan Jr. at live parties held by Errol Flynn at his Navy Island.

During the 1950's, the American rhythm and blues hits were made popular in Jamaica with the advent of transistor radios. This was due to the fact that the recording companies in United States of America did not possess the technical equipment with which to record mento.

On the north coast, the Hilton Band (The Hiltonaires) was very popular. Some of the music they recorded included the albums *Big Bamboo, Mento Hilton Band-The Hiltonaires* and *Ska Motion In Ska Lipso*.

Ivan Chin did massive efforts to put together some Mento and Calypso music (80 tracks) from the 50s. Most of the songs were originals composed by EF Williams and Alerth Bedasse from 1955 to 1957.

The Chin's calypso sextet band consisted of a rumba box, a bamboo saxophone, a bamboo flute, a banjo, a bass guitar with four strings, two heavy sticks called clave (which are knocked together) and a pair of maracas. The instruments were made mostly from local materials; the maracas were made from the calabash fruit with some John Crow beans put in as the shaker.

The recording machine cut grooves into ten-inch 78 rpm vinyl resign discs with a needle. They recorded the music in Chin's Radio Service Store at nights after the store closed for the day. After 40 years they sent the discs to Decca Records in England where they got transferred into CD format at a four-CD set in 2003. The fifth CD became avaiable in 2005 with some experimental stereo recordings of 1957.

Beside the mento bands appearing at hotels to perform for the tourists, mento is mainly performed in the rural parishes by groups such as the Hatfield Cultural Group; The Blue Glads, which originated from St. Christopher and the Littitz mento band from south St. Elizabeth. The playing of folk music is strongly encouraged by the Jamaica Cultural Development Commission (JCDC). Several of the songs that have won the National Popular Song competition are firmly based in the foundations of the folk genres of mento and revival.

the jolly boys

$108.50

The radio stations located in the southern parts of the United States of America, in particular Miami and New Orleans, have made this genre of music quite popular, not only in the USA, but also in Jamaica. The artistes that were quite popular among the Jamaican audiences included Louis Jordan, Roscoe Gordon, Fats Domino, Amos Milburn, Johnny Ace, Chuck Berry, Sam Cooke, The Drifters and Clovers. The songs were transmitted via the American radio station WINZ.

R & B - THE SOUND SYSTEMS

Rhythm and blues is somewhat similar to mento, in respect of the main beat on the second and fourth cycle and the after beat. When R & B came over from the States to Jamaica, mento's golden age ended, but it was still played and recorded.

Despite its relative similarity to mento, R & B became more popular and successful, largely due to the fact that it was heavily promoted by big sound systems, which carried the music throughout the country. The local musicians had to adapt their songs to the R & B rhythms, with the result that there were recordings made especially for the American market,

and included songs from artistes, such as, Laurel Aitken, Derrick Morgan and Owen Gray. These artistes were strongly influenced by R & B.

The three most notable big sound system disc jockeys were Duke Reid (The Trojan, Treasure Isle label), Stan "The Great" Sebastian, who used to repair radios and amplifiers for domestic and sound system uses, and Sir Coxsone, who worked on sugar cane estates prior to starting his career in the music industry.

Sir Coxsone

One of the first sound system owners was Clement Seymour Dodd, popularly known as Sir Coxsone, who started to play records to the customers in his parents' shop. During a spell in the south of the United States he became familiar with the rhythm and blues music, which was popular there at the time.

In 1954, back in Jamaica, he set up the Downbeat Sound System, starting out with a PA, a turntable and some U.S. records which he imported from New Orleans and Miami. With the great success of his sound system, and in a highly competitive environment, Dodd would make trips through the States looking for new tunes to attract the Jamaican public. Dodd opened five different sound systems, each playing every night. To run his sound systems, he appointed people like Lee "Scratch" Perry (who was Dodd's right-hand man during his early career), U-Roy and Prince Buster.

The traditional DJ style, characterised by mixing and commenting on a song by the disc jockey, evolved out of sound system street parties. These guys would endow themselves with regal titles, such as "Lord" or "Sir". Sir Clement "Coxsone" Dodd is credited with facilitating the evolution and popularity of the genre of deejaying. He was influenced by the lyrics and sounds of legendary bebop and R & B artistes such as Jacko Henderson and Poppa Stoppa. He took the lyrics and sounds, and with the assistance of Count Winston Machouki he transformed them into what has become a very popular genre of music known as deejaying. Unfortunately, there is no recorded evidence of Machouki's work, even though he has played such an instrumental role in the evolution of this now popular genre.

A number of aspiring musicians, such as Sir Lord Comic, King Stitt, U-Roy and Dennis Alcapone were inspired by the work of Sir Coxsone, and he taught them well.

These songs, produced specifically for the sound systems, were produced in his studio, but not without many challenges. At one point, during the late 1960s, he had to hire a young boxer, Prince Buster, to protect him from men like Duke Reid and a young DJ called Lee 'Little' Perry. Sir Coxsone had to come up with a number of creative ways to protect his interest and business. For example, he would release the records six months after they were produced, and often without any title or recording label. By 1971, however, he had to change his tactics as it was stipulated that all records being released should have the label of the recording company. The omission of same was only permitted when the record was pre-released, but for no longer than two months.

Sir Coxsone's first recording studio was Federal Records Studio, located at 220 Marcus Garvey Drive, now the home of Tuff Gong Studios. In 1963, he opened Studio One at 13 Grandfurt Road, now renamed Studio One Boulevard.

Sir Coxsone later lived in Brooklyn, New York, where he owned and operated another branch of Studio One and stored the entire collection of his old recordings there. He died in May 2004 from a heart attack.

Prince Buster

The king of the sound systems was Prince Buster (born Roy Campbell), also known as The Master. He first worked as a security guard for Coxsone, after which he operated his own business. Prince Buster is credited with making popular tracks such as "Al Capone", "One Step Beyond", and "Judge Dread".

It was during the late 1950's that Sir Coxsone, Duke Reid and Prince Buster started their own recording studios.

But of the three, Prince Buster was the only one who owned a sound system and could sing. He learnt a lot about lyrics from listening to a man named "Wallace", who would sit on Orange Street, and sing his own songs to the beat of his guitar.

Many musicians fine-tuned their skills there, in addition to performing in the many hotels on the north coast. Most of these musicians, such as Roland

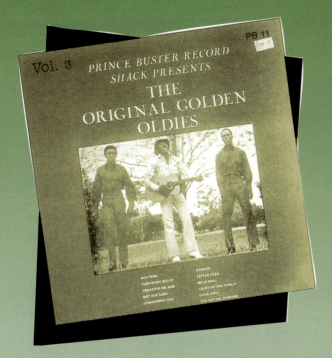

Alphonso, Jackie Mittoo and singer Leroy Smart, came out of the Alpha Boys' School (the Alpha Boys' Band started in 1892), and went on to become top entertainers.

Prince Buster became involved in the music business in 1959, when ska was becoming quite popular. His record company, with the tag line *Real Blue Beat With The King of Ska Prince Buster,* also faced numerous challenges, as there was constant competition between his studio and that of Sir Coxsone and Duke Reid. Despite the constant war, evidenced by a huge scar on his skull from a concrete brick and an ice-pick wound in his side from fights with Reid's men, Buster persisted.

His success was not long in coming, and with the assistance of Lloyd the Matador from East Kingston, and Lloyd Bell in West Kingston his "Bup Bup" music (Bup was a nickname he earned as a teenage boxer, which described his left hook) began to dominate the local sound system scene.

It should also be noted that Prince Buster was the first producer to do

recordings of Count Ossie. The Blue Beat Company in London became quite interested in Prince Buster, and every year since 1963, he has toured England. It was in that same year, while on tour with Derrick Morgan, that he recorded the song "Wash Wash", which became quite popular in Jamaica, and even reached the number one spot on the music chart. He rightly earned the nickname "Mr. Wash Wash". He also topped the charts in 1964. Other popular songs by Prince Buster include "Bad Minded People", "Time Longer Than Rope", "They Got To Go" and "Run Man Run", which shocked Jamaicans. These songs were no doubt influenced by his experiences with dons and bad men. Price Buster's biggest hit was "Ten Commandments".

An LP of historical note, which was released under Prince Buster's label, is *Pain In My Belly*. In addition to his own tracks, it consists of songs by other musicians and groups, such as the Maytals, Don Drummond, Tommy McCook & The Skatalites, Eric Morris and The Ska Busters. Today, Prince Buster lives in Miami.

THE BIRTH OF SKA

Music in Jamaica was now moving between rhythm and blues and boogie woogie. And then ska was created, some say by accident. It is alleged that Theophilus Beckford, who was accompanied on guitar, was playing "Easy Snappin" to a boogie rhythm on the piano characterised by a first and second beat. The bass guitarist consistently kept a four-fourth rhythm while the percussion underlined the first

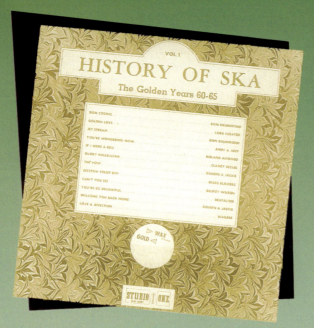

and the second beat, followed by the horns. It was very much similar to jazz. And the ska was born!

The ska was a vibrating, cutting and happy rhythm, with the trumpet providing its distinctive sound. The after beats on the guitar were more pulsating than reggae, which emerged later. The dance to this lively instrumental music closely resembles a drunkard, whose arms move like a robot.

Ska developed as an indigenous music genre. The music had the power to move the dancing feet of Jamaicans and visitors alike. The new tunes and rhythm imparted a real Jamaican feeling. Possibly, the first ska single was "Little Sheila" by Laurel Aitken, recorded in 1958 at Chris Blackwell's studio.

Later, there were two compilations of ska on LP's; the first released under the Studio One label in 1966 called *Calypso Ska Jump Up Vol. 1*, which included songs by the Soul Brothers; the Wailers with "Rolling Stone" and "Let Him Go"; the Soulettes and the Gaylads with "Falling In Love. The next was called *This Is Jamaican Ska*, with the Wailers'

track "Simmer Down" and "Go, Jimmy, Go"; the Gaylads with "Stop Making Love"; Don Drummond and Roland Alphonso with "Roll On Sweet On"; Roland Alphonso with "Bonga Tonga", "Sucu Sucu" and "20-75" and the Skatalites with "Salt Lane Gal".

Don Drummond

Don Drummond, accompanied by his trombone and his musical rendition of "Jet Stream", arrived on the music scene during the 1950s when ska was born. It was also during the time when jazz was becoming popular in Jamaica, and Ernest Ranglin with his guitar, Cecil Lloyd on the piano, Billy Cooke with his trumpet, Tommy McCook and Roland Alphonso with their saxophones, Lloyd Mason on bass and Carl McLeod on drums, were the musicians who were instrumental in establishing and incorporating this highly sophisticated genre into the local music industry. Don Drummond first played with Eric Dean All Stars during the 1950s, and later with Kenny Williams during the '60s.

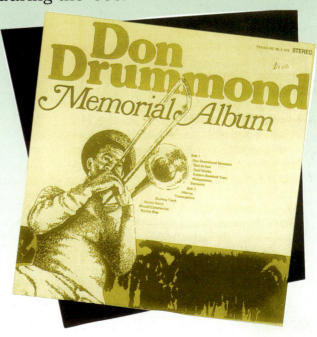

Don Drummond was adept at playing the trombone, and was famous for playing it on a high note, as if it were a horn or trumpet, or heavy and deep like a baritone. When playing, he was like a machine gun in full action.

His first recording, "On the Beach", was released in 1956, followed later by "Scrap Iron", "This man is Back", "Far East", "Green Island", "Occupation", and "Reburial", which were classic Jamaican songs, especially in an era when the recording techniques were less sophisticated.

Drummond's composition of original, simple blues songs, symbolised an act of protest against the establishment. He later became a Rastafarian and had tremendous influence over the young musicians who were around during his time. His life story was often portrayed in his songs, examples of which can be found on the LPs *The Best of Don Drummond*, released under the Studio One label, with tracks such as "The Reburial", "Heavenless", and "African Beat"; and *Don Drummond Memorial Album*, released under the Treasure Isle Label, with tracks such as "Cool Smoke", "Stampede and Alipang".

Don Drummond, happy but thoughtful, sincere and communicative, was a real son of Africa, born in Jamaica. He died tragically on May 6, 1969.

Count Ossie

Count Ossie, drummer extraordinaire, also arrived on the music scene during this time. He also had a great influence on the Skatalites.

Count Ossie learnt the "burru" rhythm or Rasta music, and created the riddims, which refers to the music created by the simultaneous playing of three drums – the bass, fundeh and repeater.

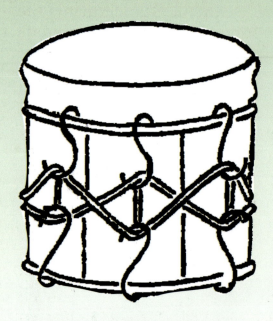

- **The bass drum** is the biggest of the three and is played in a similar manner as the fundeh. The distinction, however, lies in the variations in rhythm and sound.

  It is made from two pieces of goat skin, which are attached to a barrel (about 30 centimetres in diameter), and are held in place with a metal frame with six hooks. Pieces of rope are then passed through the hooks and tightened to create a tension in the middle of the drum. The resulting sound is determined by the degree of tension of the goat skin. The drum is either placed on the knees or suspended from the neck, and played with a stick wrapped in linen.

- **The fundeh drum**, or the middle drum, has a standing rhythm, also referred to as life-line-riddim.

  It is made from an old tin and goat skin, held in place with five metal sticks, and is tuned by screws. The fundeh drum is played on the first or third beat, depending on the type of music.

- **The repeater drum,** the smallest drum of the three, is the sole instrument responsible for creating the melody.

  It closely resembles the fundeh drum, but is made from an excavated coconut tree trunk, inside of which are two wooden rings attached with nails.

Count Ossie also created music with the flute, saxophone, bass guitar and trombone beside the drums. He taught Don Drummond, Roland Alphonso, Cedric Brooks and Tommy McCook.

Count Ossie's contribution to the evolution of Jamaican music is quite invaluable, so much so that one can conclude that without him, neither ska nor reggae would be part of Jamaica's music landscape. He even taught his orchestra, The Mystic Revelation of Rastafari, to electrically play the different drums.

In 1962, Harry A. Moodie produced the tracks "Babylon Gone" and "So Long", which featured Count Ossie on drums and Wilton Gaynair on saxophone.

Millie Small

In 1956, 15-year-old American singer Barbie Gaye recorded on the 78 record label the song "My Boy Lollipop", written by Bobby Spencer.

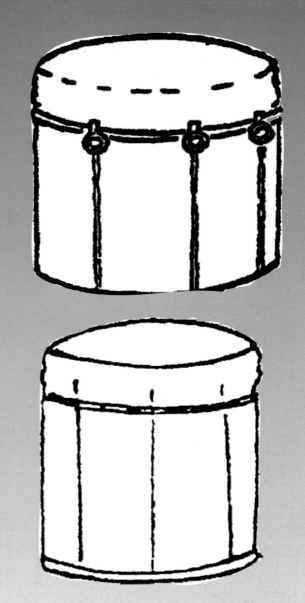

In 1964, ska exploded with Millie Small's (first international ska) version of the hit single, "My Boy Lollipop", a Chris Blackwell production. It was one of the first songs from the West Indies to reach number one on the English charts, with over six million copies sold. The song was accompanied by Ernest Ranglin on guitar and, according to persitent rumour, Rod Stewart on the mouth organ. Pete Hogman of the Pete Hogman Blues Band and Hoggie & The Sharptones said, "The backing for 'My Boy Lollypop' was recorded live in the studio. I played harmonica and Ernest Ranglin played a black Gibson. Rod Stewart has never claimed to have played that solo."

Owen Gray

Owen Gray, born in 1939 in Kingston, was like Laurel Aitken, Jackie Edwards and Derrick Morgan, an upcoming artiste during the 1950s. They all went on to become very popular and successful musicians, who packed the various night clubs scattered across the island. Their popularity was no doubt influenced by the success of the sound systems, which carried their music far and wide.

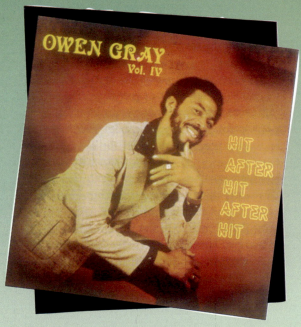

There are recordings by Owen Gray, originally done for the sound system market, but which were strongly influenced by R & B.

Owen Gray has been credited as Jamaica's first home-grown singing star. His success started in 1962 with his first hit single, "Darling Patricia", which was produced by Lesley Kong, the owner of Beverley Records. It was also during that same year that Jimmy Cliff had his hit single, "Miss Jamaica".

Gray went on to record several hits with Millie Small, performing as a duet. Prince Buster was also persuaded by Count Ossie to do several recordings of Gray playing the piano. Gray also worked with Ernest Ranglin, guitarist for The Skatalites.

He had a number of hits on his LP series, which consisted of four LPs entitled *Hit After Hit*, released under English labels. The songs were produced by Sydney Crooks (backing vocalist), with Gray on piano.

Bunny Lee produced a ten-song LP entitled *Room At The Top*, released under the American World Enterprise label, of which eight of the ten songs were written by Gray.

Later, Gray toured the USA, Canada and Europe and was so successful in England that he stayed there and worked with Island Records, after which he returned to Jamaica to improve his recordings. Gray, together with Clem "Bushranger" Bushey, produced and arranged the album *Something Good Going On* on the Weed Beat label in 1990.

Laurel Aitken

Laurel (Lorenzo) Aitken, also known as The Originator, was born in 1927 in Cuba. At the age of eleven years he and his parents, together with his five brothers and sisters, migrated to Jamaica. When he was 15 years old, he won his first song competition performing a jazz piece entitled "Pennies From Heaven".

One of his first jobs was with the Jamaica Tourist Board, where he, with a calypso band, welcomed tourists to the island at a cruise ship pier.

Aitken's first recording was "Roll Jordan Roll", recorded in 1957 for Caribbean Distributing. It sounded similar to ska, but it had a more spiritual feeling. In fact, it was recorded long before Coxsone and Duke Reid started recordings of ska.

Towards the end of September 1959, Aitken recorded "Sweet Little Sheila" under the Starlite label for Chris Blackwell (who later founded Island Record). This song reached number one on the Jamaican charts and remained on the charts until 1960. "Boogie Rock" and "Heavenly Angel" followed successfully.

Aitken was one of the biggest stars in Jamaica, and was around long before Prince Buster, who was mainly a leader rather than a solo artiste, emerged on the music scene.

After becoming successful in the local music industry, Aitken went on to England like many musicians before him did.

While in Jamaica, he only received five English pounds for each of his recordings. But when he realised that they sold a lot of bootleg copies of "Little Sheila" in England, from which he did not profit, he signed a contract with Melodisc (Blue Beat label), which was the only recording company at the time which produced ska. He subsequently recorded seventeen singles under the Blue Beat label - four for Dice, three for the Kalypso and Rainbow labels, as well as for Emi, Ska Beat, Direct and Dr. Bird Recording label.

Most of his recordings, however, were done under the Pama label, which included songs such as "Skinhead Train", "Jesse James", "Landlords And Tenants", "Mr. Popcorn", "Pussy Price" and "Fire In My Wire". His later songs, were described as 'rude reggae' style because, according to Aiken, "Jamaicans like indecent songs".

Songs from his calypso recordings, such as "Night Food", "Rise & Fall" and "Pussy Price" were banned by the BBC. "The Beat" and "Judge Dread" were also banned because the lyrics were deemed too offensive for airplay by the English people.

Despite his many hits, Laurel got little financial reward from his recordings with Blue Beat or Rio. In the 1970s, he worked in his hometown of Leicester, during which he had his only hit single on the UK chart to date entitled "Rudy Got Married", with Rico on horns and released under the I-Spy- (Arista) label. The song tells the story of Yagga Yagga, a Jamaican who did not know anything, but who was lucky with one pound when others were lucky with one hundred.

Aitken toured throughout England with the groups Secret Affair and The Beat, with whom he did a number of remarkable recordings.

He produced two songs locally, "Oneness" and "Cabana," in the early 1980s and later. During the mid-80s, he joined the band Potato 5 as a lead singer, and together they performed the "Original Jamaican Ska".

This partnership also produced singles such as "Sally Brown" and "Sahara", as well as the UB40 classic hit "Guilty" and the album *Floyd Lloyd And The Potato 5 Meet Laurel Aitken*, all of which were released by Gaz's Rockin' Records.

The group eventually disbanded, after which Laurel founded a new band, The Pressure Tenants. He also sang with other ska bands, such as The Loafers; the hit group The Manners; the German reggae bands The Busters and No Sports and the French Beurk's band.

In 1989, Laurel staged a big performance at the London International Ska Festival. He also performed with The Busters at other concerts held in Germany, the USA and Canada.

In January 1990, he performed with the Busters in Holland, Pressure Tenants in Italy, and the Beurks Band in France, and again with the Pressure Tenants in Germany. He even turned to dancehall in the 1990s. In addition to the stage shows and tours, he also recorded a number of albums.

After six decades of recording and performing, Laurel Aitken, called the "Godfather of Ska", died in 2005 from a heart attack.

In 2007, a CD and DVD, *The Very Last Concert*, was released.

Derrick Morgan

Derrick Morgan was born on March 27, 1940 in Stewarton in the parish of Clarendon. At age sixteen, he left school to work in the accounting department of the parish welfare office.

In 1957, he entered the Vere John's Opportunity Hour Talent Contest held at the Palace Theatre in Kingston. He won with a performance of "Long Tall Sally", originally done by Little Richard. Shortly after, he was recruited to perform around the island with the popular Jamaican comedy team Bim and Bam. For two years he performed Little Richard songs at various shows staged by the group.

In 1959, Morgan entered the recording studio for the first time. Duke Reid, the acclaimed sound sysyem boss, was looking for talent to record for his Treasure Isle label. Derrick Morgan cut two popular shuffle-boogie sides, "Lover Rock Boy" aka "S-Corner Rock" and "Oh My". "Lover Boy" was later renamed "Escona Rock". However, Reid did not release the song. Instead, he kept it for his sound system, resulting in he and Morgan going their separate ways.

Soon after, Morgan cut the bolero-tinged boogie "Hey You Fat Man," released under the Little Wonder label, which also became a hit. He also found time to record for Coxsone Dodd.

It was during this time that Prince Buster asked Morgan to assist him with his recordings. They collaborated on numerous recordings, a partnership which lasted up to 1962, and included such songs as, "They Got To Go" and "Shake A Leg".

Morgan then met a young man (who later became known as Jimmy Cliff), who asked him to listen to a song he had recorded for Beverley's Records entitled "Dearest Beverley". But Morgan found the song to be too slow for the ska rhythm at the time. After some rehearsals, they recorded two tracks for Beverley's: "Hurricane Hattie" and "The Lion Say I'm King And I Reign". Following the recording of these two songs, Morgan switched to Lesley Kong, and started to produce records under the Beverley Record label.

His first recordings at Beverly's were "Be Still" and "Sunday Monday", after which he recorded "Forward March", which was the song that won the first Independence Song Competition in Jamaica. It should be noted that "Black-head Chinaman", which was a big hit for Prince Buster, was made from the same melody as "Forward March".

Morgan then responded with the song entitled "Blazing Fire". It was then that a rivalry developed between Morgan and Buster, with Morgan releasing "Tougher Than Tough" followed by Prince Buster's "Judge Dread", followed again by Morgan's "I Am The Ruler", to which Prince Buster responded with "Walking Up Orange Street I Am The Ruler Too".

During this time, Morgan became interested in other artistes, such as Toots Hibbert and Desmond Dekker (Desmond Dacres), who started his singing career after two years of hanging around the studios. Even though Dekker did not have a good singing voice or a good song, he and Morgan became friends, and they often talked and drank together. It was not long before Dekker finally came up with a relatively good song entitled "Honour Your Mother and Father".

Between 1962 and 1963, Morgan had seven songs in the top ten of the local music charts, largely due to the fact that at that time he did not have a contract with any music producer. He then recorded "My Heart I Feel Like A King" for Count Bell's; "Be Still" for Beverly's; and "Housewives", 80,000 copies of which were sold under the Island Record label, owned by Chris Blackwell.

Around this time a young boy named Robert Nesta Marley came to Morgan, who recorded his first song entitled "Judge Not Before You Judge Yourself".

Both Morgan and Buster were producing such good music that fans from all over started fighting over the question of who was the better musician – Prince Buster or Derrick Morgan. To end the fight, they both started a show in 1963. Bob Marley first appeared on stage at this show, but according to eyewitness reports, he danced more than he sang. It is believed that it was Morgan who suggested to Bob Marley that he should first sing, then dance and sing again. He continued training him until he started working with Coxsone Dodd.

Derrick Morgan went to London with Prince Buster and signed at Eugene Shalet from Melodisc, where he recorded "Telephone" with Georgie Fame and "Wash Wash" with Prince Buster on the same day.

After six months, they left the cold England. Back in Jamaica he recorded "Back On The Track" to show he was back in business. In 1969, he brought in his brother-in-law Bunny Lee as a producer in the music business and recorded several songs.

In England Bunny met Carl Palmer and opened a branch of his Pama Records in Jamaica. They produced some songs like "Moon Hop" and Owen Gray's "Girl What You Doing To Me". But Bunny caused one problem by issuing the song "Seven Letters" in England on his Jackpot label and gave a license to Pama for their Crab label, and gave another license to Trojan. This led to some trouble because Goodhall issued the same song with the title changed to "Skinhead Moonstomp". In 1975, Morgan recorded the song "Some Woman Must Cry" as a contrast to Bob Marley's "No Woman No Cry".

Even today, Derrick Morgan is one of the most active performers of ska, rocksteady and reggae. Since 1987, he has been living in Miami with his family. In July 2002, in Toronto, Canada, a two-night 'Legends of Ska' concert was held. Appearing on stage were The Skatalites, Lloyd Knibbs, Rico Rodriguez, Lloyd Brevett, Lester Sterling, Johnny Moore and Lynn Taitt. Other performers included Prince Buster, Alton Ellis, Owen Gray, Lord Creator, Justin Hinds, Derrick Harriott, Winston Samuels, Roy Wilson, Patsy Todd, Doreen Shaffer, Stranger Cole, Lord Tanamo and Derrick Morgan.

In 2007, Morgan appeared on the bill at the annual Augustibuller festival. His song "Tougher Than Tough" was featured in the video game *Scarface: The World is Yours*.

The Skatalites

The Skatalites were the top ska instrumental group from the early to mid-1960s.

The group consisted of Don Drummond (died in 1969), Tommy McCook (died in 1998) and Roland Alphonso (died in 1998), Lloyd Knibb on bass, Lester Sterling, Lloyd Brevitt on drums, Bobby Aitken and Lynn Taitt on guitar, Jacie Opel (died 1970), Jah Jerry Hynes (died 2007) and Jackie Mittoo (died 1990), Johnny Moore (died 2008).

The success of this group was largely due to the trombonist Don Drummond. According to the pianist George Shearing, Don Drummond was one of the best trombonists in the world, which was confirmed by his recording of the track "Confucius" in 1964. Even though many will contend that this was a recording by the Skatalites, it was in fact an original recording by Drummond. The Skatalites however went on to record some of their best tracks on the LP *Ska Authentic: Presenting The Original Skatalites*. The group disbanded in 1964, when Drummond was hospitalised.

In July 1983, The Skatalites did a reunion performance at the Sunsplash festival in Montego Bay with great success. They recorded their reunion album in April 1984 called *The Return of The Big Guns*, released on Mango Records in the U.K.

In the 90s, they toured the USA and Europe. In 2002, their World Tour which touched USA, Europe, Mexico, Venezuela, Puerto Rico, Russia and Japan lasted nine months. In 2004 and 2005, their 40th anniversary tour took them to Colombia, Greece and Singapore.

In July 2007 The Skatalites were rejoined by tenor saxophonist Cedric "IM" Brooks, who was on hiatus, studying in Ethiopia for a few years.

The current band members are Lloyd Knibb, Doreen Shaffer, Lester Sterling, Devon James, Kevin Batchelor and Cedric "IM" Brooks.

Justin Hinds

Justin Hinds was born on May 7, 1942 in Steer Town, St. Ann. At age fifteen, he worked with his friend Dennis Sinclair, who had a boat which provided round-trip transportation for tourists from the then Jamaica Hilton Hotel in Kingston to Port Antonio or Montego Bay. From time to time they would earn money by performing songs while transporting the tourists. One day, when Elizabeth Taylor and Eddie Fisher were guests on the boat, they suggested that Hinds and

Sinclair should record their songs, which later led to the discovery of Hinds by Duke Reid. He did some test recordings with The Skatalites, which produced the hit song "Carry Go Bring Come" in 1963. The song went to number one in Jamaica and remained in the top ten on the music charts in Jamaica for seven weeks. Hinds recorded 70 singles on Duke Reid's Treasure Isle label between 1964 and 1966 and was the most popular artiste on the label.

Later, Hinds, together with Dennis Sinclair and Junior Dixon, founded the group the Dominoes, which was later re-named Fats Domino.

Together, they recorded about sixty songs for Duke Reid, and continued to work with him until the early 1960s, when Duke, because of his deteriorating health, turned over the management and operation of his studio to Sonia Pottinger. Hinds did some recordings under the tutelage of Pottinger, but she preferred his older recordings.

In 1976, Jack Ruby of Island Records asked Hinds to do some recordings for him. This collaboration produced two LP's called *Jezebel* and *Just In Time*. A financial misunderstanding eventually ended their relationship, and Hinds went back to his farm in Steer Town.

In 1981, Bob Schoenfeld, a music producer from Nighthawk (who was also the producer for The Itals and Gladiators), together with Hinds, produced the album *Travel With Love*, which consisted of a song with the same name, and other tracks, such as "Get Ready Rocksteady" and "Book of History".

The excellent musicians who collaborated on this project included the Barrett brothers (Carly and Family Man) on bass and drums, Chinna Smith as lead

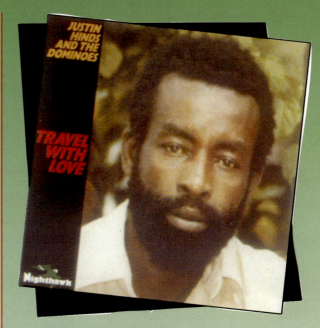

guitarist, and Tommy McCook on trombone. In 1989, they released "Picking Up Chips" on the Wonder label. It was a song that dealt with everyday issues: from the collecting of wood for the stove to cooking.

In 1991, Hinds founded the group The Revivers, which consisted of Derrick Reid, "Deadley" Headley Bennett, Ceanne Arthur, Jonathan Arthur, Maurice Gregory, Vin Gordon, Bernard Fagan and his son Maxwell. The group went on to record the album, *One Day*. Justin Hinds died of lung cancer on March 16, 2005.

The Ethiopians

The Ethiopians, which consisted of Leonard "Sparrow" Dillon, who was born in 1942 in Port Antonio; and Aston Morris and Stephen Taylor, emerged on the music scene in 1966 with the songs "Owe Me No Pay", "Live Good", "Free Man" and "What To Do", which were produced by Studio One. In 1965, Leonard recorded four songs with Coxsone Dodd. At the end of 1966, Morris left the Ethiopians, reducing them to a duo.

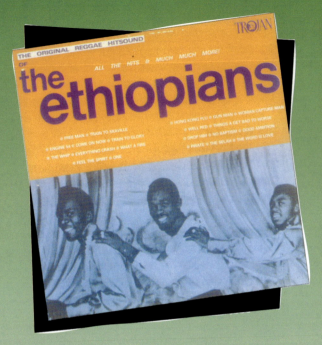

During this time, Leonard was working in Kingston as a bricklayer. In 1967, he met Albert Griffiths, who had just founded his own vocal group The Gladiators. They persuaded their employer, Lee Robertson, to do a recording session in the WIRL studio. The result was not only the first hit song for The Ethiopians entitled "Train To Skaville", but also the first recording for Albert Griffiths, "You Are The Girl", released on the WIRL label, and on which, he was the harmony singer.

In 1968, the Ethiopians entered the music charts with "The Whip" and "Train To Glory", which was produced for Sonia Pottinger on the Gay Feet label.

During the late 60's and early 70's, they did recordings for Carl Johnson's Sir JJ label, and produced such songs as "Selah", "Everything Crash", "Hong Kong Flu", "What A Fire" and "Woman Capture Man", on which Melvin Reid was the harmony singer.

Justin Hinds did some of his recordings with the Ethiopians, with whom he also toured England in 1969. Their song "Everything Crash" was one of the biggest selling records of 1968, which spoke to the social unrest that was happening on the island at that time. There was much instability, characterised by frequent strikes, food and water shortages, as well as conflicts between the police force and citizens of the country.

The Ethiopians worked with a number of producers and record labels. They also had a number of impressive hits, such as "Prophecy", which they recorded for Lee Perry; "Pirate" for Duke Reid; "Satan Gal" for Lloyd the Matador; "No Baptism" for Derrick Harriott; "Leave My Business" for Coxsone Dodd; "Jump Up" for Joe Gibbs; "Solid As A Rock" for Rupie Edwards; You Are For Me" for Prince Buster and "Them A Wicked" for Chin Randys. They also did recordings for Winston Riley, Alvin Ranglin, Bunny Lee and some lesser known producers.

The partnership ended when Stephen Taylor died in 1975 in a car accident. In 1981, Dillon went back to Studio One to record the *Everything Crash* LP. He is well known for recording songs with Rastafarianism as the main subject. The song "Open The Gate" is a good example.

At the end of the millenium, Leonard formed a new Ethiopians lineup with female backing vocalists Jennifer Lara and Merlene Webber, who appeared on the 1999 album *Tuffer Than Stone*.

FROM ROCKSTEADY TO REGGAE

In the summer of 1966, a new sound emerged. The change came about due to the influence of Motown, Memphis and Philly International and R&B music. They needed a slower rhythm to sing those kinds of R&B songs as they could not be sung to a ska rhythm. The speed change was slower and the rhythm more relaxed. The singer came more to the foreground, and singing and rhythm fit better together. It was called rocksteady.

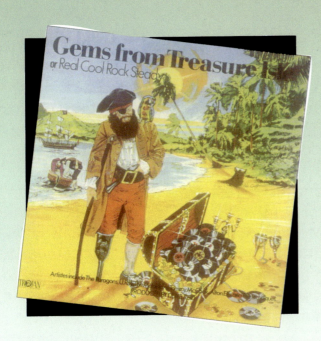

The dancers, who wanted a change, often complained to the producers to reduce the speed of the rhythm. With the reduction in speed, the rhythm and by extension, the dancing, was also slower, with the result that the dancers literally remained on one spot.

Others also attributed the birth of rocksteady to the disbanding of The Skatalites, which resulted when Don Drummond, the trombonist and one of Jamaica's musical legends, was hospitalised in August 1964.

Good examples were songs that were released towards the end of the ska era, such as "Dance Crasher" by Alton Ellis and "Dog War" by The Maytals. The voice was a natural expression and there was more space in the music, which helped the vocal trios to display their range and talent.

The drums were now stronger, and the trombones, trumpets and tenor saxophones faded into the background. The guitar was used more to play a mento-like rhythm, and the bass was used to play the melody for the solo singer.

Because of the chief role that the bass now attained in the musical composition, it is said that rocksteady set the stage for the emergence of reggae.

THE BANDS

There were four important bands during the rocksteady era: Lynn Taitt & The Jets, Tommy McCook & The Supersonics, Bobby Aitken & The Carib

Beats and Roland Alphonso & The Soul Brothers.

When The Skatalites disbanded, saxophonists Tommy McCook and Roland Alphonso formed their own new bands. Prior to the emergence of the rocksteady era, Tommy McCook and the Supersonics did a number of recordings, which were released under the Cal Tone label, owned by Ken Lack, and included some ska songs, such as "Ska Jam". The Skatalites drummer remained with McCook, until he found a job on a cruise ship, after which, Hugh Malcolm joined the band and Jackie Jackson played the electric bass.

Roland Alphonso formed The Soul Brothers, later called Soul Vendors, with Jackie Mittoo on keyboard, Joe Isaacs on the drums, Harry Haughton on guitar, Brian Atkinson on bass and Frank "Ska" Campbell, who periodically played the tenor saxophone.

Bobby Aitken also had his own band, the Carib Beats, with himself as the lead singer and on guitar, Bobby Kalphat on keyboard, Dave Parks as the trombonist, Mark Lewis on trumpet, Alphonso Henry as the saxophonist, Winston Grennan on drums and Vincent White on bass. Together, they recorded songs for Ewan McDermott on the Jolly label in his West Indies Studios, until they started their own studio and pressed their own records.

The Jets, led by guitarist Lynn Taitt, comprised Jackie Jackson on bass, Joe Isaacs on drums, Leslie Butler on piano, Hux Brown as rhythm guitarist and Gladstone Anderson on keyboard. They were managed by Federal Studios, which was the main studio in Jamaica at that time.

One of the better rocksteady compilation LPs is entitled *Come And Rock Me*

In Jamaica on the Treasure Isle Label, with Alton Ellis, Tommy McCook, The Paragons and Phyllis Dillon.

There were other bands during this time, which consisted mainly of studio musicians, who were appointed by the producers at the time of recording of the songs. These included The Virtues, The Vagabonds, The Fugitives and The Mighty Vikings.

Then, there was Byron Lee with his band, who had several number one hits. Byron Lee and the Dragonaires, however, was not a roots-rock reggae band. They played calypso, merengue, ska and cha-cha. (See section called *Soca and Carnival.*)

SINGERS

In addition to Alton Ellis, Delroy Wilson and Derrick Harriott, there was Bob Andy with "I've Got To Go Back Home" and Hopeton Lewis with "Sounds & Pressure". Stranger Cole and Clancy Eccles sang and produced. Max Romeo and Junior Byles with the Versatiles, and Peter Tosh, who recorded "Simpleton" for Prince Buster. There was also Ewan McDermott, producer for the Jolly label, and Jerry Matthias from The Maytals, who came together to form the vocal duo Ewan & Jerry, and who also had some hit songs during that time.

Also present on the music scene were The Heptones, Ken Boothe, Dobby Dobson, Marcia Griffiths, Phyllis Dillon and Judy Mowatt & The Gayletts. Dawn Penn achieved phenomenal success with the cover of a Dionne Warwick original entitled "You'll Never Get To Heaven If You Break My Heart" and also

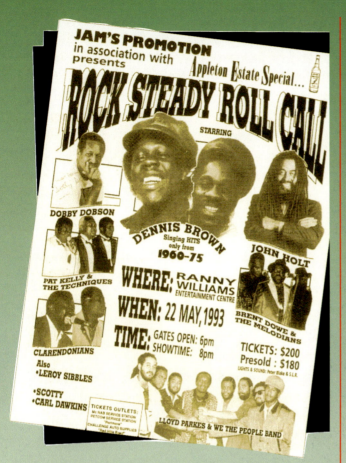

even though Federal still had more records, it was WIRL that all the producers turned to, to do their recordings. They included, Leslie Kong (he died in 1971 of a heart attack), Bunny Lee, Sonia Pottinger, Prince Buster and Byron Lee (he bought WIRL in 1962 from Edward Seaga and renamed it Dynamic Sounds Recording Inc.)

Later, Federal purchased its own four-track machine, and Duke Reid, who had been operating his Treasure Isle Studio since 1966, also purchased a four-track machine in 1970. Sir Coxsone, who had started Studio One in 1964, also purchased a four-track recording machine with which he did a number of recordings with Ken Boothe, John Holt, The Gaylads, The Heptones and The Wailers.

With the four-track recording machines, the producers could incorporate more instruments. In other words, they could place bass and drums on one track, and keyboards and guitar on the other.

Despite the heavy competition, Federal remained the leading studio, pressing from five hundred copies of a recorded song (classified as a hit) to fifteen thousand copies (classified as a big hit). Most of the songs were licensed for release in England, where they could have sold more records, but the producers were often too lazy.

with her own song "Blue Yes Blue". The Clarendonians, Delroy Wilson and Derrick Harriott were also some of the top musicians during this period. Also, one cannot forget Hopeton Lewis, John Holt, Bob Andy, Lloyd Parks, The Gaylads and Desmond Dekker, who all had number one hits.

In fact, Federal Studio and its producers, Keith Scott and Samuel Mitchell, were kept quite busy.

STUDIOS

At the beginning of the rocksteady era, Federal Studio was the number one studio in Jamaica. But soon thereafter, WIRL and its owner Edward Seaga, bought the first four-track recording machine to be used in Jamaica. And

PRODUCERS

As time went on, more and more producers were producing high quality talents. When Federal (Keith Scott and Samuel Mitchell) started out as producers, the company was not a household name.

It was not until they bought the name Merritone from Winston Blake, who was well known in the middle and upper class, that they became fully recognised.

Other well-known producers at the time included Ken Lack, with his Tone Label. J.J. Johnson also recorded at WIRL and at Studio One.

Sonia Pottinger did most of her recordings at the WIRL and the Treasure Isle Studios. In 1974 (after Duke Reid's death) Sonia Pottinger took over the Treasure Isle catalogue and facilities. She had already been heavily involved in the business for many years with her High Note, Gayfeet and Rainbow labels.

There were Bunny Lee, with his Lee's Label; Joe Gibbs with Amalgamated and Pressure Beat Label, which produced songs for Lee Perry; and Lloyd Daley with the Matador Label (formerly the Astronauts label). The Wailers also started their own labels –Wail'N and Soul'M. In England, there were the Trojan and Pama Labels, which achieved great success in the sale of records during that time.

There was a revival of the rocksteady era on May 22, 1993, with the staging of *Rock Steady Roll Call* at the Ranny Williams Entertainment Centre in Kingston. Dennis Brown, one of the performers, only sang songs from the 1960s to 1975. The Techniques performed hits such as "Ain't Too Proud To Beg", "Travelling Man" and "You Don't Care For Me"; Leroy Sibbles naturally sang his "Fatty Fatty", "Sea Of Love", "Only Sixteen" and "Why Did You Leave?" Then there was Alton Ellis, with "Ain't That Loving You"; John Holt with "Tonight", "Ali Baba", "Happy Go Lucky Girl", "On The Beach" and "Wear You To The Ball"; Dobby

Dobson with "Loving Pauper", and Carl Dawkins with "Satisfaction", "Bumpy Road", "Get Together", "Part Time Love" and "Baby I Love You". There were also performances from The Clarendonians, Brent Dowe and The Melodians.

A combination of creativity, the prolific-ness of producers and other persons who were interested in the further develop-ment of music in Jamaica, together with a willingness to adapt to the changing times, resulted in the emergence of a new genre of music called reggae. Most of the earlier artistes, who by then were forgotten, emerged as important con-tributors to the development of this new genre of music.

Most of these artistes started their music career during the ska-instrumental era. Those who achieved huge success included The Melodians with "Come on Little Girl"; The Sensations with "I'll Never Fall in Love Again", The Clarendonians with "Sho Be-Do Be Do"; Byron Lee with "Rocksteady", and The Paragons with "The Tide Is High".

Reggae gradually emerged as the lyrics, rather than the rhythm, took centre stage, becoming the focal point of the song.

In addition, it took the mild protests of the rocksteady poets and moulded them into social protest. The bass was the dominating instrument in rocksteady. The special sound and drive of reggae is comprised of the typical after beats of the guitar, the strength of the rhythm and the offbeat. The reggae beat usually starts with a short solo on percussions, which is quite different from that of ska with the result that the percussion instrument remains or fades into the background.

The Abyssinians

The group was formed in 1968 by Bernard Collins and Donald and Linford Manning, who had both previously been members of their brother Carlton Manning's group Carlton and the Shoes. They emerged on the music scene with their first LP *Satta Massagana*, which was recorded at Studio One, but released on their Clinch label. The title song is a Rastafarian hymn sung partly in the ancient Ethiopian Amharic language.

While other groups went international, and during the process changed their music style, the Abyssinians remained true to their Rastafarian faith, which was not only found in their music, but

also in their lifestyle.

The harmony and hypnotic rhythm and the lyrics of the songs on the LP made it unique, especially when compared to other records in Jamaica at the time. This record remained on the music charts in Jamaica for two years. It was and still is a favourite in the dancehall.

The Abyssinians became quite popular, and the track "Satta" became one of their most covered songs. There were versions from Peter Tosh, Third World, Johnny Clarke and "toasts" from Big Youth and Dillinger.

The group did a number of recordings for several different labels, such as Sound Dimension, Secret Agent, Antrim, Clinch and Sound Tracs, which where released during the mid-70s. This material should have been released on a follow-up LP under the Clinch label, but it fell into the wrong hands, with the result that it was sold illegally.

But Bernard, Donald and Linford went back into the studio and re-recorded the tracks, which produced the album *Arise* in 1978. It was released in England under the Front Line label, but not in Jamaica. One year later, in 1979, the group had a phenomenal performance at Sunsplash.

With recordings at the studios of Dynamic, Joe Gibbs and Harry J's, such as "Peculiar Number", "This Is Not The End", "Praise Him", "Prophesy" and "Forward Jah", The Abyssinians proved that they had not lost any of their roots nor their charismatic talent. The members of the group later went their separate ways but reunited in 1990. They recorded new material, including the singles "African Princess" and "Swing Low".

Alton Ellis O.D.

Alton Nehemiah Ellis O.D., was born in 1939 in Kingston, Jamaica. He attended Boys Town School, where he often broke into the music room in order to play the piano. After numerous break-ins, the security decided to just allow him access to the room.

As a youth, he was also fascinated with American soul artistes, and spent much of his time studying them. He was quite a good dancer, and won many competitions, and talent shows, such as Vere John's Opportunity Hour Talent Contest, until he decided that he was tired of dancing and started to sing.

In 1958, he had the privilege of performing for the then Governor General of Jamaica, Sir Hugh Foote, who visited Boys Town. He was so impressed with Alton's performance that he met with him after the show. Alton decided to start a full-time singing career. He later founded the Coxsone Dodd Recording Organisation. His first song, "Muriel" was recorded on a one-track machine at the Federal Studios. For payment, he received fifteen pounds and three T-shirts. After this incident, he started to record at Duke Reid's studio.

Three weeks later, he recorded his second song, "My Heaven," with Eddie Perkins. This song also featured Roland Alphonso, on the tenor saxophone. In almost all his songs, Alton Ellis sang about a girl called Pearl, including hits such as "I'm Still In Love", "Girl I've Got A Date" and "I'm Just a Guy".

In 1966, he recorded "Dance Crasher" and "Cry Tough". In an interview, when asked about the difference between Coxsone and Reid, Ellis stated that Coxsone was more musically-oriented, younger and more sociable. For example, he would join them at rehearsals during the night, and even gave them money to buy food and ganja. Reid's only concern was business. Coxsone also danced with the artistes, but Reid never did. Coxsone Dodd also had the better artistes and the better songs.

In 1966, Alton Ellis went on a tour of England for several months with Ken Boothe and the Soul Brothers band. On his LP *Mr. Soul Of Jamaica*, Alton Ellis

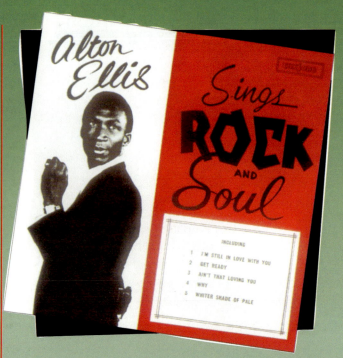

is supported musically by Tommy McCook and The Supersonics. The track "Chatty Chatty" is quite excellent.

In 1993, Alton celebrated his thirtieth anniversary at The Palais, Hammersmith, which became an annual event. With an evergreen voice, Alton Ellis was the undisputed King of rocksteady. In 2006, he was inducted into the International Reggae And World Music Awards Hall Of Fame. He died on October 10, 2008, of cancer. His death prompted a statement from Jamaica's Culture Minister Olivia 'Babsy' Grange, who said, "Even as we mourn the great Alton Ellis, we must give thanks for his monumental contribution to the development of Jamaica's popular music."

The Paragons

The Paragons were originally Garth "Tyrone" Evans (the chief writer and producer), Bob Andy, Junior Menz and Leroy Stamp. In 1964, Stamp was replaced by John Holt, and Howart Barret replaced Menz.

The early Paragons sound was heavily influenced by American soul music and used the tight vocal harmonies of Jamaican groups of the early 1960s. In 1964, the group caught the attention of the record producer Duke Reid, and they cut a succession of popular singles for his Treasure Isle label.

After this early success Bob Andy quit the group, and the Paragons abandoned their soulful sound to become the most popular rocksteady act in Jamaica, but disagreements over money led to the band's breakup in 1970. Of the band members only John Holt went on to have a solo career.

The group's impressive collection of songs were recorded at Dodd's studio One and Duke Reid's Treasure Isle studio. In fact, fifteen of the songs recorded at Studio One later became massive hits, including "The Tide Is High", which was later made popular by the American group Blondie.

On the rocksteady album *On the Beach*, the group was backed by Tommy McCook and the Supersonics. The title song, "On the Beach", painted a picture of holiday in Jamaica. This song is followed by "Island in the Sun". Also included on this album is the song "Yellow Bird" which is a favourite among tourists.

The Clarendonians

The Clarendonians, named after the Jamaican parish of Clarendon, consisted of Fitzroy "Ernest" Wilson and Peter Austin, coming together as duo in 1963. They also recorded as part of the Soul Lads. Clement Dodd expanded the group to a trio with seven-year-old Freddie McGregor. They worked often as a duo, with McGregor and Wilson recording as Freddie & Fitzie, and McGregor and Austin recording as Freddie & Peter.

Together, the duo Austin and Wilson has been performing for over thirty-five years. They represent the voices of the depressed people of the world, with remarkable lyrics, such as those contained in the song, "Rules Of Life", released in 1966: *"I will teach my people and liberate them, lead them to victory, let them know that they have*

rights and that they have to struggle for their rights".

Ernest Wilson was the first member who started a solo career. Freddie McGregor took some more time to establish himself in a solo career, but since the late 1970s, he has been one of the biggest names in reggae.

Since the days of ska to rocksteady, and even to reggae, the Clarendonians have performed at some classic shows, including Jamaica's Golden Oldie Part 3, which was a nostalgic show with performances from Alton Ellis, Ken Parker and Leroy Brown.

They recorded their first song, "A Day Will Come", which was released under Leslie Kong's Beverley label, followed by "Muy Bien" and "You Are A Fool", released under Duke Reid's Treasure Isle label.

In addition, they have recorded numerous other songs at Studio One, which are worthy of mention, as they enjoyed frequent airplay on the radio stations in Jamaica. These include "You Can't Keep A Good Man Down", Won't See Me", "Rude Boy Gone A Jail", "Sho Be-Do Be Do", "Rudie Bam Bam", "Tables Gonna Turn" and "Good Buy Forever". These songs are also on the first and only Studio One album *The Best Of The Clarendonians*.

The tracks were accompanied by musicians such as Sly Dunbar, Leroy Smart, Ranchie McLean, Bo Peep Bowen and Scully Sims. The engineer for the project was Sylvan Morris.

The Techniques

The Techniques is a rocksteady group, which originated from West Kingston. The members were discovered at the Jamaica Festival Competition in 1964, when they performed as members of the Victors Youth Band, which won the Ska and Mento competition.

The group was formed by Winston Riley, Slim Smith, Frederick Waite and Franklin White. Smith left the group in 1966 and was replaced by Pat Kelly.

In 1966, they recorded a cover of Fats Domino's hit "Oh Babe" for Duke Reid. An excellent example of their musical achievements is the LP entitled *Little Did You Know*, released under Duke Reid's Treasure Isle label.

The group left Treasure Isle in 1968, when Riley set up his own Techniques label.

The group members changed regularly, with Riley as the only constant member. Other members in the late 1960s were Lloyd Parks, Bruce Ruffin, Dave Barker and the veteran trumpeter Baba Brooks. Kelly returned for a time, recording lead vocals on "What am I to do?"

Later Lloyd Parkes and his We The People Band started working very successful on stage shows. On May 22, 1993, The Techniques performed songs from the rocksteady era at the Ranny Williams Entertainment Centre, located in Kingston. They performed hits such as "Ain't Too Proud To Beg", "Travelling Man" and "You Don't Care For Me".

The Melodians

The Melodians consisted of lead singer Tony Brevett and Brent Dowe and the harmony singer Trevor McNorton. They were not only good singers, but also good songwriters. Renford Cogle assisted with writing and arranging material.

As a rocksteady group during the 60's, their producer was Leslie Kong and between 1969 and 1972, they recorded and released some timeless reggae hits. Two of their biggest hits were "Sweet Sensations", later covered by UB40 and "Rivers of Babylon", released under the Island Label, and later covered by the German group, Boney M. It should be mentioned that the producer Frank Farian sang it himself, as it was alleged that Boney M did not have a good singing voice. "*Rivers Of Babylon*" became an anthem for the Rastafarian movement and was

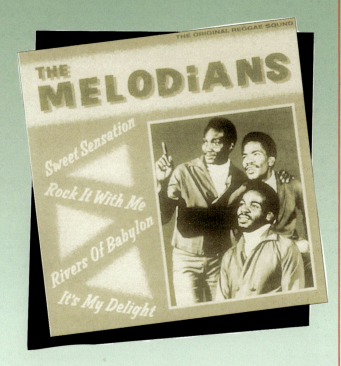

featured on a sondtrack for the movie *The Harder they Come*.

In 1973, Brent Dowe left the group for a solo career. The group reformed briefly a few years later and again in the early 1980s.

The Melodians regrouped again in the 1990s as part of the roots revival and continue to perform and record. In 1992, they recorded "Song of Love" on the Tapper Zukie label.

In 1993, a collectors' CD was released under the Heartbeat label, with songs such as "Come On Little Girl", "You Have Caught Me", I'll Get Along Without You", "Rivers Of Babylon", "Sweet Sensation"; the classics, "You Don't Need Me", and "Little Nut Tree"; and the title song, "Swing And Dine". It was Duke Reid and Sonia Pottinger (the producers), who made the compilation of this CD possible, as they had collected the old tapes and re-engineered them for release.

Throughout the late 1990s, The Melodians continued touring internationally, appearing at the Sierra Nevada World Music Festival in California in 2002. In November 2005, they embarked on a West Coast tour.

On January 28, 2006, Brent Dowe suffered a fatal heart attack at the age of 59. The remaining original members Tony Brevett and Trevor McNaughton continued touring in Europe and the U.S., backed by the Yellow Wall Dub Squad.

Ken Boothe

Ken Boothe, born in 1948 in Kingston, and popularly known as "Mr. Rocksteady", started his music career at the age of twelve years with Delroy Wilson. He did his first recording "Uno Dos" with Duke Reid, after which he started working with Coxsone Dodd. Together with Stranger Cole, they formed a duet. They did not earn much money at the time, as they only received clothes, in lieu of monetary profit for their recordings.

Boothe toured with Alton Ellis and the Soul Brothers Band for a month in England. He achieved his biggest hit in 1967 with the song "Puppet On A String". It should be mentioned that Sandie

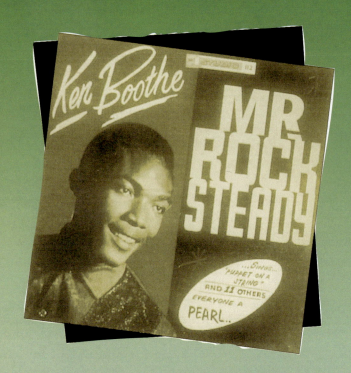

Shaw won first prize for performing this song as England's song during the Grand Prix Eurovision in 1967.

On his return to Jamaica, Boothe sang with Delroy Wilson and Marcia Griffiths. Ken Boothe had a number one hit for four weeks on the United Kingdom charts in 1974 with a version of David Gates' hit "Everything I Own". This Lloyd Charmers arrangement was copied in 1987 by Boy George, and again it reached the number one spot.

In 2003, Ken Boothe received the Order Of Distinction (OD) from the Jamaican Government. His biggest success as a solo artiste was achieved between 1966 and 1968. He released more than 40 albums throughout his career.

Delroy Wilson

Delroy Wilson was born in 1948 in Kingston. From the age of eight years, he was obsessed with music, which led to him becoming a singer. He developed his own music style from a combination of soul, jazz, funk and rock.

From the age of thirteen years, he achieved much success because of his versatility and his willingness to cooperate, which later earned him the nickname, Dean of Reggae.

He was first managed by Clement Coxsone Dodd, with whom he did his first recording entitled "Emmy Lou". This song was successfully followed by "Beautiful Baby", "I Shall Not Remove", "Joe Liges" and "I Don't Want To Cry", all of which were written by him and released on the LP, *I Shall Not Remove*. One of his earlier, well-known songs was "Sammy Dead", which was released at the beginning of the 1960s. He also had another LP entitled *Good All Over*, on which he told entertaining stories on each track.

The LP *Delroy Wilson: Collection of 22 Magnificent Hits* represents an excellent collection of his work as a singer and a songwriter. It was produced by Bunny "Striker" Lee. In 1972, he released one of his most popular songs "Cool Operator", which later became his nickname.

In his later years, with nostalgic music on the rise, Wilson became a fixture on every stage show of that type and was in demand as an entertainer, not only locally but also internationally.

In March 1995, after returning from the UK, he fell ill, and later died from cirrhosis of the liver, after spending more than two weeks in the hospital.

Byron Lee

Byron Lee and his friend Carl Brady formed the band The Dragonaires in

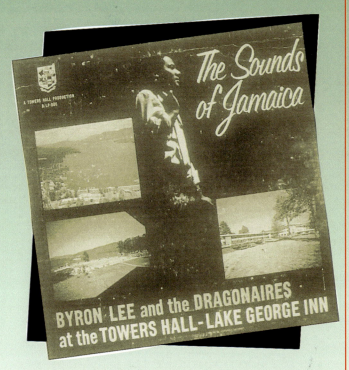

1950. Byron Lee's first song "Dumplings", released in 1950 under the WIRL Label, was an instant hit.

By 1956, Byron Lee And The Dragonaires became a fixture in the hotels. In 1962, Byron Lee, recognising the commercial possibilities and profitability of the WIRL label, bought it from Edward Seaga, and later renamed it Dynamic Sounds Recording, Inc., from which he built a distribution network.

He and his band produced several ska and rocksteady LPs. An example of the latter is the LP *Rocksteady Explosion*, which was released under the Trojan label. They released both reggae and carnival-oriented albums throughout the 1970s, and in 1975 took in another genre with the *Disco Reggae* album, released on Mercury Records in the U.S.

The group has released some 80-plus albums. *Byron Lee & The Dragonaires – 50th Anniversary*, a 3-CD set, released in 2000, is a commemorative collection boasting 60 hot tracks that memories are made of. The band also performed with Kevin Lyttle at the Cricket World Cup opening ceremony in 2007.

Byron Lee died on November 4, 2008, in Jamaica after a long battle with cancer. The band changed its name to "Byron Lee's Dragonaires" and continues to perform.

Derrick Harriott

Derrick Clinton Harriott was born in 1939. He started his singing career during the ska era with a vocal group called the Jiving Juniors, which did numerous recordings for Sir Clement Coxsone Dodd's Studio One. He is credited with inventing lover's rock.

Later, in 1962, he sang with the Vagabonds, and from 1965 to 1969, with the Mighty Vikings. He also did solo recordings, such as "What Can I Do" (a Donnie Elbert original), "I'm Only A Human", "My Three Lovers", "Close To Me", "Walk The Streets", "I Won't Cry" and "The Jerk and The Solomon".

He also performed on shows with Fats Domino and Sam Cooke.

At first, he produced and distributed records for Mr. Pottinger (Sonia Pottinger's

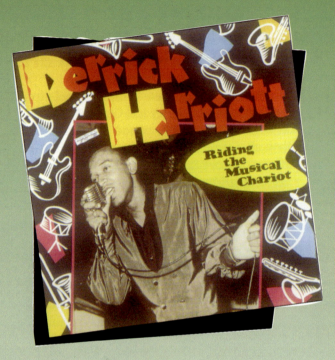

husband). At the time, Mr. Pottinger owned the Tip Top record label and also managed a record shop located on Orange Street in downtown Kingston.

In 1966, Harriott started his own record shop in Kingston, located at 125 King Street, where he started to distribute records for himself.

Today, he owns and operates a record shop at shop number 10 in Twin Gates Plaza, located on Constant Spring Road, Kingston.

Throughout his career, Derrick Harriott was multifaceted. He has performed at close to four theatres in Kingston, including the Ward, Carib, Regal and Star, where he often did more than one performance on any given day. He is also a producer.

In 1968, he produced "Stop That Train" with Keith and Tex (Keith Row and Texas Dixon). A later version was made popular by Peter Tosh. He also produced "Don't Look Back", released under the Electrola label, which was also made popular by Peter Tosh and Mick Jagger. Derrick Harriott also produced for himself and for Dennis Brown. He also had his own disco during the 1970s and often staged many dance shows.

Derrick Harriott owned numerous recording labels, such as Crystal, Crystal D, Moove And Groove and Rusty Dusty. His disco was called Musical Chariot. After decades in the music business, he cannot be described as a "rusty dusty" or "pick of the past" as one would say in Jamaica, as the numerous recordings that he has produced are symbols of his musical genius.

In July 2002, Derrick Harriott performed at the two-night Legends of Ska festival in Toronto, Canada, with other performers such as: The Skatalites, Rico Rodriguez, Lester Sterling, Johnny Moore, Lynn Taitt, Prince Buster, Alton Ellis, Lord Creator, Justin Hinds, Roy Wilson, Derrick Morgan and Lord Tanamo.

John Holt

John Kenneth Holt was born in July 1947 in Kingston. He was lead singer of The Paragons but left them at the beginning of 1970 to start his solo career at Studio One. He had hits such as "Ok Fred", "Strange Things", "I Can't Get You Off My Mind" (a cover of the Bob Andy hit) and "I Don't Want To See You Cry", which was also a hit for Ken Boothe.

At the beginning of the 1980s, he recorded a reunion LP with the Paragons, *The Paragons Return*, produced by Bunny Lee and Tyrone Evans.

John Holt's biggest success was his album *1000 Volts Of John Holt*, released in 1973 on the Trojan label. This album included hits such as "Help Me Make It Through The Night", originally recorded by Kris Kristofferson.

The album *Dusty Roads* was released a year later and was followed by the LP *2000 Volts Of John Holt*, also released under the Trojan label, and included such songs as "I'll Take A Melody", "Peace And

Love", "Yester-Me, Yester-You, Yesterday" and a cover version of Bob Marley's "Keep On Moving".

In 1982, he again had big hits with "Queen Of The Ghetto" and "Sweetie Come Brush Me". Later in that same year, he performed at Reggae Sunsplash, where his performance was well received by his adoring fans, and where he also made new converts. He again performed at Reggae Sunsplash in 1992.

John Holt is one of the most productive artistes in the business, with over fifty LPs to his credit, which have all been successful. Today, he lives and works in Miami.

Freddie McGregor

Born in 1956 in Clarendon, Jamaica, Freddie McGregor started singing at the age of seven with the Clarendonians (which later became known for songs such as "Ten Guitars", "Do Good", "It Will Follow You", "Why Did You Do It", "Hey Girl" and "Sho-Be Do Be-Do"), even though he was not a formal member of the group.

According to group member Peter Austin (at a press conference held in September 1992 for the Rocksteady Reunion) from time to time, Freddie would travel with them to concerts, from Clarendon to Kingston, often singing duets with a member of the band.

Growing up, Freddie McGregor had a crisp, clear and refreshing voice. While at school, he learnt to play the guitar, piano and drums. His formal musical education, however, arguably started at Studio One, where he eventually made his solo debut with the album *Bobby Baylon*. The album was released in

1980 under the Studio One label, and consisted of songs that went back as far as 1973, such as "I Am A Revolutionist".

He did recordings with Jackie Mittoo, The Heptones, The Gaylads, Bob Marley and The Wailers and The Skatalites. He also worked as a producer on Judy Mowatt's album *Black Woman*.

He did some additional recordings with Studio One, after which he worked with Niney The Observer and Linval Thompson, before returning to Studio One. In 1983, he became Ras Record's first artiste and became internationally known with the songs "Guantanamera" and "To Be Poor Is A Crime".

McGregor has had a number of other hits, including songs such as "Big Ship" and "Push Come To Shove", as well as his cover version of "I Just Don't Want To Be Lonely", released in 1987, under the Ras Records label. All of these songs appeared on the music charts in England.

To date, he has recorded fifteen LPs for Polydor, a partnership that lasted until 1989. Freddie performed at Reggae Sunsplash in 1984, 1988, 1990, 1992 and every year since.

He is untiring as a music producer and singer and performer. His LPs entitled *Sings Jamaican Classics: Volume Two*, released in 1992, under the America-based VP Label and *Hard To Get*, released under the England-based Greensleeves label, are testimonies to this fact.

On May 22, 1993, he performed at the White River Reggae Bash, a reggae concert sponsored by Jamaica's only reggae radio station, IRIE-FM, and held in Ocho Rios, located on Jamaica's north coast.

He established the Big Ship Recording Studio and has produced records for many artistes, including Luciano and Mikey Spice. Today, his sons Chino and Stephen help to carry on his legacy.

REGGAE: FROM JIMMY CLIFF TO BOB MARLEY

JIMMY CLIFF

James Chambers, more popularly known as Jimmy Cliff, was born in April 1948 in Sommerton, St. Catherine. At the age of 14 years, he persuaded Leslie Kong to let him record at his Beverly's Recording Studio. By 1962, under the new name, Jimmy Cliff, he released his first song, "Hurricane Hattie", which tells the story of a hurricane that was approaching Jamaica. The song later became a number one hit. This recording was then followed by "Miss Jamaica" and "King of Kings", and a tour of the Caribbean with Byron Lee and The Dragonaires. It was also during this period that he recorded "Many Rivers To Cross".

He migrated to England in 1964, where he recorded "Many Rivers To Cross", which was released under the Island label. But he was not as successful there. Cliff, however, attained success in Brazil, where he won second place in a song festival competition with the song, "Waterfall". He subsequently toured North America for nine months.

On his return to Jamaica in 1968, he recorded "Vietnam" with Byron Lee at Lee's Dynamic Studio, followed by "Wonderful World, Beautiful People", and "You Can Get It If You Really Want", which was recorded at Leslie Kong's studio.

In 1971, he became a big movie star, when he played the role of Ivan Martin in the classic Jamaican film *The Harder They Come*. The movie also featured some of his songs, including "You Can Get It If You Really Want", "Many Rivers To Cross", "The Harder They Come", and "Sitting In Limbo", all of which he produced.

As reggae became internationally recognised throughout the world, Cliff worked more as a composer. But he did not forget his first love, singing, and by 1974, he again had another hit song entitled "Don't Let It Die".

He later signed a contract with Sarner Brothers, located in California, United States of America but has done most of his recordings in Jamaica, with Jamaican artistes and musicians.

With the 1985 album *Cliff Hanger* he won a Grammy Award for Best Reggae Album.

Ironically, Jimmy Cliff is better known for his film appearances than for his music. He, however, remains one of Jamaica's best composers and singers.

The government of Jamaica honoured Cliff on October 20, 2003 with the Order Of Merit, the nation's third highest honour, in recognition of his contributions to the film and music of Jamaica.

In 2007, Cliff performed at the opening ceremony of the Cricket World Cup. In 2008, he appeared at the Jazz World Stage at the Glastonbury Festival.

CULTURE

Culture was a roots reggae trio founded in 1976 with lead singer Joseph Hill and his brothers-in- law Albert Wagner and Kenneth (Roy) Dayes as backing vocalists.

The group was first formed under the name "The African Disciples". In 1973,

they recorded their first LP entitled *Two Sevens Clash* at Joe Gibbs' studio. This album came out on the Joe Gibbs label in 1977. During this time, only groups that had contracts with producers were respected. In other words, no contract, no respect.

Even as reggae developed and changed, largely due to the use of synthesizers, the group remained committed to their roots, producing spiritually-oriented Rasta chants, as well as socially conscious anthems, which has filled their adoring fans with much enthusiasm.

According to Hill, "Roots is a legend and will remain a legend for the people who take part in it. Our message is conscious, decent and true."

The group's most recent LP is entitled *Wings Of A Dove*. The lyrics speak to the history of Jamaica, Columbus, Henry Morgan, pirates and looters.

It was promoted as passionate, inspiring, and excellent. But the proof, however, is in the listening. The record is surprisingly good, maybe because many expect the classic roots-harmony to become boring, which has happened to many groups. In fact, only a very few have survived the competition and the evolution of reggae over the last decade.

The group has identified Bob Marley, Burning Spear, Gregory Isaacs, Frankie Paul, Cocoa Tea and Beres Hammond as the singers they like most. According to the members, "these artistes do not stay on the indecent side (of the music). They do not sing slack lyrics, which do not fit roots reggae. An intelligent world should have respect for women. Culture plays decent music than can even be played in churches."

The musical style on the LP is more modern, quicker and more suited for dancing. There is even a song that could be classified as rub-a-dub/gospel-reggae.

The group does not like to travel much. As they often state, "when Jah is sleeping, we are doing the same."

In 1982 the three singers went their separate ways and did their own recordings, but in 1986, the original members reunited to record two highly regarded albums – *Culture in Culture* and *Culture at Work*. These releases marked the beginning of a very busy period for the group, including annual albums and countless tours.

Ire'lano Malomo temporarely replaced Kenneth Dayes, who left the group in 1993. Telford Nelson joined on harmony vocals in 1999. Their *World Peace* CD came out on Heartbeat Records in June 2003.

Joseph Hill, who came to symbolise the face of Culture, died in Germany on August 19, 2006, while the group was on tour. Now his son, Kenyatta Hill, sings with the band.

The Mighty Diamonds

The Mighty Diamonds are a roots reggae trio with a strong Rastafarian influence. The group, which comprises Donald "Tabby" Shaw as lead singer, Fitzroy "Bunny" Simpson and Lloyd "Judge" Ferguson, was formed in 1969. Earlier on, they produced their own records, including "Just Can't Figure Out", before they went to Studio One. They are best known for their 1976 debut album *Right Time*, produced by Joseph Hoo Kim on the Channel One label. The title song, done in Rockers style, was their first big hit. Other tracks were "Have Mercy, Africa" and "I Need A Roof", which demonstrated the group's harmonious style. In 1979 they released "Deeper

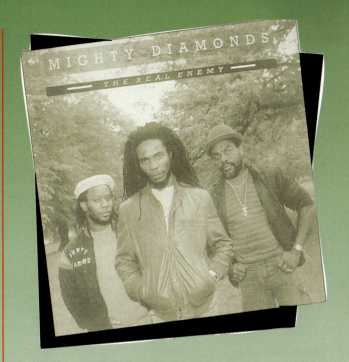

Roots" and also their first singles "Country Living" and "Hey Girl" were recorded on the Channel One label.

"Pass The Kutchie" became an international hit when first released and again when it was covered by the Musical Youth and released as "Pass The Dutchie".

At concerts, the Mighty Diamonds sings silky-soft harmonies and conscious lyrics, but the music is as tough as their name suggests, with lots of energy and power. Though music in general has changed over the years, The Mighty Diamonds have remained consistent.

Tabby, Bunny and Judge have produced over 40 albums in their long career, including *The Moment Of Truth* released under the Island label in 1992.

"Funky Kingston" and "Pressure Drop" were featured on the reggae radio station K-JAH Radio West in the video game *Grand Theft Auto San Andreas*, released in October 2004.

"Funky Kingston" was also featured in the video game *Scarface: The World Is Yours*.

Max Romeo

Maxie (Maxwell Livingston) Smith was born in 1947 in St. D'Acre, St James, Jamaica. He started recording while working as a salesman for producer B.K. Calnek, at the Jamaican-English Calton label. Together, they recorded about twenty-five singles under the name The Emotions with Max Romeo as a lead singer. Their first song "A Rainbow", released in 1967, reached number two on the music charts on both radio stations in Jamaica at the time. Five additional songs were released in 1968 under the Calton label, after which Max was produced by Bunny Lee.

Back then, Max Romeo was known primarily for his sex-oriented songs. One of his first songs with Bunny, "Wet Dreams", was a hit in England in 1968 and 1969, but shortly thereafter, was blacklisted by the BBC because it was deemed too indecent, with the result that it could not be played on the radio stations or in public. Despite this, however, the sales figures rose to 500,000, and the song remained on the English charts for twenty-six weeks. It is interesting to note that this song again appeared in 1980, and became a big hit in England. But this time, no one cared about the lyrics.

Max Romeo went on tour in England between 1969 and 1971, after which he returned to Jamaica. He worked with Bunny Lee until 1975, followed by Lee Perry, to record the album *War inna Babylon.* He changed his reputation from playboy to dread, and released numerous songs for many different producers.

In 1972, his song "Let the Power Fall" was used as a rally song for the People's National Party (PNP) during that year's General Elections. Again, it is interesting to note that it was the same political party that banned his song "War in a Babylon" during the 1976 elections. Max Romeo, as a Rastafarian, was one of the first members of that sect to criticize, using his song "Rasta Bandwagon" to lash out at people who became Rastafarians only because it was fashionable to do so.

He owned and operated a sound system named Ro-Max Hi-Fi and produced his own records on the Romax Label. In 1977, Mango Records released for the first time a record that was produced by Max Romeo himself. The album, *Reconstruction,* was recorded in the Harry J Studios. In the ensuing years, he wrote songs for the Broadway musical *Reggae* with producer Michael Butler. During this time, he traveled to New York, where he remained until the musical ended. He also did several interviews while there.

In 1981, he released the album *Holding Out My Love To You* under the Shanachie label, on which Keith Richards of the Rolling Stones played lead guitar, and Sly and Robbie on bass and drums respectively. The album was produced by Geoffrey Chung and Earl Chin, and recorded at Channel One. Sly and Robbie played the bass and drums. In 1990, he returned to Jamaica and toured and recorded regularly.

His track "I Chase the Devil" was featured on the US reggae radio station K-JAH Radio West in the popular video game *Grand Theft Auto San Andreas*, released in October 2004.

Toots & The Maytals

In 1962, Frederick "Toots" Hibbert (born in 1945 in May Pen, Clarendon, Jamaica), Nathaniel "Jerry" Matthias and Ralphus "Raleigh" Gordon founded The Vikings. They first worked with Coxsone Dodd, with whom they recorded and released their first ska hit entitled "Hallelujah". Their next song, "Six and Seven Books of Moses", for the same producer also became a hit.

In 1963, they changed producers and started recording for Prince Buster's Orange Street Studios. It was while there that the group changed its name to The Maytals.

Songs recorded for Prince Buster included "Pain In My Belly", "Bet You Lied" and "Little Flea". They also recorded songs for Byron Lee, including "It's You", "Daddy" and "Never You Change".

In 1966, the group for the first time won the Jamaica Festival Song Competition with the song "Bam Bam". They eventually won this competition two more times.

The second version of "Bam Bam" was also produced for the movie *Countryman,* which was released in 1982. All recordings produced for Leslie Kong were released on three LPs under the Trojan Label One was entitled, "Monkey Man", which contained a track of the same title. It was quite successful in England.

Frederick "Toots" Hibbert can arguably be credited for inventing the word reggae, which was introduced into the English language in 1968, with the song "Do the Reggae". He may have even created the musical style for this genre of music. Toots has survived all the highs and lows in the music industry/business in Jamaica; and together with The Maytals, they released "Six and Seven Books", which was one of their first hits.

According to Toots, he was influenced by the music legends, Sam Cooke and Otis Redding.

Stephen Davis in his book *Reggae Bloodlines*, quoted Toots as saying, "(I) invented the reggae. Reggae means simply, it comes from the people: all the music, the rhythm, but also the people's poverty and the suffering."

One of the best studio LPs by Toots and the Maytals was released in 1980 under the Island label. It consists of songs going back to the ska era and the early years.

In 1980, the group performed at the London Hammersmith Palais. The live LP produced from that concert is considered one of the best live LPs to date.

The LPs that were produced by Warrick Lynn, Joe Boyd and Chris Blackwell, after the death of Leslie Kong in 1971, were different. Among those that were very successful were *Funky Kingston* (on Island and Trojan), "In The Dark" (on the Trojan label), and *Reggae Got Soul*, on the Dynamic label and released in 1976.

The Heptones

The Heptones was founded in 1965 with members Earl Morgan (born in 1945), Barry Llewellyn (1947) and Leroy Sibbles (1949). They grew up in Trench Town, Kingston.

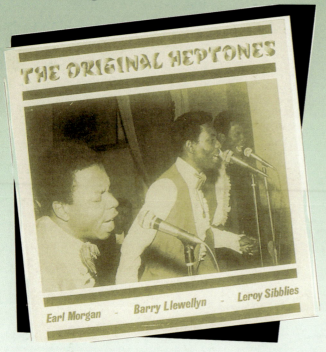

Earl Morgan   Barry Llewellyn   Leroy Sibblies

They worked with Coxsone Dodd for his Studio One label. Their first hit in 1966 was "Fatty Fatty". Other hits followed, such as "Baby", "Why Did You Leave", "Let's Fall In Love" and "Cry Baby Cry". From 1970 until 1973, they worked with numerous other producers.

They supported the People's National Party during the election campaign with "Hypocrite" and "Freedom for the People", which was recorded for Joe Gibbs in 1972. "I Miss You" was recorded for Geoffrey Chung.

In 1973, they had a big hit with "Book of Rules". That track, recorded for the producer Harry Johnson, entered the English charts. Leroy Sibbles emigrated Canada in 1973, and the group ceased recording until 1976.

In 1976, H. Johnson produced the albums, *Cool Rasta*, released under the Trojan Label and *Night Food* under the Island-Label.

In 1977, when the group was revived, Lee Perry produced the album *Party-Time* (released under the Mango Label, a United States-based subsidiary of Island Records).

Leroy Sibbles left the Heptones again in 1981 to start his solo career. The original trio reunited in 1995 and recorded the album *Pressure!*, produced by Tapper Zukie.

Inner Circle

Inner Circle was formed by the brothers Ian and Roger Lewis in 1968.

Michael "Ibo" Cooper (keyboards), Stephen "Cat" Coore (guitar), Willie Steward (drums) and Bunny "Rugs" Clarke (vocals), Funky Brown (vocals) and Prilly (vocals) completed the original Inner Circle band.

In 1973, there were some changes, and Cooper, Steward and Coore founded Third World.

Jacob Miller, the Caruso of the Caribbean, and a friend of the musicians, took over the band, and together with Lewis brothers (Roger and Ian "Munty" Lewis), continued to perform under the same name.

Inner Circle was one of the first reggae groups to record and perform songs that were non-critical of social events. Rather, their music was more on the lighter side and easy on the ears.

Jacob Miller had his own singing style, vibrating in the tune, sometimes even trembling, and where he often repeated several syllables like a staccato. He was a master of the vocal parody, as captured by his cover version of the song "Delilah", a Tom Jones original, which he performed very well.

The first two LPs released by the group consisted mostly of songs previously done by other reggae artistes. They were recorded for the English Trojan label. These were then followed by another two LPs recorded for the United States-based Capitol label.

The group eventually returned to their original roots style, and produced the LP *Killer Miller*, released under the RAS and Island Labels.

Jacob Miller started his singing career at Coxsone Dodd's studios at the age of twelve years. At the age of twenty years (in 1975) he was awarded "Singer Of

The Year" by the Guinness Brewery. Apart from his singing, he became known as a dancer who bared his belly with a ganja joint in his hand, on stage at a public performance of the song "Tenement Yard".

Joe Ortiz joined the group for the European tour from 1978-1980.

Jacob Miller died on March 23, 1980, at the age of twenty-five years, in a car crash. Some days later, the album *Tenement Yard* was re-released with several of the tracks from 1976 album, *Reggae Thing*. The album *Jacob Killer Miller* was also released.

One of the best Jacob Miller productions was a solo LP entitled *Wanted*, backed by the Inner Circle band.

In 1986, when the new lead singer Carlton Coffie joined Inner Circle, the group again became popular. They jumped to the top of the charts in 1992, both in Jamaica and Europe, with the songs "Sweat" and "Bad Boys"; the latter of which was the title song for the American television series *Cops*. Both songs remained for several weeks on both the R & B and Pop Charts in the United States.

They also remained for several weeks at the top of the charts in Germany, largely due to their successful Germany tour. Both songs are on the LP/CD *Bad To The Bone*.

Carlton Coffie performs on stage with a lot of energy and action. Inner Circle were the featured group at the White River Reggae Bash, held in Ocho Rios, Jamaica, on May 22, 1993, where they performed for the second time in Jamaica after fifteen years.

Coffie was ill for a long period in 1995 and decided after his recuperation to start a solo career. He was later

replaced by Kris Bentley.

The members of the group have been residing in Florida since 1983, where they are contracted to Big Beat/Atlantic Label. In 2008, Junior Jazz became the lead singer.

Inner Circle today consists of the two Lewis Brothers, Ian and Roger; Junior Jazz, Lancelot Hall, Bernard Touter Harvey and Lancelot Hall.

Today, the members of the group run Circle House, one of the most popular and respected recording studios in Miami.

Third World

In 1973, Stephen "Cat" Coore, and Michael "Ibo" Cooper founded the group Third World, after they had separated from Inner Circle.

Their search for a new sound started with the formation of the new band. But success only came after they moved to London, where they stayed for an extended period.

The band went through a number of changes with its members. Initially it consisted of Stephen "Cat" Coore; Michael "Ibo" Cooper, who later left the group; Richard Daley (bass), Cornell Marshall (who later joined the Wailers Band) Willy "Root" Stewart, who was later replaced by Milton "Prilly" Hamilton (lead vocals), and who was in turn, replaced with Bunny "Rugs" Clark; and Carrot Jarret (percussion), who also joined the Wailers Band in 1988.

Their debut album *Kumina*, on which they performed the St. Thomas Kumina-style of drumming, was released in 1976. They also do this performance on stage as a salute to the African roots of this popular Jamaican music.

The musical background of the members is quite diverse, but they are unified by their training in the playing of classical music and instruments. For example, "Cat" Coore plays the cello, "Ibo" Cooper, who has trained in classical music, and Willie Stewart was educated at the Billy Moe's Percussion and Drum School in Los Angeles. In this regard, the group does not see itself as a group out of one bag, but rather they "created the bag".

To date, Third World performs some of the most innovative roots rockin' reggae

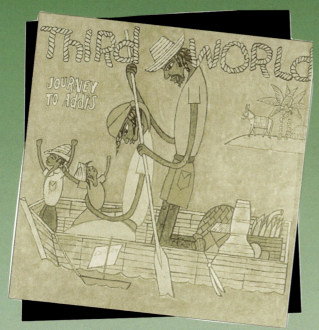

music of all time, which is characterised by a mixture of roots, soul, pop and hip hop. The group also likes to mix reggae with runk, African and Latin music.

In 1989, Third World signed a contract with Mercury records. Three years later, in the summer of 1992, they released their thirteenth album and the second for Polygram/Mercury, entitled *Committed*. It was well-received and quite successful.

The album consists of a range of musical genres, including the nostalgic "Give The People What They Need" from the ska era, to "Mi Legal", which has a more contemporary sound. Never has a reggae band achieved such international success as the Reggae Ambassadors, as the group is popularly called. Their repertoire includes such mega hits as the cover version of Gamble and Huff's, "We've Found Love" and "Try Jah Love", which was done in collaboration with Stevie Wonder. They have covered a wide range of subject matters in their lyrics. All members of the band are Rastafarians, so naturally, the subject of Rastafarianism is featured in most of their songs. They have written and recorded a number of songs, which are critical of the social problems in Jamaica, as well as several love ballads.

In addition to their recordings, Third World has toured from Africa to Japan, Europe to North America and from Australia to the Caribbean, several times over.

Their most balanced album to date, and possibly the most commercially successful, was their fourth LP entitled *The Story's Been Told*, which was produced by the group and released in 1979.

In 1980, they released *Arise in Harmony*, the first album that was recorded entirely in Jamaica at Tuff Gong studios.

There is, however, a big difference between the live performances and the studio recordings. For example, while on stage, the group likes to experiment and is livelier.

According to Michael "Ibo" Cooper, "You have reggae, you have soul and you have the Third World sound."

Despite several lineup changes, including the departures of Cooper and Stewart, the band is still performing and recording today. They appeared at the Cricket World Cup 2007 Opening Ceremony in Jamaica.

The Meditations

The Meditations, a vocal trio, was formed in 1974 by Ansel Cridland, a native of Savannah-La-Mar, St. Elizabeth; and Danny Clarke and Winston Watson, both from Trench Town, Kingston.

All three member of the group were experienced musicians prior to starting the Meditations. Danny Clarke was former member of Alton Ellis and the Flames, Ansel Cridland led the vocal group Ansel and the -Linkers and had recorded songs such as, "Bongo Man" and "Nyaman Story" and Winston was a former vocalist Lloyd Parkes and the Termites.

Together, as the Meditations, however, they recorded their three first singles with Dobby Dobson in 1975. They were "Babylon Trap Them", led by Danny, who arrived some measure of success; "Woman Piabba", led by Winston, and which attained the No. 1 spot on the local music charts; and "Rome" led by Ansel.

In the following year, they recorded and released their first album entitled *Message From The Meditations*. It was from this album that they achieved their first international hit, with a song entitled "Woman Is Like A Shadow" – a song that contained some controversial lyrics about heterosexual relationships.

Their second album *Wake Up*, was released in 1977, and contained the hit song, "Fly Your Natty Dread", produced by Dobby Dobson and recorded in Harry J's Studio. There were other hits on this album, such as "Wake Up", "Turn Me Loose" and "Lucifer". After the success of the album, the group toured Bermuda and New York, where they performed at Madison Square Garden, The Beacon Theatre and the popular nightclub, My Father's Place.

They also performed at the now legendary One Love Concert in 1978.

As backing vocalists, they supported The Congo, Junior Marvin, and Gregory Isaacs In 1980, they were also the backing vocals for Bob Marley's "Rastaman Live Up", "Punky Reggae Party" and "Black Man Redemption".

Their next album *Guidance,* released in 1980, was the group's first production. It contained tracks such as "Marriage", a song that was a hit in New York;

"Warmongers", "Life Is Not Easy On Ya" and "Hard Live".

"No More Friend" was the title of their fourth album in 1983 and was also the first dance album produced by the trio. It was done in collaboration with the Roots Radics Band, which played the rhythm, and was produced by Linval Thompson.

In August 1985, Danny and Winston stayed in New York, while Ansel left the group and returned to Jamaica. He later renamed himself Ansel Meditation.

Despite the separation, in 1988, they released the LP, *For The Good Of Man* under the Greensleeves Label.

They reunited in 1993 to record the album *The Return of The Meditations*. All three group members later emigrated to The United States.

Lee "Scratch" Perry

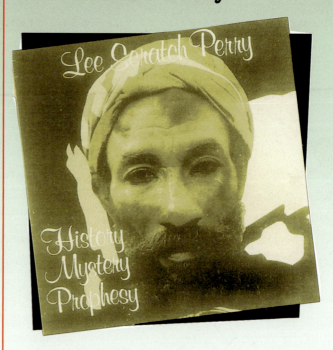

Rainford Hugh Perry was born in 1936 in Kendal, Jamaica. He has used some psuedonyms, such as Pipecock Jaxxon and The Upsetter.

In 1955, at the age of 16, Lee Perry started his career in the Jamaican music industry at Clement Dodd's Downbeat Sound System. In 1959, when Dodd started to press his own records, Perry was employed as a producer. From time to time, he would persuade Dodd to do recordings with Toots and The Maytals, which resulted in him working on their first single, "6 and 7 Books".

Initially, he co-produced a number of singles, before he became an independent producer. The Wailers LPs, *Soul Rebels* and *African Herbsman* are excellent examples of his work.

At the beginning of the 1960s, Jamaica was experiencing a number of social and political problems. There were frequent battles between the supporters of the two major political parties, the People's National Party (PNP) and the Jamaica Labour Party (JLP).

Street Gangs, who referred to themselves as "rude bwoys", were largely responsible for the violence, as they were often unemployed and literally had nothing else to do. Lee Perry and Bob Marley tried to use their music in an effort to return peace and calm to the troubled island.

It was during this time that the witch doctor himself, Lee Perry, produced some of his most memorable instrumental hits, such as, "Return of Django", "Clint Eastwood", "Man From M.I.5" and "Drugs and Poison", which were a tribute to reggae music.

Perry also has been a source of great support and assistance to the Wailers on their journey to the top. In addition to Bob Marley and the Wailers, he has produced for other artistes, such as Delroy Wilson, Junior Byles, U-Roy, I-Roy, Dennis Alcapone, Dillinger, The Mighty Diamonds,

The Heptones, Max Romeo and Gregory Isaacs.

Whether he is called Little, Scratch, Doctor Dick, King Perry, The Upsetter, Wonderman, or Super Ape, Lee "Scratch" Perry has been an inspiration to Jamaican musicians and artistes for more than thirty-five years.

In 1994, I saw him performing in Munich, Germany. He looked amazing despite all that he was wearing and what was hanging on him, but the performance was absolutely great.

In 2008, he released his album *Repentance*, coproduced by Andrew W.K. on Narrack Records.

Lee Perry now lives in Switzerland with his family.

Junior Byles

Kerrie Byles (Junior), also known as King Chubby and Junior Byles, was born in 1948 in Kingston. He worked with the Jamaica Fire Brigade until 1967, when he founded the group, The Versatiles with Louis Davis and a young

Asian called Dudley. They started recording for producer Joel Gibson (Joe Gibbs), which included songs such as "Just Can't Win", "Trust The Book", "The Time Has Come", "Push It In", "Lu Lu Ball" and "Long Long Time", all of which were released under the Amalgamated Label, a subsidiary of the Trojan label.

When he left The Versatiles in 1970, he recorded his first solo single for Lee Perry (who also produced for Joe Gibbs) entitled, "What's The World Coming To?", which was released by King Chubby under the Pama Supreme Label. Other recordings done with Perry were also successful, and he also won the Jamaica Festival Song Competition in 1972 with his song, "Da Da", which was later released on the LP *Beat Down Babylon: The Upsetter Years*, under the Trojan label.

The year 1972 was also a politically charged year in Jamaica. Prime Minister Hugh Shearer of the Jamaica Labour Party (JLP) and the Opposition People's National Party (PNP) led by Michael Manley, were campaigning vigorously against each other, which often led to street violence.

Michael Manley was at the forefront of the call for political change, and he started a musical campaign with the song "Prophet Joshua". Manley had a good rapport with producer Clancy Eccles, and Eccles together with Byles, produced and recorded the song, "Pharaoh Hiding", which suggested that Shearer should run away and let Manley "release the people from the oppression of the JLP".

There were other popular songs during the election campaign, including "King Babylon", featuring Shearer as "King Nebuchadnezzar of Babylon who leads a corrupt land". The most famous song of that campaign was Delroy Wilson's "Better Must Come".

The best song for the JLP was Leo Graham's "A Win Them", which accused the PNP of lying.

In 1973, Byles released his first album, *Beat Down Babylon*, which consisted of ten tracks, including the above-mentioned songs, released under the Trojan Label. In 1987, Trojan re-released the album as *Beat Down Babylon: The Upsetter Years*, but this time it consisted of fourteen tracks.

In 1974, Junior Byles recorded a version of Delroy Wilson's "Better Must Come", with the title "When Will Better Come". He also released "Curley Locks", under the DIP label (England), and Magnet label (rest of the world), which was relatively successful; two hundred and fifty thousand copies having been sold. This was followed by "The Long Way", also for DIP in 1975.

He has recorded for producers such as JoJo HooKim from Channel One; and Leroy Hollet and Duley Swaby's Ja-Man-Label.

His second LP *Jordan*, included songs such as "Chant Down Babylon", "Remember Me", "Lorna Banana" and "Ain't Too Proud to Beg" and also a version of the Folkes Brothers hit "Oh Carolina".

Byles recorded songs for Lloyd F. Campbell and Niney the Observer until 1976. Among these were "Run Run" (for Niney), which was an old Studio One hit, originally done by Delroy Wilson.

In 1979, Byles stopped recording because of illness. But seven years later, in 1996, he released the album, *Rasta No Pick Pocket*.

In the ensuing years, he worked on an album for Youth Promotion that was released in 1988, entitled *When Will Better Come*.

The Wailers (and others)

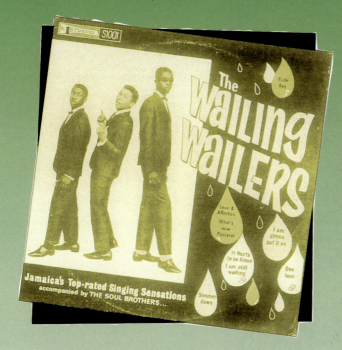

The Wailing Rude Bwoys, later called the Wailing Wailers, then shortened to The Wailers, consisted of Robert Nesta Marley, Bunny Livingston and Peter McIntosh. The name was a reflection of the time during which the group was formed. Later, Junior Braithwaite, Alwin "Secco" Patterson and the singer, Beverly Kelso joined the group.

Under the influence of Joe Higgs, who taught the Wailers, especially Bob Marley, the intricacies of the ska sound, the group began to write their own songs.

When they were matured musically, Higgs encouraged Coxsone Dodd to invest in them. Their first single, "It Hurts To Be Alone" was recorded for the sound systems, of which three hundred copies were distributed amongst Prince Buster, Lee Perry and Jack Mittoo, who was the keyboard player and arranger in Coxsone's Studio.

The next single, "Simmer Down", a ska mega hit, with Bob Marley as the lead singer, was recorded towards the end of 1963 and the start of 1964. The lyrics called on the young rowdies to calm their temper and stop the gang wars.

Also in 1964, the Wailers performed live, and had some number one hits with songs such as "Mr. Talkative", "I Don't Need Your Love", "Donna", Lonesome Feelings" and "Wings of Love."

Three years later, in 1967, Junior Braithwaite and Beverly Kelso left the group. By 1969, the group had recorded and released about thirty singles, including "Rude Boy", "Put It On" and "One Love" – a mixture of rhythm and blues and ska which was recorded with the Skatalites (Don Drummond and Rico Rodriguez) and the Soul Brothers (with Jackie Mittoo) as backing bands.

The group then released the album *The Wailing Wailers*, accompanied by the Soul Brothers, and released under the Studio One label.

Due to financial difficulties (the group did not earn much from the thirty or more singles which were released, as most of the monies remained with the recording companies) the group left Jamaica in 1967.

Bob Marley went to the United States of America. His American dream, however, was not realised at the conveyor belts of the Chrysler Company, where he was employed.

Subsequently, he was drafted into the army to go to Vietnam, but instead he returned to Kingston, Jamaica in 1968 and rejoined the Wailers.

He achieved much success with the Wailers, but his own productions were not as successful, largely due to the fact that there was not enough money to publish and promote the records.

They recorded only one song for Bunny Lee, "Mr. Chatterbox", which can be found on some collection LPs under the Trojan label.

In 1969, the Wailers teamed up with Lee Perry and produced the classic reggae LPs, *Soul Revolution Part Two* and *Soul Rebel*, on which was recorded the song, "Duppy Conqueror". With Perry's support and creativity, the now famous Wailers' sound began to evolve.

Later, Aston "Family Man" Barrett (bass) and Carlton Barrett (percussion) joined the Wailers, and became integral to the Wailers' concept.

Together, the group achieved much financial success, which allowed them to operate their own record shop, The Soul Shack, located on the King Street, Down Town Kingston; and their own recording company/studio, Tuff Gong. In 1971, they released their biggest hit at that time "Trench Town Rock".

Drummer Carlton Barrtett died in 1987.

It should be mentioned that it was from Tuff Gong that Bob Marley got the nickname Gong.

When the group became famous around the world, with Chris Blackwell as their producer, they often recorded with Lee Perry's studio band, the Upsetters.

With Chris Blackwell, a white Jamaican, and owner of the Island Label, and the use of modern studio facilities, the members of the band began realising their musical dreams for the first time.

The first two albums produced by Chris Blackwell under the Island Label were *Catch a Fire* and *Burnin'*, which were revolutionary productions, and which helped chart the course for the positive evolution of Jamaican music.

In 1973, the *Original Wailers* separated, and Peter Tosh, Bunny Wailer and Bob Marley started their solo careers. After Bob Marley left, the Wailers band continued successfully, especially as a touring band.

Elan Atias, discovered by guitarist Al Anderson, injected fresh excitement into the band.

Chris Blackwell eventually left Island Records in 1997 because of differences with Polygram, which had bought the label in 1989.

The Wailers have sold more than 250 million albums worldwide.

The new band members today are Junior Marvin, Al Anderson, Earl "Wya" Lindo, Rohan Reid, George Kouakou, Christian Cowlin, Papaa Nyarcoh, Erica Newell and Rochelle Bradshaw.

TIME WILL TELL

BOB MARLEY O.M.

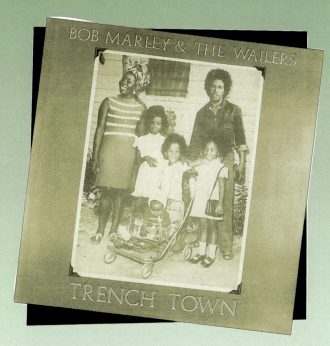

Robert "Bob" Nesta Marley O.M. was born in 1945 in Nine Mile in St. Ann.

His first two singles, "Judge Not" and "Do You Still Love Me?", were recorded for Leslie Kong in 1962, but they were released with his surname incorrectly spelt; *"Morley"* instead of *"Marley"*. In addition, the songs were not successful.

He played music and did rehearsals together with Bunny Livingston and Peter McIntosh.

During this time, he recorded five more songs for Leslie Kong, of which only "Terror" and "One Cup of Coffee" achieved marginal success.

Bob eventually left Kong when he realised that he was not paid for the last two songs that he had recorded for Kong.

On February 10,1966 he married Alpharita Anderson, more famously known as Rita Marley.

Bob Marley, together with Bunny Wailer and Peter Tosh, performed as the Wailers, and were very successful. But Marley's personality was too overpowering, with the result that both Peter Tosh and Bunny Wailer left the group to launch their solo careers.

Bob Marley then hired other musicians, including Al Anderson and Julian "Junior" Marvin (guitar), Tyrone Downie and Earl Lindo (keyboard), and from time to time Donald Kinsey (guitar), Chinna Smith and Joe Higgs to join him while he was on tour. There was also the back up vocalists, The "I-Three", which consisted of his wife Rita Marley, Marcia Griffiths and Judy Mowatt.

Sometime after 1970, Bob Marley joined the Rastafarian faith, typified by

the wearing of dreadlocks and the use of colours red, orange and green.

The LPs *African Herbsman* and *Rasta Revolution*, which were released outside of Jamaica in 1973, reflected his development and transformation.

Soon success was achieved with the release of the album *Natty Dread* at the beginning of 1975, which contained some of his best songs to date, including "Lively Up Yourself", "Them Belly Full" and "No Woman, No Cry".

By then, Bob Marley had accomplished almost all his goals. He was an excellent musician and a socio-cultural commentator. But it was his engaging performance while on stage, and the simply remarkable LPs that were released between 1975 and 1980, which earned him the title of the greatest reggae artiste of all time. These LPs were *Bob Marley And The Wailers Live!* (1975); *Rastaman Vibration* (1976); *Exodus* (1977); *Survival*, which consist of his now famous songs, "Natural Mystic", "Jammin" and "Positive Vibration"; and "Uprising" (1980).

Uprising was Bob Marley's last studio album and one of his most religious productions.

From Jamaica, his music conquered a top place in the world of rock music, largely due to his guttural, earthy voice and poetic lyrics.

One of his most emotional songs to date is "No Woman, No Cry", and the best known is the classic "I Shot The Sheriff".

Marley was instrumental in bringing together both leaders of the two major political parties, Prime Minister Michael Manley and Leader of the Opposition Edward Seaga, during the period of political hostility that characterised the late 1970s. In his inimitable style, Bob Marley, while on stage at the now legendary One Love Peace Concert, held on April 2, 1978 in Kingston, invited both men on stage where they shook hands, symbolizing a political truce, while he sang "Jah Live". Bob Marley was presented with the United Nations Peace Prize for the Third World for his efforts.

Other artistes who performed at this concert included Peter Tosh, Jacob Miller, Dennis Brown, Judy Mowatt, U-Roy, Junior Tucker and Althea & Donna.

Bob Marley died at the age of 36 on May 11, 1981 from cancer, at the peak of his popularity.

He, however, has left the world his courage, power and music, which continue to influence the lives of many people throughout the world.

Jamaica honoured him a month before his death with Order of Merit, the country's third highest honour.

In the same year of his death, his picture, together with the titles of some of his albums and songs ("Survival", "Exodus", "Is This Love","Comin' In From The Cold", "Positive Vibration", "War" and "Could You Be Loved") were featured on a series of seven stamps (with a value of one cent to three dollars).

In addition, there was an oval drawing of him, and a souvenir sheet measuring approximately 11 x 13.5 cm, with a stamp, valuing J$5.25, with his portrait in the middle, surrounded by music notes from his many record covers.

In London, there is a place called the "Marley Walk", which was named in his honour.

Bob Marley was inducted into the Rock and Roll Hall of Fame in 1994. *Time* magazine chose Bob Marley & The Wailers' album *Exodus* as the greatest album of the 20th century.

Island Records released a limited edition (10,000 copies) box set, which represented a compilation of nine LPs, with each containing a picture of Bob Marley on the front cover, and the lyrics to the songs on the back. In addition, there is a booklet, "Bob Marley: Soul Rebel-Natural Mystic", with photographs and texts by Adrian Boot and Vivian Goldman.

After his death, Rita Marley assumed management of Tuff Gong Studios, and also launched her solo career. Of the ten Marley children, Ziggy Marley And The Melody Makers have achieved much success in the music industry, both locally and overseas. Kymani started his musical career in 1997 and had a big hit with the song "Sensimillia". Damian "Junior Gong" made his breakthrough, in 1997 with his debut CD, *Mr. Marley*, which consisted of a mixture of his father's songs and new songs composed by his half-brothers Stephen and Kymani. Julian's debut album, *Lion In The Morning* was released in October 1996.

In September 1992, a four-CD-set entitled *Songs Of Freedom* with a total of seventy-eight songs was released. The first single released after his death was "Iron, Lion, Zion", which was not published until the CD-set was released. Apparently, it was found by Rita Marley in a cupboard at her home.

There is also an interesting book, which was published in 1983, and written by Timothy White, with the American title *Catch A Fire: The Life of Bob Marley*. It contains a lot of background information on Bob Marley, and a comprehensive discography.

Dennis Morris, from Epoch Productions Limited, London, in 1988 published a remarkable photographic essay entitled "Bob Marley Rebel With A Cause". It is photographic journey of the vision and message of the King of Reggae, from *Natty Dread* to *Exodus*". And for those who loved Bob Marley's words, there is a book written by Ian McCann, entitled, "Bob Marley in his own words", published by Omnibus Press in 1993.

The compilation album *Legend* was released in 1984, three years after Bob Marleys death, was the best selling reggae album ever with 10 times platinum in the US (sales of more than 20 million copies).

Songs Of Freedom

The 4-CD-set *Songs Of Freedom* with seventy-eight songs by Bob Marley, and a sixty-four-page booklet, contain Bob Marley's musical recordings from his first single during the golden ska and rocksteady eras, to his last concert in Pittsburgh in 1980.

The booklet contains short biographical notes on each of the songs, and the preface was written by Rita Marley. Authors such as Timothy White, publisher of the Billboard Magazine, and John "Rabbit" Bundrick, the keyboard player, who worked with Bob Marley during the 1970s, also contributed to the booklet. It also contains an anecdote in Jamaican patois, written by Derrick Morgan.

The booklet lists all the musicians and back-up singers who worked with Bob Marley, which really represents a "Who's Who" of Jamaican musicians.

The first CD, covered by a photograph of a young, short-haired Bob Marley, during his "rude boy days", consists of twenty-four of his songs recorded during the ska and rocksteady era (1962 to 1970), with Peter Tosh and Bunny Wailer. It was during this time that they worked with members of the Skatalites band and recorded with studio pioneers Clement "Coxsone" Dodd and Lee "Scratch" Perry.

These three "ghetto-youngsters" launched the reggae explosion of the 1970s. Many experts on reggae lovers are grateful to Bob Marley and the Wailers for their music from this period; especially for the tracks that Lee Perry, the innovative, eccentric studio genius recorded. They were arguably Bob's best recordings to date, including, "Judge Not" and "One Cup Of Coffee", both recorded for Leslie Kong in 1962; and the tracks "Bus Dem Shut", "Hypocrites", "Hammer", "Do It Twice", "Caution", "Back Out" and "I'm Still Waiting", "Mr. Brown" and the excellent tracks produced by the Wailers, "Duppy Conqueror", "Small Axe", "Don't Rock The Boat" and "Sun Is Shining".

The second CD, with eighteen songs, illustrated by a photograph of a young, short, curly-haired Bob Marley, takes us through another creative period of the Wailers and also through that period when the trio separated and launched their solo careers.

The best tracks on this CD are "Screw Face", "Craven Choke Puppy" and the suggestive "Lick Samba". There is also the previously unpublished medley recorded for Rabbit Bundrick in 1971 and two new songs the "High Tide Or Low Tide" and the reggae rocker "Iron, Lion, Zion", that had been on the British, Jamaican and German charts for a long time and was played often by the radio stations, both locally and overseas.

The third CD shows Bob as a reggae rebel during the period of his *Rastaman Vibration*, which contains very popular songs such as, "Who The Cap Fit", "War", "Rat Race", "Natural Mystic" and "Easy Shanking". There are also some rare tracks and previously unpublished versions of the hymn "Jah Live" and "Countryman" which, until the CD set was launched, was just a song on the soundtrack for the movie of the same name. There is also a jazz-like song entitled "Smile Jamaica" and a live version of Marley's first big hit, "No Woman No Cry", recorded at the Roxy in Los Angeles in 1976, which is very different from the popular version recorded at the Lyceum in London.

In addition, there is another version of the Wailer's classic "Keep On Moving", which was recorded in 1977 in London, where Bob Marley lived at that time.

The fourth CD, illustrated by a photograph of long, curly-haired Bob, during the 1980s, consists mainly of songs which demonstrates that Bob Marley was and still is one of the greatest song writer of the Twentieth Century. The lyrics offer insight into general problems of the world and especially Africa.

On this CD one can find the classics "Africa Unite", "So Much Trouble", "Zimbabwe", "Real Situation", "Survival", and "Babylon System", "Songs of Freedom"; the previously unpublished "Why Should", and the excellent "Redemption Song", which was recorded on September 23, 1980, when Bob told his band that he was too ill to continue the tour. He died eight month later in May, 1981.

Songs Of Freedom, which achieved platinum status in January 1993, is also available on cassette.

BUNNY WAILER

Neville O'Riley Livingston, famously known as Bunny Wailer, was born in Kingston in 1947. After leaving the Wailers in 1974, he withdrew from the music scene for two years, and on his return, he released the LP, *Blackheart*, with the tag line, "(that) one might preserve the strength and the fame of the Blackheart Man". It was named the best reggae album in 1976 by the English journal *Melody Maker*.

Songs such as "Rasta Man", "Reincarnation Souls", "The Oppressed Song" and "Armagedeon" showed Bunny Wailer's vocal quality and range.

For the LP, he was composer, lead singer and musician, using conga drums and bongo drum. Both vocally and instrumentally, he imitated Bob Marley, Peter Tosh, Aston "Family Man" Barrett, Carlton Barrett and Tyrone Downey Carlton.

The LP, produced by Bunny Wailer for his Solomonic label, was different in mixing, recording and the length of the songs from the one produced for Island label and released in the European market.

In 1977, the album *Protest* was released. It examined the social problems in Jamaica, and two years later, in 1979, as a follow-up LP, Wailer released *Struggle*.

The album *Bunny Wailer: Sings the Wailers*, was released in 1981. This album, which was done in collaboration with Sly Dunbar, Robbie Shakespeare and Earl (Chinna) Smith, consisted of previously published material from the 1960s.

On his next album entitled *Tribute*, all the songs were written by Bob Marley, except "War", the lyrics of which was a speech given by Haile Selassie to the United Nation's General Assembly on October 4, 1943.

After sevens years of absence from the stage, Bunny Wailer returned to perform live at the Youth Consciousness Reggae Festival on December 12, 1982 at the National Stadium in Kingston, at which he performed, amongst others, the song

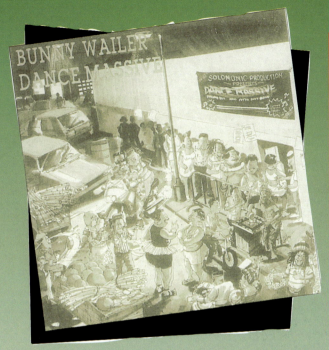

"Blackheart Man". The LP *Live,* was released a year later in 1983.

In 1986, Bunny Wailer performed at a huge concert at Madison Square Garden in New York in front of more than fourteen thousand people.

Bunny Wailer is credited with keeping himself musically current, and by 1986, with the new wave of reggae and dance-hall music taking over the local scene, he went to work in the studio. The result was the production of a dancehall-style album entitled *Rule Dance Hall,* which was released in 1987.

However, with the release of the album *Liberation,* some time later, he returned to his original style of music and lyrics. Three years later in 1990, he won the Grammy Award for Best Reggae Album.

Shortly before the death of Peter Tosh in 1987, Bunny Wailer and Tosh recorded the album *Together Again.*

Bunny Wailer has also produced for other artistes and groups, including the album *Take A Stand,* for the group, Wadada, formed between 1980 and 1981, and consisting of Denzil Williams, Kenneth Roxborough and Franklin Thompson.

He is currently working on a book on the history of the Wailers, to be titled *Old Fire Stick,* together with Roger Steffens and Jodie Pierson.

In 1995, Bunny Wailer signed a 10-year worldwide licensing and distribution deal with Japan's Nippon Columbia Label. The deal includes five albums to be released by the original Wailers, as well as some original solo material from Peter Tosh and Bunny Wailer.

PETER TOSH

Winston Hubert McIntosh, who was popularly known as Peter Tosh, was born in 1944 in the small fishing village of Belmont in Westmoreland.

He became an international star with the albums *Bush Doctor* and *Legalize It.*

Peter Tosh protested against political grievances and the adverse state of the economy in his songs. In one of his songs, "The Day the Dollar Died", he sang about the dependence of Jamaica on the American dollar.

On his last LP, the Grammy-winning *No Nuclear War,* released in 1987, he wrote, composed, sang and played the lead and keyboard.

Whereas Peter Tosh did not have the profile of Bob Marley, he nevertheless wrote some classic songs, such as I'm The Toughest", "Maga Dog", "When The Well Dry" and "Can't You See".

The collection set One Love, which consisted of forty songs by the Wailers, and released under the Heartbeat Label in 1992, contains some of his early recordings, most of which were previously released under the Studio One label.

On this collection set, one can listen to Tosh's imperious voice, his use of many common proverbs and the colourful language of the common people, which brought the Wailers close to the people.

On *Equal Rights*, also released under the Columbia Label in 1977, for the first time, Tosh had his own backing band, Word, Sound and Power, and in addition to lead guitarist and keyboard player,

Sly Dunbar and Robbie Shakespeare, there were other musicians who assisted. The musical sound of the group was more firm and direct than that on *Legalize It.*

In the first song on this album, which was a remake of "Get Up Stand Up", one can hear the inimitable voice of Peter Tosh and his rock-sounding guitar.

The songs, "Equal Rights", "Africans", "Apartheid" and "Stepping Razor" were the highlights of Tosh's career, and the album *Equal Rights* probably his best.

Some time later, Mick Jagger and Keith Richards from the Rolling Stones became interested in him. He signed a recording contract with Rolling Stones Records, and his debut album for this label was the start of his international career.

The first track of the album, "Don't, Look Back", was a duet with Mick Jagger. It was released as a disco single. "Don't Look Back", was an old original Temptations song, which was previously recorded on a reggae rhythm at Studio One, with Keith and Tex, Busty Brown and Tosh. The song combined the strength of the lyrics with the sounds of the horns and supplemented by the backing vocals of the Tamlins. It had a full guitar and keyboard arrangement, and was accompanied by a Sly and Robbie rhythm.

The album *Mystic Man* followed, thanks to Sly and Robbie, which consist of one of his best songs, "Buk-In-Ham-Palace" which was also released as a disco single.

The last LP recorded for Rolling Stones Records, *Wanted Dread And Alive*, was released in 1981. It was possibly the weakest of all. It was after the release of this album that Sly and Robbie started to work with Black Uhuru, and Peter Tosh, once again, started to form a new band.

No new record was released until 1987 when he dropped his last album *No Nuclear War.*

On September 11, 1987, three armed men on motorcycles broke into his house on Plymouth Avenue in Barbican, Kingston. During the alleged robbery, gunshots were fired. Two visitors, including veteran broadcaster and disc jockey, Jeff "Free I" Dixon, and Peter Tosh were shot to death. Tosh's girlfriend, Marlene Brown, and four other persons were also injured. The crime was never solved, but there are different versions of the story.

Following Peter Tosh's death, Jamaica, and by extension the music world, lost one its most vigorous and uncompromising voices. A musician who was not afraid to denounce the evil acts of the government.

From the time he was a member of the Wailers, Tosh was unyielding and the most radical of the group.

One memorable occasion was at the One Love Concert, held on April 22, 1978. When Bob Marley held the hands of both Michael Manley and Edward Seaga, Tosh exclaimed: *"I want no peace, I want equality! I am no politician. I must only suffer from the consequences!"*

He still lives on in the hearts of Jamaicans and reggae fans around the world.

THE I-THREE

The I-Three consists of Rita Marley, Marcia Griffiths and Judy Mowatt. Formed in 1973, they were the backing vocals for Bob Marley on all live performances while he was on tour. They assumed this role after the Wailers separated.

Their harmony, costumes and dance (choreographed by Judy Mowatt) were the highlights of Bob Marley's performances.

In addition to some singles, the I-Three also released the LP *Beginning* in 1986 under the EMI label. It was produced and arranged by Grub Cooper and Ricky Walters of Fabulous Five and Thom Bell.

The I-Three reunited for a performance on March 26, 2009 in London at the Island Records 50th anniversary concert. The concert was hosted by Sly and Robbie with some special guests like Grace Jones, Aswad, VV Brown, and current United Kingdom chart-topping artists. Proceeds from the show went to Amnesty and the Oracabessa Foundation.

Rita Marley

Rita Marley was born in 1950 as Alpharita Constantia Anderson in Cuba. She was three months old when her parents migrated to Jamaica. When she was eight years old, her parents migrated to England, and Rita and her brothers and sisters went to live with relatives. She was employed as a nurse during her spare time after school.

Rita began her singing career in 1964 with the singing trio, The Soulettes, which also consisted of her cousin Constantine "Dream" Walker and Marlene "Precious" Gifford. Her first solo recording was for Coxsone Dodd. She also recorded some solo singles, under the name Esete or Ganete. The first titles were cover versions of the Soulettes' songs.

On February 10, 1966, she married Bob Marley.

Her first solo album, *Who Feels It Knows It*, was released in 1980. It was produced by Grub Cooper, Bob Marley and herself.

Rita Marley achieved great success in 1983 with the song "One Draw" that was written and arranged by Grub Cooper and Ricky Walters of Fabulous Five. This song can be found on Rita Marley's LP, *Harambe,* released in 1982. Grub Cooper and Rocky Walters also wrote most of the songs for this LP, and they were also the backing vocals and musicians.

The third album *We Must Carry On,* released under her own Rita Marley Music Label, was dedicated to Bob. It was inspired by the words that Bob often repeated to Rita, *"I know a place ... we must carry on",* and was also the title track on the album.

Marcia Griffiths

Marcia Griffiths was born and grew up in western Kingston. She sang at concerts and in choruses at schools.

She began her career in the music business in 1964, when she performed the song "No Time to Lose" (a Carla Thomas original) at an Easter concert with Byron Lee.

Both Byron Lee and Coxsone Dodd wanted to sign her to their labels, but she chose Coxsone Dodd.

In addition to many other artistes and musicians, she met Bob and Rita Marley, Peter Tosh and also Bunny Wailer while working with Coxsone. They often worked together until 1969, when she teamed up with Bob Andy.

In 1970, she had a big hit with Bob Andy called "Young, Gifted And Black", that became quite popular because of a tour in Europe. In the following year, her song "Pied Piper" (a Crispian St. Peter original, recorded in 1966) went to number 11 on the British charts.

Her first number one single for Studio One was "Feel Like Jumpin'". Later, Coxsone was able to release two LPs from the cache of recorded materials she had done for him. The first of which was entitled *The Best Of Marcia Griffiths,* and consisted of songs that were all written by Bob Andy. Griffiths and Andy

also recorded an album for Harry J called *Young, Gifted And Black*.

Later, there was some confusion when songs from *The Best of Marcia Griffiths* album also appeared on an album released by Sonia Pottinger under her High Mark Label. Some of the titles that were duplicated included "Naturally", "Melody Life", "Truly", "Mark My Words" and "Feel Like Jumpin'".

It is the single "Electric Boogie", however, which is still her greatest hit. The original song was written and produced by Bunny Wailer in 1982, and several cover versions have been released since. The song is also on her album, *Electric Slide.*

The dance to the song *Electric Slide,* which started a dance revolution in February 1989 in the USA, quickly spread far and wide in two short years. It became quite popular at parties, largely due to the dance steps, which were easy to learn: (three steps to the right, three steps to the left, three steps back, twice squat down, a turn and then you simply start all over again).

Judy Mowatt

Judy Mowatt was the first female reggae singer to be nominated for a Grammy. In 1986, her LP *Working Wonders*, was nominated for the prestigious award.

Her LP *Black Woman*, was the first reggae album produced solely by a woman.

The significance, vulnerability, and meaningfulness of her lyrics made her songs connect with women all across the globe, and were instrumental in the African freedom movement.

Judy was born to a poor family in a district near Kingston. Even though they did not have to suffer hunger, there was not even a radio in the home.

As a child, she sang a lot and was often selected as the soloist for the choir. In 1965, she got the opportunity to join the group, The Gaylettes, also known as the Gaytones, which consisted of Bery Lawsone and Merle Clemenson.

The Gaytones quickly became one of the most popular song groups in the island and had their first hits soon after they started to record at Federal Records. They were influenced by Aretha Franklin, Otis Redding, Curtis Mayfield and Dustin Springfield.

When the other members of the group migrated to the USA at the beginning of the 1970s, Judy launched her solo career, singing soul ballads and reggae songs.

Her first solo was "I Shall Sing", which was written by Miriam Makeba. She also had a number of hit singles, including "I Shall Sing", later covered by Art Garfunkel; "Way Over There" and "Emergency".

During the mid-1970s, she established her own record label, Ashandan. Her best solo song "Mellow Mood", a Bob Marley composition, was the title hit of her first LP. On her second LP, *Black Woman*, produced by herself, she dedicated some poignant songs to Bob Marley, such as "Joseph". The LP also consisted of "Sisters Chant", "Strength To Go Through" and the title song "Black Woman". The album included songs written by Mowatt, as well as songs written by Bob Marley and Freddie McGregor.

The LP was an ode to the dignity and power of the black woman and is easily one of the best reggae LP's ever recorded by a woman.

Her third LP, *Only A Woman*, solidified her position as a spokesperson on behalf of women. The fourth LP, however, took her further into the realm of popular music, where she began to sing about current issues within the society. These included songs such as, "Lovemaking"; a forceful cover version of Taj Mahal's "Black Man, Brown Man"; "Hush Baby Mother", which describes the problems faced by single mothers, and "Mother Africa", the subject of which is repatriation to Africa.

Judy was not only a singer, but also an actor. She was featured in the movie *Heartland Reggae* and was a guest on many television talk shows in the US, such as "Night Line" and "Late Night with David Letterman". She has performed with Herbie Hancock, Joe Cocker, Wilson Picket, Peter Frampton Grover Washington, Freddie Hubbard and others.

On her 1986 LP *Love Is Overdue*, she extended her musical range, and in addition to new, strong reggae songs, she did a cover version of Otis Redding's "Try A Little Tenderness"; the Anti-Apartheid song "Sing Your Own Song", written by UB40; "Hold the Jah", a Dancehall title; a song written by Marley entitled, "Screwface" and the covers of two pop songs originally by Richard Ace entitled "Long Long Time" and "Love Is Overdue".

In 1991, the album *Look At Love*, was released on her own Judy M Label. This album addressed the fundamental issues affecting women.

Judy was formerly a member of the Twelve Tribes of Israel. But in 1996, she became a born-again Christian, and started to worship at the Holiness Christian Church. In changing from Rastafarianism to Christianity, she has acknowledged Jesus Christ as her Saviour, but she continues to wear her locks.

With reference to Marcia Griffiths and Rita Marley she has noted, *"Nothing has changed between us, we are closer than before"*.

SLY AND ROBBIE

The duo of Lowell Charles Dunbar, nickname Sly, born in 1952 in Kingston, and Robbie Shakespeare, born in 1953 in Kingston, can easily be described as the best rhythm group in reggae. They started working in the mid-1970s.

Sly Dunbar's excellent percussion skill is a model for young percussionists. He has collaborated with Robbie Shakespeare on more than one hundred LPs, and has also done his own recordings, such as *Simple Sly Man* and *Sly, Wicked and Slick*. These LPs, incorporate a mixture of soul, reggae and folklore, with a touch of oriental music.

Sly and Robbie are actively involved in producing. Their record label, Taxi, feature some top reggae artistes and groups, such as Black Uhuru, Jimmy E. Riley and The Viceroys, among others.

The drum and the bass are integral to the roots reggae, and as a result, a musical style has evolved in reggae that utilises only the drum and bass called "Dub". Over the years, roots reggae has had many bass players, such as Leroy Sibbles, Earl "Bagga" Walker, Lloyd Parkes, Boris Gardiner and Ian Lewis; and many top drummers, such as Leroy "Horsemouth" Wallace, Mikey "Boo" Richards and Desi Jones.

Robbie can be described as a self-taught musician, whose talent has been developed through the efforts and assistance of others. One such individual is "Family Man" Barrett. He has collaborated on songs such as Slim Smith's "Watch This Sound", and has also played with studio bands such as Hippie Boys, Sound Foundation and the Upsetters.

He worked with the Hippie Boys at the Evil People Club in 1972. Later, he was invited by "Touter" Harvey (whose is now a member of Inner Circle) to listen to the band, Skin Flesh & Bone, which was performing at the Tit For Club nearby.

Apparently, it was here that Robbie first met Sly Dunbar, whom he was very impressed with. Later, when Robbie worked with Slim Smith, Johnny Clarke and Bunny Lee's Aggravators Band, a drummer was required during a recording session, and Robbie asked Sly fill the position.

They soon played together for Joe Gibbs, but separately and under different names for Channel One. The best known album from Channel One was entitled *Revolutionaries*. Robbie has also played with Peter Tosh's World Sound & Power Band, and whenever another drummer was required, he would always ask Sly to fill the spot.

Sly and Robbie have been playing together over since, and have played for artistes both within and outside of the reggae fraternity. They have played for rock and R & B singers, such Grace Jones, Joan Armatrading, Joe Cocker, Gwen Guthrie, Herbie Hancock, Bob Dylan, Mick Jagger, Fela Kuti, Manu Dibandu and many others, who respected and appreciated the talent the Taxi Twins.

During the 1970s, they established their own label, Taxi Records, and it was here that they developed their inimitable and unique Taxi sound.

Artistes signed to the Taxi label include Gregory Isaacs, Black Uhuru, The Tamlins, Horace Andy, The Mighty Diamonds, Bunny Wailer, Sugar Minott, Dennis Brown, Half Pint and Ini Kamoze, among many others. These artistes were very satisfied with their work and worked repeatedly with the duo.

When Bob Marley, Jimmy Cliff and Peter Tosh began to present their music to a wider audience, Sly & Robbie were contracted to play. They also started to play and produce roots reggae.

In retrospect, one can say that the job which Marley and Tosh started, would have ended if there were no Sly & Robbie.

Far from restricting themselves to the Jamaican scene, they have been one of pop music's most sought after rhythm producers, playing for and producing for superstars such as Ben Harper, Bob Dylan, Mick Jagger, the Rolling Stones, Grace Jones, Joan Armatrading, Gilberto Gil, Joe Cocker, Serge Gainsbourg, Simply Red, Michael Franti, Sting, Khaled, Mey

Vidal, Tricky, Doug E. Fresh, Carlos Santana, Sinéad O'Connor, and many more.

After 30 years together, they still tour and record. In early 2005, they toured with Tony Rebel and Half Pint. During the summer of 2005, they toured Europe and the UK with Bunny Rugs, lead singer for Third World. At the end of 2005, they were on the road with Sinéad O'Connor. In August 2006, they appeared with Don Carlos at the Reggae on the River Festival, and in August 2007 they performed on a tour of the western United States and Canada along with Taxi label artiste Cherine Anderson.

SLY & ROBBIE
A dub experience

They have produced several new Jamaican artistes for their Taxi label, including Kibaki, Mynimoo and Zennlocc, as well as entertainers such as Elephant Man and Buju Banton, for whom they re-used their 1982 instrumental mega-hit "Unmetered Taxi". In 2006, they recorded with their original group, the Revolutionaries, to produce Horace Andy's new album *Livin' it up* and also produced several hits for Cherine Anderson.

In 2007, they worked with the Italian rapper Jovanotti for his album *Safari*. They also produced tracks for Beatles member Sir Paul McCartney and Britney Spears. In 2008, Sly and Robbie collaborated with the Ecuadorian singer-songwriter Cecilia Villar Eljuri on her song "El Aire". Sung in Spanish, the song quickly charted on World Beat and Latin Alternative radio.

ISRAEL VIBRATION

The three members of the group, Israel Vibration: Cecil "Skelly" Spence, Albert "Apple" Craig and Lascelle "Wiss" Bulgin, have more than just music in common. All three are faithful Rastafarians and during their childhood, they were stricken with poliomyelitis, an infectious disease, which occurs mainly in children, and in its acute form attacks the central nervous system, and produces paralysis, muscular atrophy and often deformity.

One day, they literally hobbled to the Channel One studio, where many were skeptical as to their ability to sing. However, during the test, they proved that they could not only sing, but that they could sing very well.

Albert "Apple" Craig had already begun to write his own songs from as early as age twelve. The group's first single "Why Worry" was released in 1976 under Tommy Cowan's Top Ranking Label. One year later, their first album, *The Same Song*, was also released under the Top Ranking and also on Harvest. Almost 100,000 copies were sold in Jamaica and Europe.

In 1980, Israel Vibration performed at Sunsplash and released their second album *Unconquered People*, which was produced by Bob Marley under his Tuff Gong label.

Israel Vibration
Forever

In 1981, they migrated to Brooklyn, New York, and one year later in 1982, they produced their third album, *Why You So Craven* which was released under the Volcano label. After the release of this album, the trio separated to launch their solo careers. Despite the separation, they released the LP *The Best Of Israel Vibration* under the Sonic Label.

The year 1988 saw the beginning of a new era for the trio. They travelled to Washington DC to record their new album, Strength Of My Life, which was released under Dr. Dread's Ras Label. The album was done in collaboration with Roots Radics, whom they had previously recorded with while at Channel One and Tuff Gong in Jamaica. Two sets of three songs were recorded in both Lion and Fox Studios, with Roots Radics singing harmony.

In the ensuing months, Mallory "She Boom" Williams and Augustus Pablo were flown from Jamaica to Washington DC to complete the album by providing additional support on keyboard and melody. Brass Tax, a talented horn group, gave the album its cutting edge.

This new beginning proved successful, and by 1990 the albums, *Forever*, *Praises* and *Vibes Alive* (double LP), and other records were released under the Ras label.

In 1997, Craig left the trio to do a solo career. His debut album, *Another Moses*, featured his own backing band, the Zionists. Continuing on as a duo, Spence and Bulgin reappeared in 1999 with a new studio album, *Pay the Piper*. They later released the limited-edition *Power of the Trinity* three-CD box set each CD showing off the greatest compositions of the trio.

Dub Combo appeared in summer 2001.

THE REGGAE AFTER BOB MARLEY

It is quite easy to speak about reggae after Bob Marley because many other musicians, such as Toots and the Maytals and Jimmy Cliff, have done a lot to move this popular music genre forward.

Dennis Brown and Gregory Isaacs were able to create reggae music from the protests and voices of the youths from the inner cities of Kingston. In fact, reggae has become the music for every occasion.

The Mighty Diamonds, Toots and the Maytals, Burning Spear (born Winston Rodney), Leroy Sibbles, John Holt and Byron Lee and the Dragonaires have also been instrumental in moving the music forward and taking it to a new level.

THE WAILERS BAND

Bob Marley shared approximately fifty percent of the profits from the sale of his records with his employees and band members, without ever signing a single contract or writing a single receipt.

After his death, the sale of his records, increased to approximately US $1.5 million. But the Wailers did not have access to these monies, neither could they substantiate the amount of money that they had received from Bob when they worked together.

The Wailers band now consist of some of the original members, as well as new members. In the case of the former, these include Aston "Family Man" Barrett (bass), who is presently the bandleader; Al Anderson (guitar); Junior Marvin (lead guitar and vocals) and Earl "Wire" Lindo (keyboards). In the case of the latter, these include, Owen "Dready" Reed (lead singer) and ex-Third World member, "Carrot" Jarrett (percussion), who jumps wildly in the air, with his upper body naked, and his metre long dreadlocks flying all over the place, while performing live on stage. In fact, his act is quite similar to the late Jacob Miller's.

Tyrone Downey, Alwin Patterson and Carlton Barett are no longer a part of the band. Barett was shot and killed at the beginning of 1998. He was replaced by Cornell Marchall, who is also an ex-Third World member, and now plays drums for the group.

These reggae-playing experts incorporate sound volume and change the mix with three guitars and two keyboards, which marks the typical after beat. Family Man's unyieldingly hard bass and Cornell Marshall on drums determine the rhythm line of the Wailers songs. The rock-sounding guitar-playing style of veteran and expert Junior Marvin and good engineering can be compared with any self-proclaimed rock band.

The group has many songs in its repertoire from the days of Bob Marley, but they also recorded their own songs,

Kapo   (famous Jamaican artist)

Ken Spencer oil painting: Bob Marley, Haile Selassie, Jesus

which have been released on several LPs. These songs include "Opening Irie" and "Chasing Tomorrow". In 1980, the album *Hail H.I.M.* was done in collaboration with Burning Spear, and was co-produced by Aston Barrett. They were the backing band for the group Alpha Blondie, which produced the album *Jerusalem*. They have also worked with Alberta Jill from Brazil and Johnny Denver from Denver, Colorado, in addition to many talented newcomers to the music scene in Jamaica.

DENNIS BROWN

Dennis Brown was born in 1957, and by the age of five years, he was performing live on stage in a musical written by his father.

He began to sing at the age of nine years, under the influence of Byron Lee and the Dragonaires, and four years later, when he was thirteen years old, he released his first single "No Man is an Island", produced by Coxsone Dodd,

which achieved much success.

Other hits followed such as "Silhouette", "Baby Don't Do It" and "Money in My Pocket".

His first album *Super Reggae and Soul Hitsk*, was produced by Derrick Harriot, and released under the Greensleeves Label, when he was only sixteen years old.

In those days, he composed and arranged most of his own songs, and with his excellent on stage performance, he became well known.

In 1979, during the Montreux Jazz Festival, he had more success than Peter Tosh even though he was not the featured artiste. He has also performed regularly at Sunsplash.

Brown worked as a studio musician, providing background vocals for groups such as the Heptones, and many others. He also worked with the producer, Joe Higgs, who wrote a number of songs for him.

In addition to producing other artistes on his DEB Label, Dennis Brown has also released between two to three LPs under other Jamaica-based recording labels, on a yearly basis, starting from the 1980s. These labels include *Live Learn, Music Works, Tappa, and Ayeola*. He has also released albums under English and American-based labels, such as Blue Moon and Two Friends respectively. In fact, his LP *Overproof*, was released in 1991 under the Two Friends Label.

When he returned from his 1999 Brazil tour with his friend Gregory Isaacs, a long-term health problem turned worse. Dennis Brown died on July 1,1999 from a respiratory failure from pneumonia.

GREGORY ISAACS

Gregory Anthony Isaacs was born in Kingston in 1951. He attended the All Saints School and All Saints Church.

Towards the end of the 1960s, he worked with The Concordes and producer, Rupie Edwards, but he produced his first solo single, "Another Heartache", for himself at Dynamic Sounds Studio.

He also produced for the Cash & Carry, which had other artistes, such as Errol Dunkley, Dennis Brown. However in order to achieve his independence, he established his own African Museum label. One of the first songs produced for his new label was "One Coco", which was done in collaboration with the group, The Upsetters.

Gregory Isaacs, popularly known as the "Cool Ruler", also has an album of the same name, which was released on his African Museum Label in 1978. In 1980, he released the album, "Lonely Lover" (also his nickname), again on his label, and the English PRE label.

Gregory Isaacs is the love rock specialist, whose almost silky, unmistakable voice, is loved by women all over the world. According to the love rock specialist, *"No gun, no bayonet can conquer war, but love"*.

In addition to the above-mentioned LPs, he released, *Red Rose For Gregory* under the English-based Greensleeves Label; *Gregory In Talk* (Tappa Label); *Come Along* (Jamaica-based Jammy Label), as well as the double album *Lovers Rock* released in 1980 under the English-based PRE Label. This album consists of some of his best music to date.

In 1989, he established his own sixteen-track recording studio in Kingston, Jamaica.

He also performed at the ICC Cricket World Cup 2007 Inauguration in Jamaica.

In 2007 he collaborated with the Spanish rap group Flowklorikos for the album *Donde Duele Inspira*.

In 2008, after some 40 years as a recording artiste, Isaacs released a new studio album *Brand New Me*. The album received positive reviews from critics, such as this review from Reggae Vibes: "Gregory is back, and how! *Brand New Me* is a very suitable title for The Cool Ruler's new album. He is back in a different style, more or less like we were used to from this great 'lovers & roots' artiste."

BURNING SPEAR O.D.

Burning Spear was born in 1948 in St. Ann, as Godfrey Winston Rodney. He first worked with Rupert Willington. As a duo, they recorded their first song, entitled "Door Peep", for Coxsone in 1969.

In 1971, they had the first great success of their relatively young career with the song "Marcus Garvey", which was recorded for Lawrence Lindo, more popularly known as Jack Ruby; who, like Burning Spear, rose from a simple sound system job, to become a well-respected producer.

From 1974 to 1977, he worked with Delroy Hines, after which he worked alone. During these years, he produced for his Travelling Label, and Burning Spear Label, which were established in 1975 and 1976, respectively.

He gave an unforgettable performance with Trumpeter, Bobby Ellis, together with some members of the Aswad Band, at a concert held at the London Rainbow Theatre.

In 1979, he appeared in the reggae film "Rockers", sitting on ruins of Jamaica's first prison in Seville, St. Ann, singing the song "Jah No Dead",

Other LPs, include "Man in the Hills", the last album recorded with the background voices of Rupert Willington and Delroy Hines; "Dry And Heavy" released in 1977; "Rocking Time" and "Burning Spear", both recorded at Studio One, and the album "Hail H.I.M., recorded at Tuff Gong Studio, together with the Wailers Band. This album reminds one of the blower arrangements background instrumental music, typical of Bob Marley's recordings during the 1970s.

In the early eighties, he worked with bands, such as UB40, Talking Heads, and The Clash.

In fall of 1992, the album *The World Should Know* that was recorded in April of the same year at Grove Recording Studio, Ocho Rios (also the home of IRIE FM) was released under the Mango Label.

Burning Spear has given back much to his community. He has established and financed a youth club -the Marcus Youth Club, located in St. Ann, for the unemployed youths in the area to meet, in order to practice and play football.

For the past ten years, together with his Burning Music Production Company, and drummer, Nelson Miller, Burning Spear has been producing music for himself.

He has remained a conscious Rastafarian and roots reggae artiste. According to Spear, *"Jah is great, Jah is real, Jah is pure, and Jah is the only light that appears, the only light that appears for a man, a woman, a child. Do not let us speak about colors and races".*

In 2002 Burning Spear and his wife Sonja Rodney, who has produced a number of his albums, founded Burning Spear Records.

He advocates messages of honesty, peace, and love, which tie in with his social and religious messages of Rastafari and black unity.

Burning Spear was awarded the Order of Distinction in the rank of Officer on October 15, 2007.

FRANKIE PAUL

Frankie Paul, born Paul Blake, in 1965 in Kingston, began his singing career at the age of eight years with the group the Miami Tides, which originated from Kingston. They toured throughout Portland, St. Catherine, St. Ann, St. James and Westmoreland.

The group did their first recordings for Channel One, followed by High Times; and their first LP for Henry "Junju" Laws.

He not only sang in most of his recordings, but he also played the keyboard, which he taught himself to play.

According to Frankie Paul, both Stevie Wonder and Dennis Brown influenced him musically, especially at the beginning of his career. He has named Roger Wazair and Gail Boyde, as his best producer, and manager, respectively.

Frankie Paul has also recorded on the Techniques Label, some of the songs were released under the Jammy's Label.

His first single, "African Princess", was released under the High Times Label, in 1982. A classic song done by this lover's rock artiste is "I Need Your Loving"; and his most remarkable LP to date, *Every Nigger Is A Star*, was released in 1991.

Frankie Paul has remained a tireless entertainer and producer. In 1992, he released five LPs.

JUNIOR REID

Junior Reid started his music career at the age of thirteen years, performing at school concerts and at tourist resorts.

It was his friend, Locksley Castell and first producer, Hugh Mundell, who encouraged him, to record his first single, "Speak The Truth", released in the early eighties on the Rockers International label.

He did several recordings for Jammy's and Negus Roots, an England-based recording company, until he joined the group, Voice Of Progress.

The group released songs, such as, "Know Your Stuff" and "Mini Bus Driver".

In 1984, he recorded "A-One Lover" and "Foreign Mind", with Sugar Minott.

When Michael Rose (later known as Mykal Roze), and formerly the lead singer of Black Uhuru, left the group soon after they had won the Grammy, Junior Reid was asked to fill his position.

The first song he produced for the group was entitled "Fit Yu Ha Fi Fit", which was done in collaboration with Sly and Robbie, which later became a great hit. He also wrote six of the songs for the first album released as a member of the group entitled, "Brutal". One of the songs, "Great Train Robbery" rose to No. 6 on the British charts. Together, Junior Reid and Black Uhuru toured Europe.

After three years, they separated and Reid launched his solo career. He started to experiment, out of which evolved new materials for his songs, which can be heard in recordings such as, "Married Life", "One Blood", "When It Snows", "A No So", "Dominant" and a remix of "Eleanor Rigby". These songs were subsequently released on his album entitled, *One Blood*.

Still successful in the music recording business, Junior Reid remains a true roots-reggae singer/artistes, and a reggae ambassador.

In addition to his own recordings, he has produced a number of other artistes on his JR Productions Label, such as, Foxie Brown, Major Mackerel, Baby Wayne, whom he introduced to the music scene at his Birthday Bash held in Negril, Ocho Rios and Portmore (Kingston), in June 1993.

During the years when he was without a visa for the United States, he explored other aspects of his music industry, which led to the establishment of a recording studio and the signing of

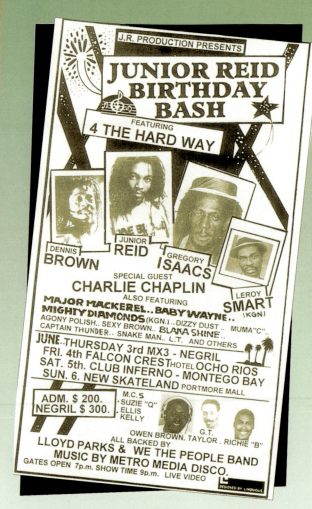

artistes to his recording label.

In recent years, his visa was reinstated, but he has still not lost his focus. Today, his major focus is still his recording studio.

He has since established his JR Label and One Blood recording studio, located on Lindsay Crescent in Kingston and has now extended his operations to the adjoining property, which houses a record shop.

DR. CARLENE DAVIS

Carlene Davis was born in Colonel's Ridge, Clarendon. At the age of thirteen years, she migrated to England, where she grew up.

She has recorded pop and reggae songs with local groups, which have appeared on the music charts in Jamaica.

Later she went to Toronto, Canada, where she developed her individual style of singing.

While residing in Toronto, where there is a large Caribbean community, Davis often attended concerts at which reggae groups and artistes, such as Toots and The Maytals and Peter Tosh performed.

These frequent visits to stage shows and concerts finally paid off when she met Bob Marley, who had gone to Toronto to perform at a reggae show. In 1980, she returned to Jamaica, and went on tour with Bob Marley. Prior to this, two years earlier, in 1978, she was invited to the inaugural staging of Reggae Sunsplash, and performed regularly at the annual staging of this event. She also tours North America every year.

In the last ten years, Davis has recorded more twenty hit songs, which earned her the nickname, "The Move".

The new directions into which reggae music was moving (Dancehall and Raggamuffin), have had an influence on her music style, which have been captured in the hit songs, "Telephone Love" and "Dial My Number".

Her gospel – reggae album *Jesus Is Only A Prayer Away* has had a positive impact on the music scene, especially as regards reggae music. One of the exceptional songs recorded on this album, is "Why Me Lord", that she performed as a duet with Ken Boothe.

In 1992, she released the LP, *Carlene*, under the Gee Street/Island/PLG label. The songs were written, arranged and produced by Mike Bennett & Two Friends.

In 1995, when Carlene released the album *Echoes Of Love* and the album *Passion And Pain,* she won the Radio Jamaica Top Female Artiste Award.

In 1996, she was diagnosed with cancer – she survived. She decided to give her life and talent to the Lord.

In the same year, she got married to Tommy Cowan, whom she met in 1980.

Today, Carlene Davis is one of the most consistent artistes in gospel music. Together with Tommy, she works with the annual gospel show Fun In The Son.

Carlene Davis, now a full-time gospel artiste, does mini tours along with her work at Fun In The Son to maintain her Christianity.

In 2006, she completed her doctorate in Pastoral Counselling from the Trinity Theological Seminary in South Florida.

JUNE C. LODGE

June Caroll Lodge was born in 1958 in London.

Her mega-hit single "Telephone Love" released in 1988, started the reggae boom in discos in New York. It was also appeared on the album, "Selfish Lover", which was released in 1991 under the Music Works Label.

Her musical achievements were highlighted in 1989, when she performed on Singers Night at the premier reggae music event, Reggae Sunsplash.

Her CD *Tropic of Love* was released in 1991 under the Tommy label. It featured sexy, soulful ballads, such as "Pillow Talk" and "Chain Of Love"; and dancehall songs, such as "Why", "Come Again" and "Love Me Baby". It also featured her mega hit, "Telephone Love".

There is a song for everyone on this CD. However, most will agree the that the dancehall songs, except "Love Me Baby", were not as good, especially when compared to the other songs on the CD, such as the "Brazilian", which has a good background rhythm, and "Where The Hurt Is", which features the classical guitar sounds of Gregory Allison, to whom the CD is dedicated.

Tyrone Downey, Cleveland, Danny and Dalton Brown have provided a technically perfect musical background for this album.

SUGAR MINOTT

Lincoln Barrington Minott was born in 1956 in Kingston. He is one of the top classic roots singer. He is an artiste who knows the heights and depths of the music business, and uses this knowledge to his advantage, with the result that he has had many hit songs.

As a natural artiste, Sugar Minott does not fit very well into the hard-core music business, but he makes the best of it.

He started his music career as a harmony singer for the group the African Brothers, who did their recordings at the Studio One.

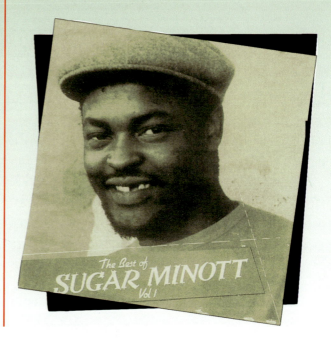

He later launched his solo career, and wrote, produced and arranged most of the songs for himself. His writing and composing skills improved with each song.

He was one of the few reggae singers/artistes who did not sign with a major recording label.

According to Sugar Minott, *"(They) who control the music industry are very rich. They don't want to be confronted with the fight of the poor and the suffering of the people in the ghetto or with religion or politics. They want to live in their illusions and their big, beautiful houses and say, everything is ok. They reluctantly support roots and culture and real, pure music".*

His expertise spans the musical spectrum, evidenced by the two nicknames he earned in music industry, "King Of The Dancehall" and "Lovers Rock Don".

He is a gifted writer, who writes music as it appears to him. According to Sugar Minott, artistes and musicians, such as Ken Boothe, Alton Ellis and Dennis have positively influenced his music career.

His greatest ambition is to work with the youth and to support them. To this end, in 1979 he started the organisation, Youth Promotion, together with other artistes, including, Little John, Tony Tuff, Junior Reid, Yami Bolo and Daddy Freddy. The organisation was later joined by Tony Rebel, and together they established a studio, record shop and a music school, where youths could learn to play an instrument free of charge. The group also recorded several songs.

In 1984, together with Junior Reid, Minott recorded "A-One Lover" and "Foreign Mind". Two years later, the collection album, *Powerhouse Presents Strictly Live Stock*, was released in 1986 under the English-based Greensleeves label, which featured artistes, such as Frankie Paul, Sugar Minott, Junior Reid, Half Pint, Michael Palmer, Wayne Smith, Echo Minott, Welton Irie, Nitty Gritty and Tenor Saw.

Prior, in 1984, he toured Japan with the Gifted Roots Band. They performed together under the name Black Roots Band. As a member of this band, they recorded the single, "Nattie Fred", which was featured on the LP, *Gifted Roots Band Presents Gifted* released in 1986 under the Abeng Label.

He has released over 60 albums and hundreds of singles.

He appeared on the 2006 record, *Radiodread*, released on the Easy Stars label, and he provided the guest vocals on the song "Exit Music".

THE REGGAE POETS

MUTABARUKA

Allan "Mutabaruka" Hope was born in Rae Town, Jamaica in 1952. Unlike most of his colleagues, he did not grow up in the ghetto. His name comes from the Rwandan language and means "one who is always victorious".

He converted from Catholicism to Rastafarian.

After four years of study, he worked as a technician at the Jamaica Telephone Company (later Cable and Wireless, now Lime).

His first book of poetry, entitled *Outcry,* was published in 1973, and was quite a success.

Another book, *Sun And Moon,* followed in 1976. It was co-authored by another poet, Faybiene.

Mutabaruka promoted himself by doing readings at schools and the Kingston Creative Arts Centre. Quickly, the name Mutabaruka became known.

Mutabaruka: The First Poems (1970-1979) was published in 1980 in Kingston.

A German Edition (translated by Christian Habekost) was published by Schwinn Verlag, Neustadt (Germany) in 1987.

The second poetry book came out in 2008 as a two-book edition together with the first poems.

In 1981, he released his first single "Evrytime A Ear De Soun". One year later, he toured Cuba with Jimmy Cliff.

In 1982, the short album *Sister Breeze*, which consisted of four dub-poems was released under the US-based Heartbeat Label. The titles were, "Drug Kulcha", Life Waste Dub", "Slip" and "African School Dub".

His first LP, *Check It*, was released in 1983 under both the US-based Alligator Label and Tuff Gong Label. It consisted of ten dub-poems, produced by himself and Earl "Chinna" Smith. The musicians, Earl "Chinna" Smith, Carlton Barrett (Wailers), Leroy "Horsemouth" Wallace Rockers), Augustus Pablo, Earl "Wire" Lindo and Dean Fraser provided the excellent musical background to the poems.

Check It was released again on the Chicago blues label Alligator Records.

Outcry followed in 1984 on the US-based Shanachie. It was produced by Mutabaruka himself, and accompanied by "Ibo" Michael Cooper (background vocals), and Mutabaruka, together with Harry, T. Powell on percussions.

His third album, *The Mystery Unfolds*, done in collaboration with Marcia Griffiths and Ibo Cooper, was also released under Shanachie. It represented one of the highlights of his career.

The album *Any Which Way...Freedom* was released in 1989.

In September 1992, Mutabaruka had a No. 1 hit with a single entitled "Johnny Drug Head". It appeared on several US-based music charts.

He appeared in two movies in 1993: *Sankofa* (Slave History) and *Blak Wi Blakk...k...k.*

In 2008, Mutabaruka was featured as part of the Jamaican episode of the television program Anthony Bourdain: *No Reservations*.

Since 1996 Mutabaruka has been on *Irie FM* every Wednesday from 10 pm to 2am with his programme "Cutting Edge". He plays African music, explains African first names, broadcasts very interesting historical and theological documentations about the different religions with partly controversial statements.

He also talks about actual social and political subjects from the week.

LINTON KWESI JOHNSON

Linton Kwesi Johnson (LKJ) was born in 1952 in Chapleton, Claredon, Jamaica.

He grew up with his grandmother, a farmer and an avid reader of the Bible. In fact, Johnson's literary experience began with the reading of the bible, which he still quotes from (particularly the Book of Psalms), even today, and reads regularly with his grandmother.

In 1963, he migrated to England to live with his mother, who had left Jamaica two years before. He literally traded the moist green climate of Jamaica for the concrete reality of Brixton, located in the south of London.

With his great quest for knowledge, he attended school where he was soon to experience the harsh reality of racism. He left school at the age of sixteen years, but returned some years later to the Goldsmith College of the London University.

He was influenced politically by the Youth League of the Black Panthers that he joined in 1970. While there he organised a workshop for writers, together with other members.

It was during this period that LKJ began to read from his works. In June 1973, he recited his poem "Voices Of The Living And The Dead" at the Keksidee Centre in London, to the background music of the Rastafarian band, *Love*. His performance at this recital set the stage for his later reggae-influenced poetry style. In the meantime, his poems were being published in the journal, *Race Today*, which also published his first book of poetry, *Voices Of The Living And The Dead*. The second book was published in 1975 at Bogle L' Ouverture.

Linton Johnson's poems are greatly influenced by his life experiences growing up as a member of the Black Panther in a hostile environment, and his commitment to fight for the black working class, which earned him the name *Poet of Brixton*.

His poems were revolutionary, but not radical. In fact, his style was quite unusual. The poems were written in the common language of the Jamaicans (patois), which millions of immigrants spoke only secretly in Great Britain. To them, he simply added the main source of his creative energy, reggae music. According to Johnson, "Always, when I write, I might have the reggae rhythm in the head." In addition to the reggae rhythm, he imitated the style and language of the reggae deejays, such as Big Youth, U-Roy and Dillinger. The next logical step was into the recording studio.

In 1970, LKJ released *Dread Beat & Blood* under the Virgin label, which was followed by *Forces of Victory*, released under the Island Records Label in 1979. Topics such as political suppression, racist politicians, the fight against British colonialism, as well as the confrontations between the government and the Black Panther, were featured in his poems. Even though speaking about these issues made him uncomfortable, he could not ignore them anymore.

The album *Bass Culture* followed a year later, which further expounded on the issues previously mentioned. One of the songs on the album, entitled "Reggae Sound", featured a combination of art and his experiences.

In his poems and songs, LKJ attempts to create a relationship between the experience of his listeners/audience and his experience, which is transmitted through the music.

In 1981, his LP entitled *LKJ in Dub* was released, followed by an extensive tour, where he initially performed to recorded background music, and later with the nine-head Dennis Bovell Dub Band.

LKJ also worked as a journalist with the magazine *Race Today*, and the BBC. Between November 1982 and January 1983, he produced a documentary entitled "From The Mento of The Lovers Skirt", which examined the history and evolution of popular music. It was broadcast in 1993 by the BBC.

Towards the end of 1983, LKJ again returned to the studio to record the album, *Making History*, which was released in 1984. This album featured a quite radical LKJ. The title song celebrated blacks residing in Britain, while "Reggae Fi Radni", paid tribute to the union leader Walter Rodney, who was murdered in Guyana and "Di Great Insohreckshan" described the riots that occurred in British cities during the summer of 1981. The work was the subject of a BBC *Radio 4* programme in 2007.

In 1991, he released the LP *Tings An' Times*, under the English-based Stern Label, which represented a triumphant return to the recording studio.

In 2004 he became an Honorary Visiting Professor of Middlesex University in London. In 2005 he was awarded a silver Musgrave medal from the Institute of Jamaica for distinguished eminence in the field of poetry.

BIBLIOGRAPHY

- *Voices of the Living and the Dead.* Race Today, 1974

- *Dread, Beat an' Blood.* Bogle L'Ouverture, 1975

- *Inglan is a Bitch.* Race Today, 1980

- *Tidings an' Times: Selected Poems.* Bloodaxe, 1991

- *Mi Revalueshanary Fren.* Penguin, 2002

NEW GROUPS

BLACK UHURU

In 1977, Michael Rose (now known as Mykal Roze) and Derrick "Duckie" Simpson (the founder of Black Uhuru), as a duo recorded the song entitled, "Sun Is Shining", which was not successful. In 1979, Puma Jones, an American, who migrated to Jamaica, joined the group and later became a Rastafarian.

Uhuru is the Swahili word for freedom. Michael Rose, with his excellent singing voice was an asset to the trio. The first LP, entitled "Showcase", and released under the Taxi Label, featured the excellent vocals of the trio, together with the inimitable rhythms of Sly and Robbie.

The album *Sinsemilla* was then successfully released in 1980, followed by the release of "Red" in 1981. Both albums, which were a tribute to Bob Marley, showcased a wide spectrum of Roots and Rastafarian music. They were both produced and accompanied musically by Sly and Robbie.

In 1984, the group won the Grammy Award for the best album in the reggae category with the album entitled *Anthem*. In that same year, lead singer Michael Rose left the group to pursue his solo career. He was replaced with Junior Reid, who assumed the role of lead singer, as well as sharing the role of songwriter. Reid remained with the group for two years, after which, he too left to pursue his solo career, but not before he wrote six of the songs that were released on an album while he was a member of the group.

The group eventually dissolved in 1994, as the then members, Derrick Simpson, Don Carlos (Ervin Spencer) and Rudolph "Garth" Dennis went their separate ways. They were motivated by the desire to establish their independent careers, and their independence in respect of their recording labels. Prior to separating, however, they recorded the album "Love crisis", which was produced by Prince Jammy, and later released under the title "Black Sounds of Freedom".

Don Carlos gained recognition as a dancehall artiste and recorded two albums for Negus Roots. He later migrated to Africa, where he also became quite popular.

Although well known internationally, Black Uhuru was not quite as popular in Jamaica. The group was not well respected by the Jamaican media, maybe due to their refusal to pay money (payola) to the disc jockeys to have their music played on the radio stations.

With the release of the albums, "Now" and "Iron, Storm" in 1990, the group experienced a rebirth in 1991.

Towards the end of May 1993, Black Uhuru completed a five-week tour of promotional tour of North America, for their new LP entitled, "Mystical Truth", which was similar in style to the previous album, entitled "Iron Storm".

Some interesting songs were featured on this album, including, Tip of the Iceberg", a duet with US-Rapper Ice T; "One Love", a duet with US-based DJ Louie Rankin and "Slipping into Darkness", a cover version of War's pop hit from 1972.

After the split, the remaining group members (without Derrick Simpson) tried to perform and do recordings under the name Black Uhuru, but Simpson sued them in a court of law, claiming that he was the sole owner of the trademark name, *Black Uhuru*, *"therefore any man who portray or present the trademark on any billboard, or in any commercial dealing, then me a go sue them (then I will sue them"*.

Simpson successfully defended his claim, as a California Supreme Court judge ruled in his favour, declaring him rightful owner of the name.

2008 has brought new life to Black Uhuru. Duckie Simpson has once again taken charge. Along with new manager Mario Lazarre of No Joke Entertainment, Black Uhuru are back in the studio recording a new album. Guest appearances of this new album include Latin superstars Aterciopelados and Jarabe De Palo.

CHALICE

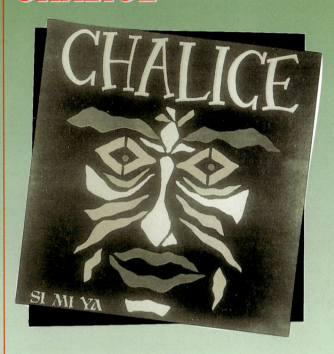

The band Chalice is one of most impressive live bands in Jamaica today. The group started in the 1980s and has also recorded several albums.

The first LP, *Blasted*, released under the English-based Pipe label in 1981, did not achieve much success. Success, however, came in 1984, following the release of two LPs, *Good To Be There* (Ariola Label) and *Stan' Up*, again released under the Pipe Label.

The next LPs, *Crossfire* released under the Jamaica-based CTS Label in 1986, and *Catch It*, released under the US-based Rohit Label in 1989, and *Si Me Ya* released under the Jamaica-based Peace Pipe label again, did not create much of an impact.

The group, however, achieved much success performing as live in Jamaica.

But success on the international stage was illusive. A new singer and drummer, Dean Stephens and Wayne "C-Sharp" Clarke, respectively have since joined the group. Together with these members, a rebirth on the international reggae scene seems imminent.

ZIGGY MARLEY AND THE MELODY MAKERS

"Ziggy" Marley was born in 1969. On his first LP, together with The Melody Makers (Cedella Marley, Sharon Marley-Prendergast, and Stephen Marley), entitled *Hey World*, he composed and arranged the songs himself – except "Give A Little Love", which was written and composed by Diane Warren and "Fools" Hammond. He also played the guitar, percussion and synthesizer, with Sly Dunbar on drums and Robbie Shakespeare on bass. The album was released under the Rita Marley music label.

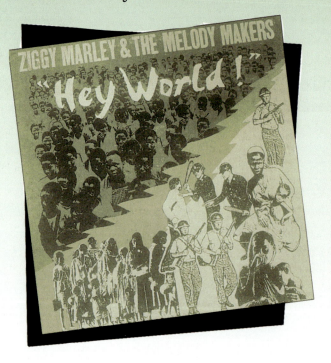

In 1988, the group released their second LP, entitled *Conscious Party* under the Virgin Recording Label. It consisted of hits, such as "Tomorrow's People ", "Lee and Molly" and "Tumblin Down", which was No. 1 in the USA on the Billboard Rhythm and Blues Charts.

This album also reached platinum status, with over one million copies sold.

The third LP, "Bright Day", was released in 1989, again under the Virgin Label. The hit song, "Black My Story" was written by both Ziggy and Stephen Marley, and was one of the best songs recorded on the album while The "Problem", which was also quite successful, was also written by Ziggy, together with his sister Sharon (Prendergast).

During the same year, the Melody Makers established their own recording label, *Ghetto Youth Label,* but still maintained some amount of control of their father's label, Tuff Gong Records.

Jahmekya was the first album to be released under the newly established Ghetto Youth label. It was released in 1991, and consisted of songs such as "Raw for Riddim", "Drastic" and "Namibia".

At the "Bob Marley Reggae in Bash" held in 1991 at the White River Reggae Park in Ocho Rios, the family performed together live on stage. There were, Ziggy with his children (who danced on the stage), the Melody Makers, Rita Marley, Marcia Griffiths and Judy Mowatt. For those who watched the performance live, it was an unforgettable musical experience. Tyrone Downey (a former member of the Wailers Band), and who now plays for Ziggy was also a part of the performance.

To promote their next album, *Joy and Blues*, which consisted of songs such as "Head Top" and "Body Contest",

Ziggy Marley and the Melody Makers embarked on a tour of South America on May 25, 1993. The tour was subsequently extended to include Europe, the USA, Japan and the Caribbean.

When Ziggy Marley and the Melody Makers received their third Grammy in February 1998, he stated, *"I did not have a Grammy on my mind. I just have the spirit to create music and make it different. Grammy is just the icing on the cake. I feel great, even though a nuh some thing weh me set me heart on. But we glad for it still"*.

While there are those in the music fraternity who are worried about the status of reggae on both the international and local scenes, Ziggy is of the view that the message in the music has changed from that which obtained in the 1980s, to something which is more conscious.

The group successfully toured the United States in 1998. They did a total of twenty-four concerts. The tour culminated with the staging of a massive concert at the Lockhardt Stadium in Fort Lauderdale, which holds twenty thousand people.

FORMS OF REGGAE: DUB AND DJ

The DJ-style was born towards the end of the 1950s. it evolved out of "toasting", a form of entertainment whereby promoters and talented DJs chant their lyrics while a rhythm or song is being played, usually by a sound system. It later became a genre of Jamaican popular music, which was eventually recorded and millions of copies sold to date.

During this time, sound systems dominated the dancehalls. One of the first and largest of the earlier sound systems DJs was Stan "The Great" Sebastian, together with Duke Vin.

Sir Coxsone Dodd of Downbeat also promoted a number of these DJs including, Count Machouki (credited for starting "toasting"), King Edwards, Count Boysie, Lord Chaos Of The Universe, Duke Reid, with V- Rocket, late Cuttins, Bells, Count Nick The Champ, Prince Buster with Voice Of The People, Supertone, and many others.

Towards the end of the 1960s, patrons of the dancehall were entertained by recorded songs or instrumental music. But this soon changed with the emergence of the modern DJ-style, where melody, song, and talk were combined, which resulted in a new form of entertainment.

The DJ version of music are usually instrumental versions of previously hit recorded songs or new independent instrumental music, to which the Disc jockey, comment on the social and political issues of the day in his lyrics.

The initial form of the DJ-style then expanded from short, crisp words by the announcer, to include the rhythm of the bass drums.

Some of the best-known DJs were Big Youth, Dillinger, I-Roy, U-Roy, Tapper Zukie and later, Yellowman, who became known at Sunsplash in 1982 and has since produced a number of hit songs.

Four track-recording studios were eventually established, and together with the installation of mixing machines in the mid to late 1960s, these new studios were able to record dub version of songs.

The dub versions of the records are instrumental versions of hits songs, recorded on the "B" side of the records. Here the melody starts in much the same way as the "A" side, and then goes through all the instruments, without any vocals. The various instruments often merge partially with each other, come in as an echo, stops or fades, or end abruptly.

Through multi-track recording technique the soundtracks could either fade in or fade, with an echo or a distorted, and the left or the right channel emphasized. The manner in which it is done is totally dependent on the DJ.

Dub LPs became big business, and the expert in this field was the indomitable, Lee "Scratch" Perry.

U-ROY O.D.

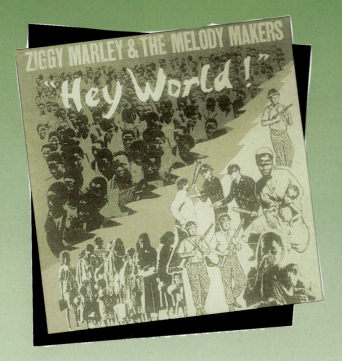

The legendary "father of deejaying" is Ewart "U-Roy" Beckford, the "Originator".

His career strted in 1961 when he began dejaying at various sound systems.

He developed his modern DJ style with technician and engineer King Tubby, who at the time had his own HI-FI equipment*, made several records for different producers also mixed songs for Duke Reid.

He discovered that he could make exciting new versions of known melodies when he altered the records, by removing or adding the bass, inserting echoes into the guitars and or by retaining or removing the vocals. For his ability he was nicknamed, 'The Dubmaster".

King Tubby made Dub versions with resonance and echo, from four of the best-known Duke Reid hits, such as "You Don't Care For Me", and recorded re-mixed versions of these songs with DJ, U-Roy; and the dance patrons were excited.

They danced for hours to these four Dub records, and were entertained by the seemingly endless fresh lyrics from U-Roy. With that, the DJ-Reggae-Style was born.

King Tubby**, U-Roy and Duke Reid, who recorded these original songs, were responsible for starting this phenomenon.

Within a year, U-Roy, with three of Duke Reid productions, were among the top ten songs on the local music charts. King Stitt, Clancy Eccles and Prince Buster also did recordings in this new DJ-style, but U-Roy outdid them all. He did records, which set the standard for others to follow, as he had the ability to move his voice with or over the rhythm, thereby extracting the original singer.

The combined styles of Shabba Ranks, Ninjaman and Cutty Ranks were influenced by U-Roy's "Version Galore", "Wear You To The Ball" and "Things You Love", where he (U-Roy) toasted the Techniques, Paragons and Melodians.

In songs, such as "Wake The Town" or "Rule The Nation", U-Roy did not use the original voices, rather he did three minutes of toasting, which was even much more creative.

This new DJ style became so popular, that many "stars in waiting", Dennis Alcapone and Prince Far-I, who had his own DJ sound system in the sixties, hurried to the microphones to get a piece of the action. Others such as Scotty were singers initially. But there were also new comers to the scene, such I-Roy and Big Youth. Except for Alcapone, whose style was authentic/original, the others utilised records previously done by U-Roy, to which they added or created their own styles. At the beginning of the 1970s, I-Roy and Big Youth also established themselves as DJs.

The following LPs are recommended for the avid collector: *"Ska Bonanza"*, released under the Heartbeat Label; "Keep On Moving Through The Door", "King Tubby's Special 1973-65" and "The Trojan Story", all of which were released under the Trojan Label; and Prince Buster's "Original Golden Oldies". Most of the best U-Roy tracks are recorded on the LP, "Version Of Wisdom" which was re-released in 1990 under the US-based Caroline Label.

In 2000, he recorded his album *Serious Matter*.

U Roy was awarded the Order of Distinction in the rank of Officer on October 15, 2007.

* Up to 1975 "Tubby's Hometown HI-FI" was the most popular sound system in Jamaica, until during the election, the police confiscated his equipment while he was staging a dance on grounds he had no license to stage the event. The years of work was literally destroyed within minutes.

** King Tubby (Osbourne Ruddock) was shot and killed in at his residence Kingston, on February 9 by a gunman. His firearm, necklace and a purse were stolen. To date, the motive is still unclear.

DILLINGER

Lester "Dillinger" Bullock was born in 1953 in Kingston. Inspired and influenced by U-Roy and Dennis Alcapone, he started in the music business with Lee Perry, but did a number of records for almost every producer in the ensuing years.

His first successful album *Bionic Dread* was recorded in the Channel One studio,

together with Sly Dunbar, Ansel Collins, Earl "Chinna" Smith and trumpeters Tommy McCook and Bobby Ellis. It was distributed in England by Island Records.

Dillinger became popular with songs such as, "Ensom City Skank", "Crashie First Socialist", "Jah Jah Dub" and "CB. 200", a song that was released on an LP of the same name in 1978 by Channel One. This LP also consisted of songs, such as "Cocaine In My Brain", which became a hit in Europe and the USA. Later, he also released an LP with the same name.

The album *Talkin' Blues*, consisted of songs that were all written by Dillinger himself. It was recorded in King Tubby's studio for producer Bunny Lee.

Dillinger was named as one of the best DJs of that time. The media often spoke about the "hottest DJ and performer".

In 1980, he recorded *Cup Of Tea*, a technically advanced album, which featured the excellent guitar-playing skills of Earl "Chinna" Smith. It also offered a concentrated range of the Roots Reggae and Disco Reggae.

His "Marijuana In My Brain", which was a number 1 hit in the Netherlands

His output dropped somewhat in the mid 1980s but he returned to recording in the early 1990s.

TAPPER ZUKIE

"*From the age of sixteen years, the pickney (little) youth, that jumped and twisted to the Viego sound system and the dub vendor; who has performed at the Four Aces, and on the Black Star Liner -the cruise ship that pulls into port*"; that is the review on the LP, entitled

"MPLA", especially for all of dreadlocks.

He also added the following message on the cover of the same LP, which was released in the international markets: "*The music business makes me happy. Not because of the money. It is because I love music. Perhaps, you might see with a purse full of money, after I have released an album, however that is not how it usually works in Jamaica. I record my music in Jamaica only for my fans. I earn money, but I also do a lot of travelling and business deals. Travelling costs a lot, as a result,, the money comes and it goes. So, to all my fans, please read one chapter of the Bible day, that keeps the sins away, that's what Zukie says.*"

Tapper Zukie was born as David Sinclair in 1955 in Kingston.

In 1973, his mother sent him to England, where he released a number of records. He was also greatly admired by the English media., which often described him as "*an existing legend*" and "England's "*hottest reggae interpreter*", a sure top ten artist and the archetypical Natty Dread".

His first LP released in England, *Man A Warrior*, was recorded during his first stay between 1974 and 1975. But it did not create much of an impact.

In 1976, while on his second trip to England, he recorded the Single "M.P.L.A." for Klik records, in which he sang about the solidarity with his black brothers in Angola. It was the best selling record for that year.

While on tour with Pattie Smith, he was the darling of the press, but this newfound status did not increase record sales.

But a contact with Virgin brought about the change. Later, three LPs entitled *Tapper Roots*, *Dub*, and *Peace In The Ghetto* were released. Since 1977, Zukie has financially supported the Peace Center, located on Ridge Street in Kingston – a meeting place not only for young people who are unemployed, but also an entertainment center for the performance of cultural music, dance and poetry.

The project is financed from the sale of his records, and also from donations received from the surrounding communities.

He also provided financial support to a general store, located on Harris Street, Kingston, which is operated by youths, who assist the elderly and poor in the inner cities.

He has a record shop on Constant Spring Road in Kingston.

BIG YOUTH

Manley Augustus Buchanan, more popularly known as Big Youth, was born in 1949 in Trench Town, Kingston. At the beginning of the 1970s, he was a member of the Wailers Band and Burning Spear, both of which dominated the reggae music scene at that time.

He dedicated his songs to the poor youths of the inner cities. "Dread Locks Dread", which was produced by Prince Tony in 1976, and later released under the Caroline Label, as well as "Reggae Phenomen" released under the Trojan label, represented Big Youth at his best. He was quite electrifying and dynamic in his style, which was influenced by the great U-Roy.

His first song, was entitled "Movie One", for which he was only paid J$20.00. it was later followed by the release of "The Killer" and "Ace 90 Shank", which is arguably one of his greatest hits.

He was named the number one DJ in Jamaica in 1973, following the overwhelming success of his LP, entitled, "Screaming Target", which was released under the Trojan Label. Having reached the peak of his music career, Big Youth made the transition from recording artiste to producer, and in the mid-1970s, he established the recording labels, Negusa and Augustus Buchanan, on which he produced and released a number of hit songs.

On his first tour of Europe, together with Dennis Brown, he was welcomed enthusiastically by the English crowd.

Later, he signed a recording contract with Island Records, which resulted in the release of his first British-based album, entitled, "Isaiah -Prophet Of Old". The British media described this LP as *"unbeatable and best reggae album produced for all times."*.

The next LP, "Dread Locks Dread", which was previously recorded in Jamaica in 1974, was also quite successful. He appears five times at Reggae Sunsplash between 1983 and 1996. His career revived in 1990, with the "Chanting" single, produced by Winston "Niney" Holness, and "Free South Africa" on the protest album One Man One Vote.

FORMS OF REGGAE:
DANCEHALL, RAGGA, RAGGAMUFFIN

Programmable drum machines, synthesizers, sequencers, samplers and desktop computers revolutionized the music recording industry in Jamaican during the 1980s, with the force of a hurricane.

Computer technology made it possible for a producer to do the work of a dozen musicians. He could now record complex rhythms, by simply pushing a couple of keys.

This had tremendous impact on Jamaican dancehalls scene, where young ambitious disc jockeys, with high expectations of making it big in the recording industry, competed for recording contracts.

During this period, therefore the Dancehall dominated the music industry, to such an extent that even traditional reggae artistes and groups, such as Ziggy Marley and Third World, in an effort to remain current, integrated the DJ-style and computer sounds into their records.

The dancehall-reggae was no longer static. In fact, the studios in Kingston were engaged both during day and night. Careers were started and ended overnight. A hit song was released on a rhythm, followed by dozens of versions "pon the same riddim" *(on the same rhythm),* and the lyrics of many DJs, influenced by the daily events which unfolded on the streets of Jamaica; whether it be comedic or tragic, about fire arms and gun shots, or about culture, love and sex, were transmitted around the world.

This new genre, referred to as dancehall, ragga or raggamuffin can best be described best as Hip Hop combined with Reggae. The lyrics, often done on a fast-paced rhythm, and in patois *(a regional dialect with a combination of African and English words),* celebrated mostly crime, guns and sex. It was the medium through which violence and the rebellious nature of the youth was expressed.

With regards to the quality, most of the 7" singles released in the Jamaican market were of a poor quality, whether played on duke boxes or on portables. The "B"-side of the records, usually consisted of the instrumental version of the song.

Tim Willis, a writer for the *Sunday Times*, based in London, in May 1993, did an article about Ragga on the British Broadcasting Corporation, which earned the ire of many, and led to much protest actions by homosexual groups.

Despite the furor over the article, it brought about much publicity for Shabba Ranks, who proclaimed the crucifixion of all homosexuals. In 1992, he reiterated in a televised interview conducted by a leading English-based music magazine that homosexuals were responsible for the spreading of diseases.

Buju Banton also earned the ire of homosexual groups, both in Britain and the United States, when he released his single "Boom Bye Bye", the lyrics of which advocated the shooting death of all homosexuals.

Despite the negative publicity, however, the sale of Ragga music was not adversely affected, and at the time, there were three ragga songs in top three positions on the British music charts. They were Shaggy's "Oh Carolina", at No. 1; Snow's (Darrin O'Brien, an Irish/ Canadian, born in Toronto in 1970) "Informer" at No. 2; and Shabba Ranks', "Mr. Loverman" at No. 3.

In the USA, during April 1993, "Informer" was No. 1 on both the Bill Board Rap Chart, as well as the pop charts. The single sold over one million copies and achieved platinum status. It should be noted that even though Snow is a white Canadian Ragga artiste, Ragga music is generally the music of the angry black subclass.

The music produced in Jamaica during this time, were highly rated. In fact, even the late Bob Marley would have been impressed. But one can state categorically that despite the high quality of the Ragga music produced during the mid-80s, and being played in the dancehalls in Kingston, they could not be compared to the songs written and recorded by Bob Marley, even though the latter songs appeared ten years before this new genre of music exploded on the scene.

THE "ENGLISH" REGGAE

Aswad

The group Aswad (from the Arabic for 'black') was formed in 1974 in West

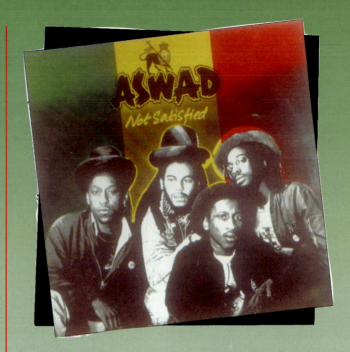

London. The group initially consisted of George "Ras" Oban (bass), Jamaican-born Courtney "Khaki" Hemmings (keyboards), and Brinsley "Chaka bar" Forde (singer, composer, rhythm guitar). Later, Jamaican-born Donald "Dee" Griffiths, lead guitarist and Angus Gaye on drums, joined the group. Tony Gad (Dennis Anthony Robinson) joined in 1980.

The band has remained unchanged since its formation and it has accompanied Burning Spear on numerous tours of England since. In fact, they were the accompanying band on the live LP released by Burning Spear, entitled "Burning Spear Live".

The first LP, entitled *Aswad* was released under the Island Record label in 1976. It featured a good mix of roots-reggae and typical British rock music, tempered with blues and flamenco elements; but it did not achieve much success.

After the release of this LP, the group went on tour with the punk band Eddie and The Hot Rods. But after a few concerts, they were dropped from the tour because of the perception that they were better that the punk band, which was very popular in England at the time. This resulted in disagreement between the punk band and the recording company.

While on tour the group, together with the punk band, had done performances in support of anti-racism, with the result that subsequent attempts by Aswad to sign recording contracts with numerous recording companies failed.

Aswad, however, remained loyal to their concept, and in 1979, they returned to Jamaica, where they released their second album "Hulet", in the spring of 1980, followed by the release of their fourth LP towards the beginning of 1981, entitled "Showcase". Both albums were weak and did not create much of an impact.

The group, however, has improved musically over the years, and to date, has released eight additional LPs.

In 1982, Aswad was featured on the soundtrack for the movie, *Countryman*.

In 1984, at a concert held in the Crystal Palace American Football Stadium, among other songs, they performed "Roots Rockin' Aswad".

An inspiring performance also followed in 1990, when they performed at Reggae Sunsplash on "International/Variety Night".

Aswad reunited for a performance on March 26, 2009 in London at the Island Records 50th anniversary concert.

Steel Pulse

The group Steel Pulse originated in Handsworth, Birmingham. David Hinds (rhythm guitar and lead vocal), Selwyn "Bumbo" Brown (keyboard and vocals) and Basil Gabbidon (lead guitar and vocals) founded the group in 1975. It was later joined by Alphonso Martin (percussion and vocals) and Steve "Grizzly" Nisbett (drums) in 1977, Alvin Ewen (bass) in 1983. Later, Jimmy "Senyah" Haynes (lead guitarist), who produced the albums *Earth Crisis* and *Babylon The Bandit*; and Tyrone Downey (keyboard and vocals) joined the group. Ronny "Stepper" McQueen (bass and percussion) was also a member. He left the group in 1983 after the release of the album "Earth Crisis", to pursue a career as a roots artiste. Basil Gabbidon was also absent from this album. Most of the songs, which were recorded on "Earth Crisis", were written by David Hinds.

In 1977, Steel Pulse returned to London and played at Punk Rock clubs and concerts, together with groups, such as Generation X, Billy Idol and The Stranglers. They were quite vocal about the issue of racism and its negative effects, with the result that they were often greeted by an angry audience, who often spat at them while they performed on stage.

The fans eventually accepted their style of music, largely due to the high quality of the lyrics and the rhythm/sound.

At the beginning, however, most club owners were disappointed with Steel Pulse, as they thought that it was a Calypso Steel Band. But overtime, the group was accepted, and it was one of the first non-punk group to perform in the Vortex Club.

Mainstream success was not far off, as shortly thereafter, the group was contracted as the opening act for Burning Spear, and continued to so do, until they signed a recording contract with Island Records.

The rock-style music, combined with the traditional Jamaican music of their parents, greatly influenced and improved their music style. They achieved a good balance, which was more aggressive than, but not as mystic as other groups.

In their lyrics, Steel Pulse not only sang of the social grievances in Jamaica, but also about issues, such as the Ku-Klux-clan, in a song of the same name released in 1978; the CIA and the many wars that were being fought around the world.

In 1978, the first album *Handsworth Revolution* was released to great reviews from the music industry. On the back of the record cover, the band acknowledged David Hinds' parents for the use of their basement during practice sessions.

In 1979, the album *Tribute To The Martyrs* was released. It consisted of very militant lyrics, advocating among other issues, the repatriation of Rastafarians to Africa.

Their live performances showcased their excellent instrumental improvisations, where one can literally hear the influence of Rock music.

With the release of their third album *Caught You* (released in the USA under the title, *Reggae Fever*), which was not so successful, Steel Pulse began to change their music style more towards the direction of disco reggae.

By the end of the 1980s, therefore, having honed their musical style, the American music market was now ripe for the picking.

A tour of Chicago, Boston, New York and Detroit followed in February 1981 on the heels of this successive tour, the group was invited to perform at the fourth staging of Reggae Sunsplash, which was in memory to Bob Marley. They played themselves into the hearts of many Jamaicans, who were astonished that an overseas band could play reggae music so well. The group has since performed every year at Reggae Sunsplash. Tours to Japan, Europe and the USA followed in 1984.

They eventually established their own recording label, "Wise Man Doctrine" in England in 1985.

In 1991, the album "Victim" was released under the America-based MCA label. Tyrone Downey had left the group by then, and Jimmy Haynes was invited to play as guest musician.

In the same year more than ten thousand reggae music fans danced enthusiastically for more than one hour to the music of Steel Pulse at the "Ben & Jerry's One World, One Heart Open Air Festival", held in New York's Central Park, at which they performed ten of their most popular songs. It was a free concert, sponsored by Ben and Jerry's, one of the largest manufacturers of ice cream in the United States.

In spring of 1992, the album, *Rastafari Centennial* (a compilation of songs performed live at a concert held in Paris) was released under the MCA Label. It represented an excellent overview of songs spanning their career, which was recorded with considerably more power than their studio recordings.

In 2007, the band released their music video for "Door Of No return", a track taken from their latest studio album *African Holocaust,* which explores themes of the Trans-Atlantic Slave Trade.

UB 40

UB 40 consists of Astro Brown (DJ and percussionist), Jim Brown (drums, synchroniser), Ali Campbell (lead vocal, rhythm guitar), Robin Campbell (vocal, lead guitar), Earl Falconer (bass), Norman "Lamount" Hassan (percussion, conga drum, vocal), Brian Travers (tenor saxophone, melodica) and Michael Virtue (keyboard, string, and organ).

The group prefers the "pop style" music form, which Ziggy Marley and the Melody Makers also plays.

Over the years, they have work with artists such as Burning Spear and Judy Mowatt, with whom they wrote the anti-apartheid song, "Sing Your Own Song".

UB 40 has recorded cover versions of a number of songs in the lovers rock style; the most popular of which are, "Red Red Wine" written by Neil Diamond; "Guilty" (Laurel Aitken), "Keep on Moving" (Bob Marley), "Cherry Oh Baby" (Eric Donaldson), "Sweet Sensations" (The Melodians) and "Many Rivers To Cross" (Jimmy Cliff).

All these songs can be found on the LP "Labour Of Love", with Jackie Mittoo on keyboard.

They have had more than 50 singles on the UK charts.

More recently, the members of the have been spending most of their time at their new residence (a nice villa on the seaside with a modern studio) near Oracabessa, St. Mary, where they relax and produce records.

In 2007, they toured South Africa and headlined the *Live Earth Concert.* They performed one of the longest sets for the event at about 54 minutes long.

Maxi Priest has toured with the band since 2007.

In 2008, Ali Campbell and Mickey Virtue left the band, and two new members, Duncan Campbell, vocals, and Tony Mullings, keyboard, joined.

SOCA

Soca (**So**ul of **Ca**lypso) music is gladly played and enjoyed by patrons at any event, including carnival and during the Christmas season. It is a cheerful mix of fast rhythms and is similar in sound and rhythm to Samba, Lambada and calypso.

Byron Lee, the owner of Dynamic Sound Studios popularized this music form in Jamaica. The artiste, Arrow and the band Fabulous Five are well-known players of soca music.

Soca emerged in Jamaica at the beginning of the 1980s. It also emerged as a popular dance in Europe, having placed second to Lambada, which was named the dance of year in 1990.

In Trinidad, the home of the Soca music, the three leading bands are, The Blue Ventures, which consist of eighteen musicians, and has played at the Orange Carnival held in Jamaica in 1989; the Brooklyn Carnival, held in New York, and at the Toronto's Caribana Festival), Charlie's Roots and Shandileer.

BYRON LEE AND THE DRAGONAIRES

Byron Lee, together with the Dragonaires, features prominently in any history written about the evolution of popular music in Jamaica, in particular the era from rock-

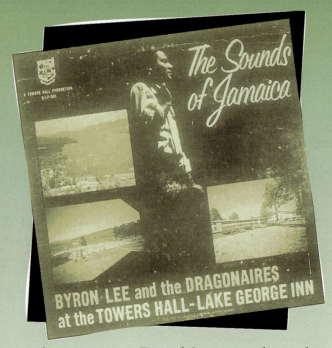

The Sounds of Jamaica

BYRON LEE and the DRAGONAIRES at the TOWERS HALL-LAKE GEORGE INN

steady to reggae. But this group has also made significant contributions to the evolution of soca music in Jamaica. In fact, when the history of soca music in Jamaica is written, Byron Lee and the Dragonaires will be credited for making this music form quite popular. It is one of, if not the best soca bands in Jamaica to date.

The album *Wine Miss Tiny* was released in 1985, and featured the hit song "Tiney Winey". It was followed by the release of the album, "De Music Hot Mama" in 1988, which also consisted of a hit song of the same name.

Each year during Jamaica Carnival, held in March and April, the group releases a compilation CD, which consists of all the popular soca songs for that year.

Examples include *Jamaica Carnival 90* and *Soca Carnival*, which was released in 1991.

FABULOUS FIVE INC.

During the mid-70s, Fab Five released an album with slow reggae rhythms under the Trojan label.

It consisted of a two-part song entitled "My Jamaican Girl", which was previously released as a single and was a big hit for the group; the Mento song, "Shaving Cream", in addition to cover version of songs, which also became hits.

They first became successful on the international scene, when they performed as the backing band on Johnny Nash's platinum album, *I Can See Clearly Now*. The songs "Guava Jelly" and "Stir It Up", written by Bob Marley were also featured on this album.

They went on tour in 1983 with Rita Marley, whose song "One Draw" was popular at the time. The song was written and arranged by band members, Grub Cooper and Ricky Walters. It was later released on Rita Marley's LP, "Harambe". For this LP, Cooper and Walters not only wrote most of the songs, but they also provided background vocals and were the backing musicians.

Fab Five emerged on the Soca scene during the mid-80s. The song entitled "Yu Safe" released in 1985, was a 7½-minute soca hit. It remained at the top of the music charts in both New York and Jamaica for weeks. An album with the same name followed a year later.

In 1987, the group released a dance-hall album entitled *Jamaican Woman* under the Stage Label. In addition to a song with the same name, the album also consisted of the previously released, "Shaving Cream".

The album *All Night Party* also released under the Stage Label in 1989, featured a wide range and variants of soca music. Latin American, Jamaican and American musical forms, were interestingly combined to create a unique soca sound. These soca creations were recorded on this album. The pace of the rhythm varied from fast to slow. For creating this musical style, Fab Five is Jamaica's best-kept secret "musical weapon".

In 1989, Fab Five was named the best upcoming band, best show band and best group.

In 2003 Fab Five received The Prime Minister's Award For excellence in the Performing Arts for their services to Jamaican music.

In addition, the bands musical director Grub Cooper, OD CD, was awarded from the Jamaican government with the Oerder Of Distinction , Officer Class (OD) and Commander Class (CD).

ARROW

Alphonso "Phonsie" Celestine Edmund Cassell, singer, composer and producer, was born in 1954 Montserrat, and was the youngest of nine children.

In 1970, *Arrow* won a calypso competition (and than 4 more times) and has since reigned as the "Calypso King" since then.

He set up his own Arrow label in 1973.

By the mid-80s, his music style had improved, as evidenced by the release of the LPs *On Target* (1974), *Instant Knock Out* (1981), and *Double Trouble* (1982), which earned him critical acclaim.

Arrow was the first Soca singer to perform on television shows such as Soul Train in the United States and the Terry Wogan Show in England.

He has one of the most successful Soca bands in Jamaica.

In 1982, the band had a massive hit with "Hot Hot Hot", which was quite popular around the world. Today, it is sung in twelve different languages, and has conquered the pop and disco music markets around the world.

The album *Soca Savage*, released under the Dynamic label in 1984, was also quite remarkable.

Over the years, the rhythm of the Arrow has become faster and fresher. A very good example is the album, Zombie Soca released in 1991.

Arrow continues to be in demand in the Caribbean, and most recently performed at the Cricket World Cup 2007 opening ceremonies with Shaggy, Byron Lee and Kevin Lyttle.

THE NINETIES

Yellowman, one of the founders of the Dancehall style, has placed contemporary reggae music into four categories:

Roots: the reggae (music) that was made popular by Bob Marley, and which Culture plays.

Dancehall: what he performs, and also Shabba Ranks, Supercat, Admiral Bailey and Charlie Chaplin

Pop: played by Ziggy Marley and UB40.

Lovers Rock: sounds similar to R & B and performed by Maxi Priest and Beres Hammond

As in the fashion industry, where cuts and colours are often repeated as time passes, so does the rhythm in music.

In Jamaica during 1992, two very hot riddims (rhythms) emerged on the music scene. The first was the "Cherry O Baby" rhythm. The song was originally recorded in the 1960s by Eric Donaldson, and was later covered during the 1970s by the Rolling Stones and in the '80s by UB40. In 1992, however, several songs by different artistes appeared on the music charts in Jamaica with the same (computer-aided) rhythm, including, Tony Rebel with the hit song, "Sweet Jamaica"; Pinchers, Marcia Griffiths, Beres Hammond, Cobra, Admiral Tibet and General Trees.

The other was the "Bam Bam" rhythm. The song was originally recorded by Toots and The Maytals in 1966, but was re-engineered by Sly Dunbar in recording studio in Kingston.

The DJ and singer Shaka Demus and Pliers had a hit single "Murder She Wrote" on this rhythm. It was produced by Jah Screw. Ziggy Marley also released "Stop Joke" on the same version.

The Bam Bam rhythm is recognised throughout the entire Caribbean and internationally. In Brazil, it is called "clave"; in Nigeria, "high life"; Dr. John, Allene Toussant and the Neville Brothers from New Orleans refer to it as "second line"; and Blues and Rock 'n' Roll fans as "Bo Diddley Beat", "Not Fade Away" and "Who Do You Love" beat. In 1992, a compilation LP was released under the Startrail Label, *Bam Bam*, which featured artistes such Beres Hammond, Tony Rebel and Gregory Isaacs.

Changes were also taking place in the world of local radio. In 1988, Bob Clarke, Programme Director for IRIE FM, applied for and was successful in obtaining a radio broadcasting/transmission license. Two years later, in July 1990, IRIE FM, a radio station dedicated solely to the playing of reggae music, started broadcasting from its studios located in Ocho Rios, St. Ann. The station takes one on a twenty-four hour journey, every day through the annals of Jamaican music. A daily dose of ska, rocksteady, reggae, dancehall, and lovers rock, in addition to soca music is offered each day.

IRIE FM has also established a record-producing studio (Grove Recording), where it also manufactures its own records. It is presently rated the second best radio station in Jamaica by the Jamaica Media Survey.

Carl Young, owner and Chairman of IRIE FM, was also one of the organisers of the reggae concert, White River Reggae Bash, held once or twice every three months, at the White River Reggae Park in Ocho Rios.

This event provided tourists, who stay outside of Kingston the opportunity to view live performances of various groups/bands and solo artistes. It was a concept that started at Little Pub, locate in Ocho Rios in the late-70s or early-80s.

During the mid-90s, new DJs, Beenie Man, Bounty Killa and Luciano emerged on the music scene, and were the top record selling artistes. Some female artistes also emerged, including Lady Saw and Nadine Sutherland.

Record sales in 1995 were relatively slow. In fact only the No. 1 song for that year, "Anything For You" (Snow and Friends), sold more than twenty thousand copies.

At the end of 1995, the top ten songs in Jamaica, were as follows:

Titles	Artiste(s)	Positions on Chart
"Anything For You"	Snow and Friends	Atlantic 21/16/4
"Untold Stories"	Buju Banton	Loose cannon 19/12/3
"Slam"	Beenie Man	Mad House 18/9/4
"Cellular Phone"	Bounty Killer	John John 17/10/3
"Big Up And Trust"	Beenie Man	Shocking Vibes 18/11/3
"Suspense"	Bounty Killer	Priceless 16/10/2
"What we need Is Love"	Spanner, Banner & Luciano	Island, Jamaica 18/8/3
"Soca Tatie"	Byron Lee & The Dragonaires with Admiral Bailey	Dynamic 19/8/3
"Book Book Book"	Bounty Killer	Jammys' 16/9/2
"Done Wife"	Mad Cobra	How Yu Fi Say Dat 20/12/-

In 1996, a new sound was emerging – a fusion of reggae and soca, now known as Soggae (pronounced *so gey*).

In February of the following year, the Soggae Carnival was launched in Kingston. One week of activities followed from April 6 to April 14, which culminated with a massive road march.

BEENIE MAN

Moses Anthony Davis, popularly known as Beenie Man, was born in 1973 in the Waterhouse district in Kingston.

In 1981, together with his older brother Little "Kirk" Davis, Beenie entered a talent contest being staged by their community, in which there were forty-two other participants.

The DJ and singing contest was won by Beenie Man and Little Kirk, respectively.

Also present at the event was popular Jamaican radio disc jockey, Barry G. He introduced Beenie Man to producer Henry "Junjo" Lawes, who produced Beenie Man's first Single "Too Fancy".

The young upcoming deejay, managed to combine school work, his music career and working on his uncle's band, "Master Blaster", at nights, until he met Patrick Roberts, the manager of Shocking Vibes Productions.

Roberts started to promote both Beenie Man and Little Kirk, until the latter left because of disciplinary problems.

At age of eight years, his first LP, "The Invincible Beenie Man: Ten Year Wonder", produced by Bunny Lee was released. It is alleged that Beenie Man was not paid for his work on this LP. After this, he returned back to Roberts' camp, where he recorded several singles.

During the 1990s, however, Beenie Man has become a household, largely due to his many great performances; (five times) at Reggae Sunsplash, Reggae Sumfest, and numerous other music events. It had taken him at least fifteen years of hard work and dedication to become one of today's DJ sensation, as well as his own backing band, *Blaze*.

Beenie Man had signed a recording contract with Jammy's, prior to signing a two album recording contract with Chris Blackwell of Island Record (Jamaica) Limited in 1995.

The first album, entitled Blessed" consisted of fourteen songs, including, "Blessed", "Slam", " Stop Living in the Past" and Modeling". The second album was entitled "Maestro".

Beenie Man has won the title of Jamaica's top deejay on many occasions. In 1994 and 1995, he won all the major deejaying awards.

In May 1996, he received the "DJ of the Year Award" at the Tamika Awards held in New York.

After his album *The Doctor* was released in 1999 on the VP label he was also called Dr. Beenie Man.

Beenie Man got married to Michelle Downer, also known as D'Angel in August 2006 in a lavish ceremony in Jamaica. A DVD of their wedding was bootlegged and sold afterwards. Their son, Marco Dean, was born in November 2006. Their relationship, however, was shortlived. In June 2007, Beenie Man separated from his wife. In a *TVJ* interview with Ian Boyne, D'Angel said the marriage was a disaster.

BOUNTY KILLER

Bounty Killer was born Rodney Basil Price in 1972 in Kingston. He emerged on the music scene during the late-80s to early-90s. Like Beenie Man, his records were also released under the Shocking Vibes label. He also his own backing band, Kaushion.

He is no doubt, one the most talented deejays in of Jamaica.

In the nineties, he became known in the USA and Europe.

At stage shows/music concerts, Bounty Killer usually performs before or after Beenie Man. But from time to time, he decides when he is to perform; and in the event that his demands are not met, he is known to leave the venue without performing, as he did at Reggae Sunsplash in 1994.

Although a talented performer, he tends to be unprofessional. However, once he enters the stage, he is known to silence his critics with a solid performance.

In 2006 he signed to VP Records.

He inspired many young artistes such as Elephant Man, Baby Cham and Vybz Kartel.

LUCIANO

Jepther McClymont, also known as Lucien Nicolet or Luciano, was born in 1978.

Luciano is one of the best talents to emerge during the 1990s. His song, "It's Me Again Jah" was one of the smash hits in 1995. During the same year, at the annual staging of Sting, he kicked things into the gear with his dynamic performance.

Luciano made his first United States appearance in November 1995 at the Reggae Cafe in Fort Lauderdale. He was supported by the Xterminator Crew, which consisted of Mikey General, Shadowman, Jesse Jendau, Ragnomposier, Sizzla, and veteran Dancehall star, Frankie Paul. He was backed by the powerful Firehouse Crew.

The Fort Lauderdale show had been scheduled for the summer, but had to be postponed after Luciano decided to go on a 40-day Sabbatical.

In December 1996, he made his New York debut.

NINJA MAN

The word *Ninja,* in Japan is a synonym for a silent death; but not the for the Jamaican Ninja. The Jamaican Ninja Man, born in 1966 as Desmond John Ballentine in Annotto Bay, is never silent.

He is a popular dancehall deejay, known for his controversial and pro-gun lyrics and his stuttering and melodramatic style. He does not hesitate to tell to any and everyone that he is the master of the Jamaican DJ scene and "will obliterate" any other DJ, who crosses his path. The song "Murder Dem" is a good example of this artiste's belief in his self-proclaimed badness.

One can state categorically that he is a gifted orator, who is known for his social protestations, as evidenced by his oft repeated statement, *"DJs are the eyes of the nation and all DJs are the*

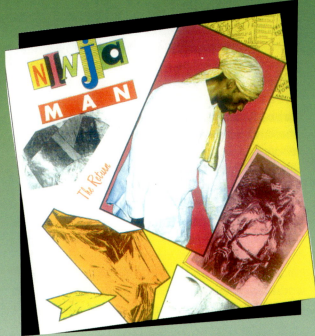

He was sentenced to one year in jail in late 1999, after being convicted of unlawfully possessing a firearm and ammunition.

In March 2009, Ninja Man was arrested and charged in connection with a murder on Marl Road, Kingston.

Irrespective of one's view of the Don Gorgon, he is one of the most exciting and controversial deejays to emerge on the music scene in Jamaica.

TONY REBEL

teachers of the nation"; or his religious insight, with the biblical statement: *"The time will come, when the world will be governed by musicians"* or, *"Reggae teaches the world and brings it peace "*; one dare not say that *"this is (not) the gospel according to Ninjaman"*.

Despite his social and religious awareness, however, He tends to use lot of "noise" and violence, both in and outside his music to put across his message.

Ninja Man is the legendary personification of the ghetto-raggamuffin. He is a gangster-rapper in the true sense of the word, who represents the hard core. In his lyrics, the machine guns are more important than the women. He sings and raps more about the negative aspects of life than the positive, is more a gangster than a lover.

Ninja Man, the most controversial DJ in the dancehalls to date, was Christened the "Don Gorgon", because of the frank and fearless manner in which he delivers his message through his music.

Because of his fearlessness, he is often in problems with the law, and seems to always attract controversy.

Tony Rebel, born Patrick George Anthony Barrett, in 1962 in Elliston, Manchester, is one of the most prolific and tireless reggae performers.

He represents the link between the older, more traditional Rastafarians, and the younger dancehall generation.

He is described as a cultural artiste, who has recorded songs such as, "Sweet Jamaica" (on the *Cherry O' Baby* rhythm). Above all, he became known in Jamaica through the reggae radio station, IRIE – FM, located in Ocho Rios, St. Ann.

After winning twice in dancehall competitions held in Manchester, both in 1983 and 84, Sugar Minott a veteran in the music industry recognised his potential, and took him to Youth Promotions, a recording company located in Kingston. But success was elusive, and due to financial difficulties, he returned to Manchester, the parish of his birth.

While there, he caved enough money to independently produce and record the single "Casino". It was an uncompromising critique of casino gambling in Jamaica. Even though the song was relatively successful, it led to much public debate on the issue of casino gambling, which is illegal, but is a feature in numerous hotels and other establishments throughout Jamaica. It also resulted in him becoming more popular, and his abilities as a serious cultural musician was becoming more recognised.

Many will argue, however, that Tony Rebel made it difficult for himself in the music industry. He was already at a disadvantage, based on the fact that he was a musician from the "country", with limited financial resources and who did not access to the modern recording facilities that DJs in Kingston were accustomed to.

In addition, he was a Rastafarian, and at that time there were literally no prominent Rastafarian DJs in the music industry who could offer guidance and support his budding career.

But more importantly, many believe that it was his refusal to perform typical dancehall music that made the situation worst, and the producers at that time, were not impressed with his cultural songs. However, he remained steadfast and refused to dishonour his name by recording or performing music that he believed did not meet his moral standards.

However, success came with the release of the single, "Music Fraternity" in 1989, and "The Amor" and "Mandela Story". in 1990.

With this newfound success, he went on a tour of the eastern Caribbean Islands, and was well received in Trinidad and Barbados.

Later, in 1992, he had other hit songs, such as, "Chatty Chatty" and "Fresh Vegetable", and the album *Rebel With A Cause*, was also a hit.

As an outsider in the large dancehall centres in Kingston, where slackness and gun lyrics dominates the music, the cultural DJ, Tony Rebel eventually found his way. It is probably not the recipe for a great success, but he did it his way.

He signed in 1992 with Columbia Records. In 1994 he founded his Flames record label. His yearly Rebel Salute shows are a must event.

SHABBA RANKS

Shabba Ranks was born in 1966 in Sturge Town, St. Ann, as Rexton Ralston Fernando Gordon.

In 1980, at the age of fourteen years, he stepped onto the music scene. One year later, in 1991, he released his first single, "Hold a Fresh", under his stage name Shabba Ranks, which was borrowed from a notorious gangster.

Several singles followed up to 1987. But it was the release of the single, "Live Blanket" that made him a household name, and put him on the international scene. It also led to a number of live performances in England, Canada and USA. "Wicked In Bed" then followed, and with this single he made his entry onto the American music charts, and in 1990, he won his first Grammy in the reggae category.

In 1991, he entered the English music charts with a cover version of "She's A Woman", a Beatles original. It was done in collaboration with the band, Scritti Politti. He had further successes in Britain with "Housecall", which was recorded with Maxi Priest.

"Mr. Loverman", as he is affectionately called, was also quite successful, and is a song about his relationship with women. He his also nicknamed "Mr. Culture".

His slackness and sex-obsessed lyrics made him to the hottest sex symbol in the dancehall scene.

In 1992, he received his second Grammy for the album *As Raw As Ever*, released under the Sony-Epic Label and produced by Bobby "Digital" Dixon and Clifton Dillon. During the same year, he recorded a song with KRS-ONE, which was described as Classic Rock *(a combination of Rap and Deejay)*.

According to Shabba Ranks, *"Music is the only thing that can make the world unite."*

After the release of the LP *Rough & Ready: Volume One*, which consisted of remixes of previous songs that were quite popular in Jamaica; he released "X-Tra Naked" and went on a promotional tour of Germany for this new album in November 1992.

The album was launched in Jamaica at the Godfather's Night Club, simultaneously with the launch of a safe-sex campaign.

Proceeds from the sale of the records (J\$50,000.00) were donated to the Jamaica A.I.D.S Fund.

Shabba Ranks is currently being managed by Leggo Recording Studio, and his producer is Flabba Holt from the Roots Radics band.

Interesting singles released in 1993, were "Daddy, Grandpa", "Wise as Ever", "Drive", "Lesbian" and "Militants", done in collaboration with Beres Hammond.

Recently less active, he did a song in 2007, "Clear The Air". He lives in New York.

His success helped pave the way for even bigger crossovers by artistes like Shaggy and Sean Paul.

"Wicked inna Bed" is featured on the reggae radio station K-JAH Radio West, in the video game, *Grand Theft Auto San Andreas.*

BUJU BANTON

Buju Banton (Mark Anthony Myrie), was born in 1973 at Salt Lane, near Kingston. He started his music career at the age of thirteen years and made his music debut with the release of three singles.

When one listens to his voice only, he sounds like a two hundred-pound giant, but he is small in stature and looks like a teenager. He speaks with the speed of a machine gun, he is quite jovial, and laughs the loudest. Politics does not interest him, but he readily and easily talks about girls.

In 1991, he recorded twenty-six singles and had up to four songs in the top ten spot on the music chart.

By 1992, he was the new dancehall star, and his songs were not popular in

Jamaica, but also in London, New York and Tokyo. On October 2, of the same year, he was one of the headline performers at the annually held Miss Universe Contest.

His series of hits started with "Love Me Browning ", which was No. 1 on the Jamaican music charts, the lyrics of which was much to the annoyance of women of a darker shade: *"I love my bike, I love my car, I love my money but most of all I love my Browning" (brown woman).*

To appease the latter, he released the single "Love Black Woman", and together both songs were in the top spots on the music chart. Buju Banton and Shabba Ranks are two DJs who appeal to women with their lyrics.

His first album, *Voice Of America,* (the first of a six-album record deal which he signed Mercury) was released in July 1993 under the American-based Mercury Label. The album featured songs such as "Deportee", which was previously released as a single; and "A Little More Time", a duet with Beres Hammond. It reportedly sold over three hundred thousand copies.

His next album, *Til Shiloh,* released in 1996 and the second for Mercury, not only defined Buju Banton as a serious and prolific reggae artiste, but it also separated him from the average DJ.

In 1998, the third album *Inna Heights,* was released by Polygram (a subsidiary of Mercury) under the Island Records Label. It sold over sixty thousand copies during the first five months.

His fourth album featured ten preciously recorded songs, which were not released until the launch of the album, and five new songs. It featured songs such as, "Good God Of my Salvation", "Stamina Daddy", "Gold Spoon", Batty Rider", and "Grudge".

In June 1998 he went on an extensive three-month tour, which took him throughout the United States of America, Europe, Africa and Japan.

At the Cricket World Cup 2007 Opening Ceremony he performed with Third World and Beres Hammond.

In 2008 he did a soca collaboration Winning Season (remix) with Machel Montano of Trinidad and Tobago on Machel's album Flame on.

In 2009, Buju released the long awaited and often delayed album, *Rasta Got Soul,* a return to strictly conscious lyrics. Included on the album is "Magic City".

BERES HAMMOND

After more than twenty years in the reggae music business, the break-through for Hugh Beresford Hammond came in 1992.

Hugh Beresford Hammond was born in 1955 in Annotto Bay, St. Mary, but spent his early years alternating between Annotto Bay, where his parents lived, and Kingston, where some of his siblings resided.

He particularly loved his trips into Kingston as they gave him the opportunity to listen to and observe the current trends in the music industry, which no doubt influenced the title for his first song, "Wanderer", which he recorded at the age of fifteen years.

He did a few recordings for Merritone in 1972, but the professional stage of his recording career started in 1975 at Aquarius Records. One year later, in 1976, his first album *Soul Reggae* was released. It was produced and arranged by Willie Lindo. The album featured the hit single, "One Step Ahead", which is still popular today.

Other singles followed, such as "I am in Love With You", "Just A One", "Groovy Little Thing", "Got To Get Away" and "What One Dance Can Do".

After a three-year break from the music business, because of financial challenges; during which he pursued other interests, he returned with a slew of hits, which earned him the nickname "soulman" because of his soulful ballads.

He has since released seven LPs and numerous singles, most of which appeared on the top ten music charts in Jamaica, and even advanced to the number one spot.

The lyrics for his songs are inspired by the people he encounters on a daily basis. He had written songs for the Virgo Label, and he has also done recordings for different labels, such as Exterminator, and Penthouse, and for his own labels (Harmony House and Star Trail Records. He has also recorded for Sly and Ronnie on their Taxi Label. But he is an independent producer, who is not signed to a recording label, as this gives him the ability to be totally independent. In other words, no one can dictate to him.

Beres is of the view that most recording companies may offer a five-year contract to an artiste, who usually has some measure of financial security during the contract period, but is usually uncertain as to his future after it ends, especially if it is not renewed. Further, he is of the view that most of these contracts, signed between recording companies/labels and artistes, place the former in a more advantageous position, than the latter.

Since 1992, Beres Hammond has been performing tirelessly on stage shows. In addition, he has had a number of hit songs on radio stations, such as, "Putting Up Resistance", "Double Trouble", "What One Dance Can Do", "She Loves Me Now", "Tempted To Touch" and "You And Me", a duet with Marcia Griffiths, as well as "Full Attention" and "Big Man Nuh Cry", recorded with Buju Banton.

He is one of the very few entertainers, who have the ability to stage a one-man show, and normally starts his shows with his greatest hits. He has been an inspiration to other artistes and audiences across the world.

If the possession or gift of talent alone could pay, Beres Hammond would have been a millionaire. But he is quite satisfied to live his life without complaints.

Beres Hammond has sung hits after hits since 1976, but financial success only came in the early 1990s. It is quite obvious that money is not his motivation, as he gets his satisfaction from knowing that he is creating beautiful music, which is appreciated by his many fans.

He is an artiste who does not make plans for the future, but lives in the present, and uses his daily experiences to create music.

The question is: When will Beres Hammond sign a contract with one of the big recording companies?

The answer probably lies in the title of one of his famous songs: he is "putting up resistance".

GARNETT SILK

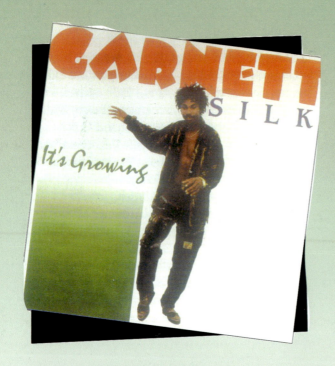

Born Garnett Damion Smith in 1966 Manchester, Garnett Silk has left a strong spiritual and musical legacy. (He got the name Silk from Steely and Clevie.)

From 1992 until 1994, he captured the public's attention, when he changed the face of the dancehall music; and the difference was not to be ignored.

Garnett started his music career as a deejay in Manchester under the name Little Bimbo.

Success came soon after he started to record with Jammy, Tubby, Germain and Steely and Clevie at the Grove Recording Studios in Ocho Rios. The songs included, a cover version of Johnny Nash's, "I Can See It Clearly Now" and the country-oldie "Seven Spanish Angels", which was produced by Courtney Cole for the Roof Label.

Both Beres Hammond and Tony Rebel were supportive of his music career, and exposed him to various aspects of the music industry, such as stage shows (Rockers Awards and White River Reggae Bash). In fact, it was Beres Hammond who introduced him to the Grove Recording Studios.

The previously mentioned hits, together with "It's Growing", were recorded by Bobby Digital, and released on an album of the same name. Other LPs included "You Are Looking Good", recorded for Germain; "Nothing Can Divide Us" for Cole and "Show A Little Mercy" for Jammy. The release and success of these LPs resulted in Garnett Silk becoming one of the most sought after entertainment artiste during the early 1990s.

Most of the above-mentioned LPs (including *It's Growing* and *Nothing Can Divide Us*), as well as *Love Is The Answer*, *Silky Mood* and his masterpiece and biggest seller, *100 Per Cent Silk*, were recorded at VP Records.

But his budding career was cut short, when he died on December 10, 1994, in a fire where he tried to save his mother. On Boxing Day, 1994, over forty thousand people bid farewell to Garnett Silk, whom many claim was the heir-apparent to Bob Marley's throne.

Tony Rebel, his friend, and mentor, has credited him for the current wave of cultural music which is now a feature of the music recording industry; but more importantly, he believes that Garnett Silk was the was the sacrificial lamb for Rastafari and reggae.

ANTHONY B

As a contemporary dancehall artiste, Anthony B has had numerous hit songs on the music charts in Jamaica since 1996. His single "Fire Pon Rome", a critical look at persons occupying leadership positions in the areas of politics and commerce, was banned by radio stations and triggered a firestorm of criticism.

His style of reggae music is consistent with the growing trends in music today and is characterised by more melody than what previously pertained in earlier dancehall music.

Born Keith Anthony Blair in 1976, in Clarks Town, Trelawny, Anthony B, together with his friends, started making music on the side of the roads in his community, where they would beat drums and "chant down Babylon" during the evenings.

Encouraged by his friends and neighbors, he decided to start a career in music. Following this decision, he went to live with an uncle in Portmore, St. Catherine.

He later went to Richard "BoBo" Bell, a producer at Star Trail Records, who was impressed with Anthony's first recording, "A De Man", and a slew of hits and popular songs followed.

Anthony B's debut album, *So Many Things*, featured sixteen songs, including "Fire Pon Rome", "Raid The Barn", Cold Feet" and "Prophecy A Reveal".

He has performed live in Jamaica on numerous occasions, including at the White River Reggae Bash, Reggae Sunsplash, Reggae Sumfest and Sting, as well as on overseas shows in Tampa, Fort Lauderdale, New York, Austria, Antigua and Trinidad.

From his earlier days, until today, Anthony B has been igniting audiences around the world with his no-holds-barred opposition to all forms of injustice.

Today, Anthony B tours extensively in Europe and North America and is known for his fiery, high-energy performances.

THE NEW MILLENNIUM

The new millennium has not given us a new reggae style, but there are a lot of new artistes coming up. When you check the ads on the Jamaican TV, radio and newspapers you find the names like Vybz Kartel, Bling Dawg, Magowan, Perfect, Chuck Fender, Turbulence, Capleton, Macka Diamond, Notorious, Spragga Benz, Terror Fabulous, Wayne Wonder, Tenor Saw, Assassin and more.

Baby Cham

Born as Dameon Beckett in 1977, Baby Cham took Jamaica by storm as one its biggest dancehall stars by the age of 20. Beckett got his stage name thanks to his baby-faced appearance, which starkly contrast his booming baritone. His albums like "Ghetto Story" and "Vitamin S" were issued in radio versions, parental advisory versions, and unedited versions to promote sales.

Growing up in the musically rich district of Waterhouse in Kingston, Baby Cham became immersed in dancehall at an early age. At the age of seven, he began watching established DJs of the day hone their skills on the mic. Son he began polishing his own deejaying abilities at school. He spent his spare time after school hanging out at recording studios and rubbing shoulders with reggae greats such as Shabba Ranks.

He has since dropped the Baby from his name but is still called Baby Cham by his fans.

Cham eventually got a gig as an opening act for Spragga Benz and then hooked up with producer Dave Kelly. Kelly and Cham collaborated for a series of hit singles, which were compiled on *Wow...the Story*, a two-disc album designed to introduce Baby Cham to a wider audience.

OUTSTANDING ARTISTES IN THE NEW MILLENNIUM

Shaggy

Born in 1968 as Orville Richard Burrell in Kingston, Shaggy, at age 18, emigrated with his family to the United States where they settled in Brooklyn.

His stage name was adopted from a character from the popular cartoon *Scooby Doo*.

In 1988, Shaggy joined the United States Marine Corps and served during Operation Desert Storm during the Persian Gulf War.

On his return from the Persian Gulf, he decided to pursue his music career and his first hit in 1993 "Oh Carolina", was a dancehall re-make of a ska hit by the Folkes Brothers. The same year, Shaggy appeared on Kenny Dope's hip hop album "The Unreleased Project". He worked together with producers such as Sting Intl., Don One (who cut his first track), Lloyd 'Spiderman' Campbell and Robert Livingston. He had further big hits, including "Boombastic" in 1995.

He is especially notable for his distinctive sub-baritone voice.

He had a major comeback in 2001, featuring worldwide number-one hit singles "It Wasn't Me" and "Angel," the latter of which was built around Merrilee Rush's 1968 hit "Angel of the Morning" (which was remade in 1981 by Juice Newton). The album *Hot Shot*, from which those cuts came, would hit number one on the Billboard 200.

However, his 2002 release *Lucky Day*, and the 2005 album *Clothes Drop* failed to match *Hot Shot*'s success.

Shaggy performed the theme for *Showtime*, a 2002 movie.

Sean Paul

Born in January 1975 in Kingston as Sean Paul Henriques, Sean Paul's lineage truly reflects Jamaica's motto, "Out Of Many, One People." On his Portuguese father's side there is a family legend about the shipwreck of horse-rustling ancestors during a daring escape from bounty hunters. Sean's mother is a renowned Jamaican painter, and both his parents were noted athletes – a tradition Sean continued as a youth, representing his country in many international swim and water polo meets. After graduation from the University of Technology (UTECH), he worked as a chef and later as a bank teller.

In his early teens, Sean Paul developed a love for dancehall and reggae. Such artists as Lt. Stitchie, Major Worries, and Supercat were important influences. Sean soon began writing his own lyrics, he made a link and busted some rhymes for Cat Coore, Bunny Rugs, and Carrot Jarret of Third World. "Cat said, 'Your voice sounds great, lets do some demos,'" Sean Paul recalls.

Sean developed his skills by making dubs and performing at barbecues. In 1996, after releasing a few singles, he made the crucial connection with then up-and-coming producer Jeremy Harding, owner of 2 Hard Records. Jeremy had just completed the Fearless riddim, and Sean voiced it with "Baby Girl", his first woman-oriented lyric. The song became a huge hit, opening doors all over Jamaica for Sean. During this time, he continued to learn the deejay trade and improve his artistry. He hooked up with the Dutty Cup Crew, a group of aspiring deejays. "We used to smoke weed, and a 'dutty' is a used pipe, but that's not what we were all about," Sean explains. "In life, if you don't work hard and dutty, you won't get nowhere. So our cup is full."

In 1998, Sean recorded "Infiltrate" on Jeremy Harding's Playground/Zim Zimma riddim. The riddim was a reggae smash, both in Jamaica and internationally. The song also became a top record in the juggling mix. "'Infiltrate' took me to enough places," Sean recalls. Charting number one in Belize, the record rocked hip-hop mix shows in New York and Miami.

Hitting next with "Excite Me," Sean's name was spreading to the rest of the Caribbean, especially Trinidad and Guyana. He then recorded "Deport Them," which became a number one record in Jamaica on Tony Kelly's Bookshelf riddim. The song received major airplay in Miami and on New York's hip-hop mix shows, later crossing over onto regular rotation on New York's Hot 97.

It was around then that Sean Paul joined forces with emerging sing-jay Mr. Vegas. Their first collaboration, "Hot Gal Today," on the Street Sweeper riddim by Steely and Clevie, became a number one record in Jamaica and throughout the Caribbean. Sean and Mr. Vegas also collaborated on the dancehall hit, "Tiger Bone," produced by Richard "Shams" Browne on the Intercourse riddim. In March of 2000, just as "Hot Gal Today" was heating up in Miami and New York, VP Records released *Stage One*, Sean Paul's debut album. Meanwhile, Sean and Mr. Vegas joined forces with producer Tony Kelly and multi-platinum rapper DMX for "Top Shotta," a song on the Belly soundtrack, further lifting Sean's rep in the States.

The infectious sounds of Sean Paul have already earned the young reggae star a permanent place in Jamaica's musical pantheon. Sean is now leading the influential hip-hop-flavored dancehall form fully into the American mainstream with his breakthrough single, "Gimme The Light." With U.S. radio stations and video channels opening their doors to the charismatic artist and his music, the song is a bona fide smash on both the national R&B/Hip-Hop and Pop charts.

"Gimme The Light" prepared he way for the November 2002 release of *Dutty Rock*, Sean's second album – and his first via a new long-term worldwide pact between Atlantic Records and VP Records, the largest independent label for new Jamaican music in the U.S. As a result, Sean joined the Atlantic roster, following a brilliant run of hit crossover singles and rapidly mounting media attention.

In 1996, Sean Paul's release of "Baby Girl" was the first of a series of undeniable reggae smashes that rocked Jamaica, quickly establishing a solid base for Sean among the island's dancehall massive. Part of the wave of mid-nineties Jamaican deejays that brought new blood into the Jamaican music scene, he quickly pulled to the front of the pack. Hardcore dancehall fans were captivated by his songwriting and rapping skills, and Sean rapidly became a favourite with ladies in the audience.

As his reputation grew in Jamaica, the rest of the Caribbean quickly picked up on Sean Paul's sound. Soon, Jamaicans in Miami, New York, and London knew the words "dutty yeah" were a signal to hit the dance floor. Record-breaking airplay on American hip-hop radio followed, and the success of "Stage One," Sean Paul's 2000 smash debut album, established him as VP Records' best-selling. With *Dutty Rock*, Sean moved from strength to greater strength.

After a wicked re-mix on the Punany riddim, "Hot Gal Today" joined "Deport Them" in rocking American hip-hop and R&B radio. Together the two tunes thrust Sean Paul's Stateside career into orbit. He became the first reggae artiste to have two singles added at the same time to a major American radio station (NYC's Hot 97), and the first reggae artiste to simultaneously chart two singles from the same album ("Hot Gal Today" at #66 and "Deport Them" at #85) on the Billboard R&B Singles chart. "Hot Gal Today" also hit #6 on the Billboard Top Rap Singles chart. With all the radio play in New

York, Sean built up a major New York City base among tastemaker disc jockeys and true hip-hop fans.

Sean was named number three Reggae Artist of the Year by Billboard and "Stage One" was named Billboard's number four Reggae Album of the Year 2000. Meanwhile, "Hot Gal Today" was featured on the *Shaft* soundtrack. The sales of "Stage One" went through the roof. At the same time, Sean continued his string of Jamaican successes with "No Bligh" for Penthouse Records, "Check It Deeply" for In The Streetz, and "My Name" for Shocking Vibes.

Notably, Sean was the first reggae artist to perform on Hot 97's Summer Jam, one of the most important annual American R&B/hip-hop concerts. "Suddenly, I was with artists who were my mentors," Sean enthuses. "I met Big Daddy Kane, Snoop, Aaliyah; there I was, talking to Funkmaster Flex. It was crazy." That summer, Sean rocked Summer Jam-type shows from Miami to Boston.

A forward-looking artiste, Sean Paul began work on his next album, while continuing to record dancehall smashes with reggae producers. Teaming with Tony Kelly he scored again with "Like Glue" on the Buyout riddim. Next, working in combination with sexy Ce'Cile, Sean voiced on the hottest riddim of 2001, the Jeremy Harding-produced Liquid, to make the hit single, "Can You Do The Work." Both songs appeared on *Dutty Rock*.

Other outstanding tracks include "I'm Still In Love With You" featuring Sasha, a romantic cover of the Alton Ellis/Marcia Akins classic, and "Gimme The Light", the album's lead single. *Dutty Rock* also boasts a fantastic Spanish version of "Punkie," a huge hit around the Caribbean and in Latin hip-hop clubs.

With his radio success in America, Sean's reputation in the U.S. hip-hop and R&B community exploded, leading to collaborations with Busta Rhymes, Jay-Z, DMX, The Neptunes, Clipse, Mya, Tony Touch, and Rahzel of the Roots, among others. "A lot of hip-hop artists have been linked to dancehall," Sean once told the *New York Times*. "It always has been, and now people can see for themselves."

Sean was named Best Reggae Artist for 2002 at the MOBO Awards in London, and he also garnered a High Times magazine 2002 Doobie Award for "Gimme The Light".

"I see dancehall-reggae and hip-hop as fused together," Sean Paul explains. "When I was a kid, they were the two kinds of music that spoke to me and said 'Move'." In August 2009, he released his fourth studio album, *Imperial Blaze*, the follow-up to his platinum-selling, *The Trinity*.

Damian Marley

Born in Kingston, Jamaica in 1978, Damian Marley is a Grammy-winning reggae artiste and the youngest son of reggae legend Bob Marley. He is also the only child born to Marley and Cindy Breakspeare, Miss World 1976. Damian's nickname is Junior Gong which is derived from his father's nickname Tuff Gong. Damian has been performing since the age of 13, and enjoys a full-time music career like most of the Marley clan. He shares with most of the Marley family a full-time career in music. But unlike his brothers and sisters, his specialty is deejaying.

Like his famous father and the rest of the Marley family, Damian is a Rastafarian whose music reflects both his beliefs and the principles of one love, one planet, and freedom for all. While he travels and tours for most of the year, he lives between Kingston, Jamaica and Miami, Florida.

In the summer of 2004, Damian participated in the 27-city Bob Marley 'Roots, Rock, Reggae Festival Tour' with his four brothers, Ziggy, Julian, Stephen and Ky-Mani, each of whom have their own professional recording careers.

On September 19, 2006 Marley became the first reggae artiste to perform on the popular PBS show Austin City Limits.

His album *Halfway Tree* was the 2002 recipient of the Grammy Award for Best Reggae Album. At the 2006 Grammy Awards, he won Best Reggae Album again for *Welcome to Jamrock* and Best Urban/Alternative Performance for the song "Welcome to Jamrock".

CHRISTMAS-REGGAE & CHRISTMAS-SOCA

Reggae music at Christmas is synonymous with cheerful music for a cheerful celebration.

Arguably one of the most beautiful Christmas Reggae LPs is *Christmas In The Tropics*, which was released in 1973 on the Dynamic label. It featured artistes and bands such as Byron Lee and the Dragonaires ("White Christmas"), Toots and The Maytals ("Happy Christmas"), Boris Gardner ("The Meaning of Christmas"), Keith Lynn ("Blue Christmas"), and Vic Taylor with a song entitled "Pretty Paper".

By the DYNAMIC SUPER STARS

A more contemporary LP, *Caribbean Christmas Cheer*, produced by Lloyd Lovindeer (also on background vocals), was released on the TSOJ label and included musicians such as Sly and Robbie and Michael 'Ibo' Cooper. One can feel the "Christmas breeze" on this album, according to the lyrics of one of the songs.

The LP *Christmas in Jamaica*, released on the Studio One label, is outstanding, because it features an interesting mix of reggae, soul and ska. In fact, no one can remain still when listening to songs by Jackie Mittoo, Horace Andy, The Cables, Alton Ellis, The Heptones, The Gaylads and The Wailers. The album invokes a genuine Christmas atmosphere.

However the rocksteady Christmas album *Sir Coxsone's Family Album Christmas Stylee*, which featured artistes such as Johnny Osbourne, Jennifer Lara, The Family Group, The Silvertones and Freddie McGregor, is not as remarkable. The rhythm is quite slow and served better as background music, for relaxation or for handing out presents.

More reflective and possibly more rhythmic, is the album *The Reggae Christmas Hits*, recorded by John Holt in 1986 on the Sonic Sounds label. It featured songs including cover versions of "White Christmas", "Blue Christmas" and "When A Child Is Born".

Two recording artistes, Jacob Miller and Ray "Weatherman" I, released two LPs on the Top Rank label: *Natty Christmas*, for the international market and "Ital Christmas" for the Jamaican market. Though both albums bear similar titles, the songs on each are arranged differently. The songs reflected Jacob Miller's typical sound, while Ray I showed more diversity.

Released in 1981 on the Rave Music label, *Yard Style Christmas* featured The Tamlins ("Silent Night"); Home T4, Barrington Levy and Carlene Davis ("Santa Claus"), and "Sensimillia" by Dean Fraser.

The American production on the Wackie label, *Wackies' Reggae Christmas*, featured a compilation of songs by different singers and musicians. Appearing under the name, Wackies' Rhythm Force, were Max Romeo, Miltone Henry and others.

In addition to a medley of Christmas songs, there is also a Christmas song done to a soca.

Also released under the Wackie Label, together with NEC in 1988, is the Japanese-American production, "Reggae Christmas", which featured Yami Bolo, 809-Band, and Tiger; and "dancehall Christmas", which featured some relatively new artistes, and bands. The Christmas songs featured on the album were recorded in DJ and dancehall-style and described as contemporary and modern.

FILM & REGGAE

THE HARDER THEY COME

Jimmy Cliff became a big movie star in 1972 with the role of Ivan Martin in the film *The Harder They Come*. He also became quite famous around the world for the songs he recorded for the film soundtrack. The songs included the title song, "You Can Get It If You Really Want", and "Sitting in Limbo".

Other songs on the soundtrack included "Rivers of Babylon" by the Melodians; "Shanty Town" by Desmond Dekker; "Johnny Too Bad" by the Slickers, and "Draw Your Brakes" by Scotty.

The soundtrack also featured the instrumental version of "Easy Ride" (also known as "Stop That Man") by Derrick Harriott, along with Keith and Tex "Pressure Drop" and "Sweet and Dandy" by Toots and the Maytals.

The Harder They Come showed a realistic view of the Jamaican music industry during the 1960s: the fast dollar, the dependence on others, usually Caucasians, for financial support, and the unscrupulousness of music producers at the time.

Set in the slums of western Kingston, the film made Cliff a bonafide star.

CLUB PARADISE

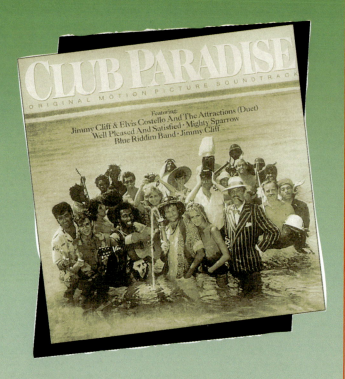

The film debuted in 1986. It was set on the fictitious Caribbean island of St. Nicholas (shot in Jamaica), and featured Jack (Robin Williams) also from the film *Good Morning Vietnam*, Ernest Reid (Jimmy Cliff) and Philadelphia Lloyd (Twiggy).

The plot surrounds Jack, a fireman, who was injured during a fire. He went on early retirement and eventually settled on the island of St. Nicholas. While living there for some months, he became friendly with Ernest, the owner and operator of Club Paradise.

A conspiracy eventually developed involving the prime minister, an Arabian businessman and the owner of the Royal Hotel, who wanted to take possession of Club Paradise in order to access the prime real estate on which it was located.

When the conspiracy was uncovered, Ernest, Jack and the patrons of the club, chased the corrupt businessmen off the island.

The soundtrack for the film featured songs by Jimmy Cliff, Elvis Costello and the Attractions, Well Pleased and Satisfied, Mighty Sparrow and the Blue Riddim Band. The LP was released under the Oneness Label.

COUNTRYMAN

Opened in 1982, the film tells the story of a Jamaican fisherman who paddles to a reef to cast his net and ends up rescuing two Americans from the wreckage of a plane crash. When he is implicated in a political scheme, he draws on his knowledge of the terrain and fighting skills to survive the ordeal. Directed by Dickie Jobson, *Countryman* is a tale of modern culture and ancient magic, starring Countryman, Carl Bradsaw, Kristina St. Clair and Munair Zacca.

The double LP soundtrack was produced by Chris Blackwell and released on Island Records. Eight songs by Bob Marley and the Wailers were featured

on the soundtrack, in addition to songs by the group Aswad, Toots and The Maytals, Steel Pulse and Fabulous Five. It also featured artistes such as Dennis Brown, Lee Perry, Jah Lion, Rico and Wally Badarou, who wrote the theme track for the movie.

KLA$H

Kla$h: Kaught Up In Da Mix was filmed entirely in Jamaica, starring Jasmine Guy (*A Different World*), and Giancarlo Esposito (*Malcolm X*), in the supporting role. It also featured Cedella Marley, Shabba Ranks, Patra, Mike McCallum, Lucien Chen, Carl Bradshaw and Snow.

The film premiered in 1995 at the Sundance Film Festival and was also featured at the Cannes Film Festival. It was one of fifty films shown at the Pan African Film Festival in Los Angeles and opened in Jamaica in February 1996 at the Carib Cinema in Kingston.

Kla$h is the story of a big music event – a electrifing clash between reggae and dancehall bands, which develops into a dramatic thriller, interwoven with live performances on stage.

The music-based film featured over forty songs on the soundtrack, including live performances recorded at the clash. The soundtrack to the music-based film featured over 40 songs, including live performances recorded at the clash.

Elements of Jamaican culture, including music and language were exposed in this film, a credit to the filmmakers, who utilised local talents to help strengthen the Jamaican film industry.

ROCKERS

Rockers is a 1978 musical adventure/comedy by Ted Bataloukos, which follows Leroy "Horsemouth" Wallace, a drummer living in the Kingston ghetto who supports himself and his family by selling music records throughout the island on a motorcycle. The motorcycle is subsequently stolen and a violent confrontation with

the thief ensues.

A very good overview of reggae music during the 1970s is featured in the film and formed the background to the action sequences. It also showed positive aspects of Jamaicans, and their interaction amongst themselves, with visitors to the island, the hotel industry, and with youths in the inner city communities of Kingston.

In addition, most of the leading reggae artistes and bands at that time were featured on the soundtrack for the film. They included Inner Circle, The Maytones, Junior Marvin ("Police and Thieves"),

The Heptones ("Book of Rules"), Peter Tosh, Jacob Miller *("Tenement Yard")*, Junior Byles, Bunny Wailer *("Rockers")*, Gregory Isaacs, Rockers All Stars, Kiddus I, Burning Spear, Third World, Justin Hinds and The Dominoes.

THE REGGAE MOVIE

The *Reggae Movie* is a concert film, which premiered in September 1995 in the United States at the United Artist Theatre Circuit in Eaglewood, Colorado. It was later shown in twenty-five cities throughout the United States, including the Criterion in Times Square, New York.

The movie captured the soul of reggae music, from the smooth ballads to the jammin' dancehall tunes.

Produced and directed by Ricardo Chin and Randy Rovins, it was shot during live performances at various venues around the world, including Japan, the United States, Australia as well as Jamaica. It took less than two years for the idea to evolve into a movie.

The film captured the performances of various artistes and bands, including performances by Dean Fraser, Shaggy ("Oh Carolina", "Boombastic") Rayvon, Buju Banton, Wayne Wonder, Luciano, Garnet Silk, Inner Circle, Steel Pulse, Third World, Shinehead, Mystic Revealers, Burning Spear, Beres Hammond, Carlene Davis, Freddie McGregor, Ziggy Marley and the Melody Makers, Chaka Demus and Pliers, Dennis Brown, Apache Indian, Yami Bolo, Maxi Priest and a special guest appearance by Sandra Bernhard.

REGGAE SUNSPLASH:
THE GREATEST REGGAE SHOW ON EARTH

A TIMELINE:

1978

The inaugural staging of Reggae Sunsplash took place at Jarrett Park in Montego Bay, St. James, in June.

People of different races and nationalities came together for ten days to celebrate reggae, and arguably, Montego Bay has never been the same since.

Some Featured Artistes and Bands: The Heptones, Joe Higgs, Lloyd Parkes and The We The People Band, Jimmy Cliff, Byron Lee And The Dragonaires and the Blues Busters.

1979

The performance by Bob Marley and The Wailers was the absolute best. Despite a huge police presence and other security personnel with dogs, to protect Bob Marley, the audience nevertheless breached the security barriers but only to get close to the reggae star.

There were also performances by Burning Spear and Third World.

1980

General Elections were held during this year, and due to the violence that ensued, not many overseas visitors attended the event.

However, there were some excellent performances from Peter Tosh, Culture, Black Uhuru, Sugar Minott, Dennis Brown, Ken Boothe and the dub artistes Oku Onuora and Michael Smith.

1981

The event was staged in honour of Bob Marley who had died in May of the same year.

Every musician of rank and name were in attendance. Among the performers were: Rita Marley, Judy Mowatt and Marcia Griffiths, who sang "Belly Full But Dem Hungry"; The Wailers: Ziggy Marley and the Melody Makers ("Sugar Pie"); Eek-A-Mouse ("Wa Do Dem"); and Dennis Brown, with ("If I Had The World").

Black Uhuru, Sheila Hylton, Gregory Isaacs, Carlene Davis, The Mighty Diamonds, and Third World also performed.

On the final evening, over fifteen thousand enthusiastic spectators came to watch Stevie Wonder, who dedicated his performance to his friend Bob Marley.

It should be noted that Steel Pulse performed for the first time in Jamaica at the staging of this event.

1982

Reggae Sunsplash was dedicated to Count Ossie and Don Drummond.

The Wednesday night was opened by Byron Lee and the Dragonaires, who backed Rita Marley on "One Draw". They then accompanied John Holt on "Sweetie Come Brush Me" and other songs. Roy Shirley, who brought the audience to laughter because of his unusual mode of dressing, started his stint with his usual acrobatics – jumping in the air while performing. U-Roy "The Godfather" followed with "Wear You To The Ball" and other songs.

Byron Lee and the Dragonaires celebrated their twentieth anniversary as a band with a performance of a ska medley. Big Youth and his band The Archangels, Tommy McCook on trombone, Burning Spear, and Toots and the Maytals ended the first night.

1983

Reggae Sunsplash was held at the Bob Marley Performing Centre, also located in Montego Bay.

There were performances from Chalice, Dennis Brown, Black Uhuru, Third World, Super Max, Ras Karbi, Musical Youth, Judy Mowatt and others.

1984

The artistes who performed included, among others, The Mighty Diamonds, Derrick Morgan who did a combination of ska and rocksteady songs, Freddie McGregor and Burning Spear, who could hardly leave the stage as the crowd wanted more.

1985

The best performances were by Third World, Michael Roze, Half Pint, Mutabaruka and Brigadier Jerry, presumably the best DJ at that time.

1986

There were performances by Carlene Davis, The Wailers, Sly & Robbie, Ini Kamoze, The Tamlins, Half Pint and Gregory Isaacs, among others,

1987

The reggae festival celebrated its ten-year anniversary in August.

Bunny Wailer performed for the first time as a solo artiste. Other artistes and bands included Burning Spear and Ziggy Marley and the Melody Makers, who were specially invited to celebrate the ten-year anniversary.

Dancehall Night, the most populous night, had over thirty-eight thousand spectators in attendance.

1988

Sunsplash was again staged at the Bob Marley Performing Centre. There were performances by Toots and the Maytals, Marcia Griffiths, The Abyssinians, Hortense Ellis (who appeared for the first time), Freddie McGregor, Foundation, A.J. Brown, Frankie Paul, Junior Delgado and Barrington Levy, among others.

1989

Reggae Sunsplash was dedicated to the legendary producers, King Tubby and Jack Ruby, who died earlier in the year.

The programme consisted of a sound system clash, a competition between four systems (Metro Media, Inner City, Electro Force and Spinners Choice), in front of five thousand spectators. The winner, according to 'the jury', was Inner City.

The Beach Party was staged on the Tuesday of the following week and became an annual feature. It catered mostly to new and upcoming artistes.

On Wednesday's "Oldies Night" draw over ten thousand spectators to the Bob Marley Performing Centre. There were performances by The Abyssinians, Delroy Wilson, Horace Andy, Culture, Justin Hinds and The Dominoes, The Mighty Diamonds, Sugar Minott, Wadada, Foundation the former Skatalites trombonist, Don Drummond, and Rico Rodriguez.

Thursday's 'Dancehall Night' attracted mostly Jamaicans spectators. There were performances from Admiral Tibet, Papa San, Tiger, Admiral Bailey, Lt. Stitchie and Josey Wales, among others.

Approximately twenty-five thousand spectators were in attendance, a marked reduction from thirty-five thousand in 1987 and thirty-eight thousand in 1999.

At "Singers Night", staged on Friday, there were performances by Lloyd Parkes & We The People Band, Nadine Sutherland, Ken Boothe, Bigga, Third World, Barrington Levy, Trevor Sparks, Dennis Brown, Frankie Paul and J.C. Lodge.

On Saturday's "Variety Night", in addition to the Sagittarius band and the Ninja Force as backing band, there were performances by deejays and singers, including Half Pint and Ebony, Marcia Griffiths, The Revealers, Ziggy Marley and the Melody Makers, Steel Pulse, Shinehead, Crucial, Robbie, Peter Metro and Charlie Chaplin.

The festival atrracted between ten thousand and thirty thousand spectators each night.

1990

Reggae Sunsplash was staged in July of this year to woo the many visitors, who visited the island for the annual Emancipation and Independence Day celebrations.

Among others, the event featured performances by UB 40, Gregory Isaacs, U2, Burning Spear and Coco Tea, who proclaimed on stage that *"Every Jamaican is a star"*.

On "Singers Night", performers included Shabba Ranks, Papa San, Lady G, Marcia Griffiths, Freddie McGregor, Dennis Brown and Maxie Priest.

"Vintage Night" saw great performances from Chalice, Alton Ellis, Inner Circle with their hit "Bad Boys". Hopeton Lewis, the ska legend, sang "Boom Shaka Laka" (the winning entry of the 1970 Jamaica Festival Song Competition). Pat Kelly, Leroy Sibbles and Eric Donaldson, were backed by Sly and Robbie.

Bunny Wailer featured two rappers during his performance, and also launched his LP *Liberation*. The title song from the LP was well received by the audience.

The last night, "International/Variety Night", saw a surprise performance from Lasana Bandele who was followed by Judy Mowatt. U-Roy, Admiral Bailey, Peter Metro, Shinehead, the group Aswad and the Skatalites also performed.

1991

The featured artistes, among others were Cocoa Tea, Ziggy Marley, Lucky Dube, The I-Three, Third World, Shabba

Ranks, Maxi Priest, Barrington Levy, Shinehead, Mutabaruka, Frankie Paul, Gregory Isaacs, and Dennis Brown.

1992

Reggae Sunsplash was again staged in Montego Bay.

It started on a Monday, with the staging of the beach party at Cornwall Beach, featuring performances by Delroy Morgan, Morgan Heritage, The Dreads, Willie One Blood, Courtney Melody, General Tree, Screwdriver, the British deejay Dominik and Cindy Breakespeare.

Tuesday's "World/Caribbean Night" featured new talents, such as the Sane band, the duo Link & Chain and the harmony trio, Foundation. There were also performances from Bankie Banks, Cidade Negra of Brazil, Chaka Demus & Pliers, Nardo Ranks, Brian & Toni Gold. In the soca segment, there were performances by Denise Plummer, a lead singer with Byron Lee and the Dragonaires, and Singing Sandra, both from Trinidad. The Mighty Sparrow also graced the stage.

Wednesday, dubbed "Vintage Night", featured Lloyd Parkes and the We The People Band, saxophonist Dean Frazer The Tamlins, Derrick Harriott, The Abyssinians, Ras Michael and the Sons Of Negus, Big Youth, Delroy Wilson, Ken Boothe Alton Ellis and a surprise performance by the Heptones with Leroy Sibbles.

During the second half of the night, Sly & Robbie and The Aggregation, provided background music for the singers.

"Dancehall Night", held the next day, started with Leroy Smart, who was followed by such artistes as, Charlie Chaplin, Tony Rebel, Cobra, Buju Banton, Ninja Man, Jack Radicks, Ed Robinson, General Degree, Professor Nut, Pinchers, Little Lennie, Wayne Wonder, Cutty Ranks, Admiral Bailey, Capleton, as well as Papa San and his brother Dirtsman.

The highlights of "Singers Night" held on Friday were the performances by Judy Mowatt, Freddie McGregor, Marcia Griffiths, John Holt, Beres Hammond, Buju Banton, Mikal Roze, The 809 Band, Steel Pulse, and Cocoa Tea accompanied by Lloyd Parkes and the We The People Band. The night culminated with two hours of non-stop reggae rocking by Dennis Brown and his son Daniel.

On Saturday night, "International Night", the show began with performances by The Dreads, Delroy Morgan, Morgan Heritage and the reggae-veteran Delroy Morgan.

They were followed by The Mystic Revealers and Carlene Davis (backed by the Skool Band) Barrington Levy and Macka B, the Wailing Souls (backed by Lloyd Parkes and the We The People Band) Lucky Dube with the Slaves Band, Junior Reid and Culture. The night culminated with a performance from Sugar Minott.

1993

The sixteenth staging of Reggae Sunsplash took place at its new venue, Jamaica's Festival Village (Jamworld), an entertainment centre located in Portmore, St. Catherine.

It was staged from August 2-7, and drew over forty thousand spectators.

For the first time in the history of Reggae Sunsplash, the festival was transmitted via satellite to the United States of America.

The annual beach party was held at Fort Clarence Beach, Portmore on a Monday, followed by World Beat/Caribbean Night,

Vintage Night, Dancehall Night and Singers Night. It culminated on the Saturday with the staging of International Night.

The artistes who performed included Garnet Silk, Freddie McGregor, Nadine Sutherland, Dennis Brown, Burning Spear, Gregory Isaacs, Shinehead, Leroy Smart, Buju Banton, Papa San and Tony Rebel.

1995-1997

The festival was held on August 1-4 at Dover in St. Ann on the grounds of the Chukka Cove Polo Club.

1998

The festival was held at the White River Reggae Park in Ocho Rios. It was staged during Bob Marley Week (February 5 to).

Through a massive promotion by MTV and Super Clubs (hotel chain in Jamaica) Reggae Sunsplash was transmitted to over one hundred million viewers in Europe thanks to a partnership between hotel chain Super Clubs and MTV.

1999

Postponed from February to May 21-23 (Labour Day Weekend in Jamaica). The festival was staged at James Bond Beach. The programme was shortened however to only two nights of live performances and a beach party, held at the same venue.

Since the demise of Reggae Sunsplash, which set the bar for the staging of reggae music festivals, much has changed in the music industry. Where the staging of music events is concerned.

In addition, a slew of new music festivals have emerged and then disappeared from the scene. There was the summer festival billed as "Vintage Classics" *(held towards the end of May)*, which was staged at the Pulse headquarters in Kingston. The dancehall/reggae show Sting, among many others, also emerged

In 1994, a hot new summer reggae festival entered the scene: *Reggae Sumfest*.

The inaugural staging featured five days of performances at Catherine Hall in Montego Bay. It also started with a beach party and followed a similar format as Reggae Sunsplash.

In 1995, for the first time at the staging of an event of this nature, a performing artiste (Grammy winner Shabba Ranks) was paid one million Jamaican dollars.

Also the "reggae bed", a piece of cardboard sold to patrons who wished to take a nap during the performances, for the first time was sold for upwards forty Jamaican dollars or more.

In 1995, in addition to the traditional reggae beds, there was a new feature – "ambition blankets" – two onion bags stitched together, which were sold for sixty Jamaican dollars.

In 1996, season armbands/tickets to the event were sold for three thousand five hundred Jamaican dollars.

For many years, towards the middle to the end of August, numerous stage shows, jerk festivals, raves, beach parties, and many other music events are staged to culminate the summer season, featuring performances by both local and foreign acts.

These include the Portland Festival held at the Crystal Springs Resort in Buff Bay, Portland; The Frenchmen, Sashi, among many others.

REGGAE GRAMMYS

YEAR*	ARTISTE	ALBUM
1984	Black Uhuru	Anthem
1985	Jimmy Cliff	Cliffhanger
1986	Steel Pulse	Babylon The Bandit
1987	Peter Tosh (posthumous)	No Nuclear War
1988	Ziggy Marley & The Melody Makers	Conscious Party
1989	Ziggy Marley & The Melody Makers	One Bright Day
1990	Bunny Wailer	Time Will Tell - A Tribute to Bob Marley

YEAR*	ARTISTE	ALBUM
1991	Shabba Ranks	As Raw As Ever
1992	Shabba Ranks	X-tra Naked
1993	Inner Circle	Bad Boys
1994	Bunny Wailer	Crucial! Roots Classics
1995	Shaggy	Boombastic
1996	Bunny Wailer	Hall of Fame: A Tribute to Bob Marley's 50th Anniversary
1997	Ziggy Marley & The Melody Makers	Fallen Is Babylon
1998	Sly Dunbar & Robbie Shakespeare	Friends
1999	Burning Spear	Calling Rastafari
2000	Beenie Man	Art And Life
2001	Damian "Junior Gong" Marley	Half Way Tree
2002	Lee "Scratch" Perry	Jamaican E.T.
2003	Sean Paul	Dutty Rock
2004	Toots Hibbert	True Love
2005	Damian "Junior Gong" Marley	Welcome to Jamrock
2006	Ziggy Marley & The Melody Makers	Love Is My Religion
2007	Stephen Marley	Mind Control
2008	Burning Spear	Jah Is Real

* Years represent album release date.

THE STEEL BANDS

Steel bands can be found all over the Caribbean – in restaurants, hotels, and even on the beaches.

They originated in Trinidad and Tobago and Barbados.

The music, including reggae, calypso, soca, R&B, and "love" songs, is played on oil barrels.

The different types of drums are:
Tenor Pan
Double Tenor
Double Seconds
Guitar Pan
Bass
Rhythm

The oil barrels are tuned by utilising a hammer and chisel. Congo drums and percussions are also included in the ensemble.

A very good example of the steel band is the Barbados Steel Orchestra, which has *Classics To Calypso*, an album featuring songs such as "House Of The Rising Sun", "The Elizabethan Serenade", "A Short Night Music" and "Chow Chow Bambino".

TOP 20 JAMAICAN POPULAR SONGS: 1957 – 2007

In April 2009, an esteemed panel of music industry insiders, academics and aficionados gathered at the University of the West Indies, Mona Campus, to present what they deemed the Top 100 reggae songs recorded between 1957 and 2007. It goes without saying that when revealed, the list stirred immense controversy, which still lingers even today.

How was the list arrived at? Reportedly, a team of 21 selectors in all made the final decision. The team included a five-member committee chaired by Dr. Omar Davis (also including Frankie Campbell, Francois St. Juste, Bunny Goodison, and Wayne Chen). The rest comprised Sly Dunbar, Robbie Lyn, Dean Fraser, Boris Gardner, Ibo Cooper, Owen Brown, Roy Black, Dwight Pinkney, Neville Wray, Garfield Hamilton, Basil Walters, Tamara Dickens, Steve Golding, Jack Scorpio, Arif Cooper and King Stitt.

In the end, the following popular songs emerged as the chosen Top 20:

1. **One Love/People Get Ready** (Bob Marley and The Wailers)
2. **Oh Carolina** (Folkes Brothers)
3. **54-46** (The Maytals)
4. **Got To Go Back Home** (Bob Andy)
5. **My Boy Lollipop** (Millie Small)
6. **Many Rivers To Cross** (Jimmy Cliff)
7. **Israelites** (Desmond Dekker and The Aces)
8. **Cherry Oh Baby** (Eric Donaldson)
9. **Simmer Down** (The Wailers)
10. **Carry Go Bring Come** (Justin Hinds and the Dominoes)
11. **The Harder They Come** (Jimmy Cliff)
12. **No Woman No Cry** (Bob Marley and the Wailers)
13. **Rivers of Babylon** (The Melodians)
14. **Redemption Song** (Bob Marley and the Wailers)
15. **Easy Snappin'** (Theophilus Beckford)
16. **Girl I've Got A Date** (Alton Ellis)
17. **Satta Massagana** (The Abyssinians)
18. **Everything I Own** (Ken Boothe)
19. **Eastern Standard Time** (Don Drummond)
20. **Wear You To The Ball** (U-Roy)

DISCOGRAPHY & VIDEOGRAPHY

LPs with the covers included in the book are identified by an asterisk (*).

KUMINA-REVIVAL-RASTAFARIAN-CALYPSO-MENTO

Compilations

Boggu Yagga Gal	Czech	2001	Interstate	HT CD 45
Calypso Ska Jump Up Vol.1	JA	1969	Studio One	103
*From Kongo to Zion	US	1983	Heartbeat	HB 17
Me Mama Never Taught Me				
Pepperpot Calypso Songs	JA		Port-O-Jam	POJ 109
*The Original Golden Oldies Vol. 3	US	1967	Prince Buster Music	PB 11

Count Ossie and The Mystic Revelation Of Rastafari

Count Ossie ... Double-LP	JA	1966	Tuff-Gong	TG 014
*Gronation	JA		Gronation	NTI 301
Tales Of Mozambique	JA		Dynamic	DY 3358

Ras Michael & The Sons Of Negus

Anthology	US	2002	Culture Press	
A Weh Dem a Go Do Wit It	US	2003	Roir, Earth	
Dadawah Peace & Love Nyabinghi	JA/GB	1974/75	Wildflower/Trojan	
Disarmament	GB	1982	Trojan	TRLS 203
Freedom Sounds	JA	1974	Dynamic/Creole	
DYLP 3004				
Iration (prod by Tommy Cowan)	JA	1977	Top Ranking	
Know Now	US	1990	Shanachie	
Kibir Am Lak - Glory To God	JA	1977	Rastafari	
Live in a Babylon: Geneva		2002	Sankova	
Live in San Franzisco	US	2003	2b1 Records	
Love Thy Neighbour	US	1979	Jah Life	JLLP 005
Lion Country	JA	1999	Roots & Culture	
Mediator	JA	1992	High Times	
Movements	JA	1978	Dynamic	
Merry Peasant	US	2004	2b1 Records	
New Name	CDN	1994	Lagoon	

Nyabinghi	GB	1974	Trojan	TRLS 113
Promised Lands Sounds - Live	CDN	1980	Lions Gate	LGR 1201
Ras Michael & The Sons Of Negus	JA		Top Ranking	
Ras Michael & Zion Train	JA	1990	SST Records	
Rally Round	US	1985	Shanachie	
Rastafari	JA	1975	Rastafari	
Rastafari In Dub	JA	1979	Top Ranking	
Revelation	GB	1982	Trojan	
Rastafari Plus Dub	CDN	1995	Lagoon	
Spiritual Roots	US	1999	VP/Universal	
Tribute To The Emperor & Jazzboe Abubaka	GB		Trojan	TRLS 132
Zion Train	JA	1985	SST Records	
Trilogie (3 CD)	JA	2006	Carol	

Prince Buster

Big Five	GB		Melodisc	MLP 12-157
Fabulous Greatest Hits	GB		Melodisc	MS 1
Greatest Hits				
I Feel The Spirit	GB		Melodisc	MS 2
It's Burke's Law Jamaica Ska Explosion	GB		Blue Beat	BBL 806
Judge Dread Featuring Prince Buster Jamaica's Pride - Rocksteady - Hush Up	GB		Blue Beat	BBL 809
Outlaw Pain in My Belly (The Prince Buster All Stars, Ska Compilation)	JA		Prince Buster Music	PB LP 804
She Was A Rough Rider	GB		Fab	BBLP 820
Sister Big Stuff	GB		Melodisc	MLP 12-156
Ten Commandments	US		RCA	LSP 3792
Tutti Frutti	GB		Melodisc	MS 6
Wreck A Bum Bum	GB		Blue Beat	BBLP 821
The Original Golden Oldies Vol 1	US	1967	Prince Puster	PB 9
The Original Golden Oldies Vol 2	US	1967	Prince Puster	PB 10
The Original Golden Oldies Vol 3	US	1967	Prince Puster	PB 11

The Hiltonaires

Big Bamboo (CD in 2001 added 4 tracks)	JA	1996	Island Records	ILP 1041
Hold Im Joe	JA		Island Records	
Meet Me In Jamaica	JA		Studio One	
Seven Bells	JA			
Ska-Motion in Ska-Lip-So	JA		Port-O-Jam	WIRL 1027
The Best Of Hiltonaires	JA		Coxsone	

The Jolly Boys (Jolly Brothers)

The Roots Of Reggae	JA	1977	Lyricords Records	
The Jolly Boys at Club Caribbean	JA	1979	High Note	
Sunshine 'n' Water	JA	1991	Ryco	
*Pop "n" Mento	JA	1989	First Warning	
Live in Tokyo		1997	Respect Records	
Beer Joint & Tailoring (CD)	JA	1991	First Warning	

Chin's Calypso Sextett

5 CD set recordings of the 50's	GB	2003-5	Chin's		registrated owners

THE SKA

Compilations

Calypso Ska Jump Up Vol.1	JA	1969	Studio One	103
Dance Crasher	GB	1988	Trojan	TRLS 260
(Ska To Rock steady)				
From 'Bam Bam To Cherry Oh: Baby'				
	JA		Dynamic	DY 3332
*History Of Ska Vol. 1	JA		Studio One	GW 0001
History Of Ska Vol. 2	JA		Studio One	GW 00011
The Birth Of Ska	JA		Treasure Isle	DSK 3542
This Is Jamaican Ska				
Presenting The Skatalites	JA		Studio One	
Treasure Ska	JA	1989	Treasure Isle	

Laurel Aitken

Clash Of The Ska Titans				
(L. versus The Skatalites)		1999	Moon Ska	
Early Days of Blue Beat, Ska and Reggae		1988	Bold Reprive	
En Espanol		2004	Liquidator	
Escapade En France (Mini)	GB		Unicorn	PHZA 69
High Priest Of Reggae		1969	Nu Beat	
Godfather Of Ska		2000	Grover	
It's Too Late	GB		Unicorn	PHZA 53
Laurel Aitken Meets Floyd Lloyd				
And the Potato Five		1987	Gaz's	
Live At Club Ska	GB	2004	Trojan	
Jamboree		2001	Grover	
Pioneer Of Jamaican Music		2000	Reggae Retro	
Rasta Man Power		1992	ROIR	
Ringo The Gringo	GB	1990	Unicorn	PHZA 50
Rocksteady Party (with Potato 5)		1996	Blue Moon	
Rise And Fall	GB	1989	Unicorn	PHZA 48
Rudi Got Married		2004	Grover	
Sally Brown (Mini)	GB	1989	Unicorn	PHZA 54
Ska With Laurel		1965	Rio	
Super Star		2005	Liqiudator	
The Blue Beat Years	GB	1996	Unicorn	PHZA 67
The Pama Years		1999	Grover	
The Long Hot Summer (with The Skatalites)		1999	Grover	
The Story So Far		1999	Grover	
The Very Last Concert (CD+DVD)		2007	Soulove	

True Fact (with Potato 5)		1988	Rackit	
With The Skatalites	GB	1963/90	Unicorn	PHZA 59
Whoppy King		1997	Tribute	

Roland Alphonso

Brighter Shades of Roots	CDN		Imperial	IC 8024
King Of Sax	JA		Studio One	
Ska Strictly for You	JA		Studio One	
The Best Of	JA		Studio One	SOL 1127

Don Drummond

100 Years After	JA		Studio One	SOL 1114
Check The Winner (& Bobby Aitken)	GB	1974/89	Greensleeves	
Dance The Ska Vol.1	NL		IBC	1A062-23953
Greatest Hits	JA/GB		Treasure Isle	
In Memory Of Don Drummond	JA		Studio One	CSL 8021
Memorial	F	1992	Esoldun	
*Memorial Album	JA		Treasure Isle	014
Ska-Boo-Da-Da	JA		Wirl	1042
The Best Of	JA		Studio One	SOL 9008

Clancy Eccles

Clancy Eccles	GB		Big Shot	BILP 101
Fatty Fatty 1967 - 1970 (& Friends)	GB	1988	Trojan	
Freedom	GB	1959	Trojan	TTL 22
Presents His Reggae Review	US	1990	Heartbeat	

The Ethiopians

*All the Hits & Much Much More	GB	1986	Trojan	TRLS 228
Clap your Hands		1993	Lagoon	
Dread Prophecy (& Gladiators)	US	1986	Nighthawk	NHM 7492
Engine '54	JA	1968	Dr. Buster Dynamic	
Everything Crash	JA	1981	Studio One	SOLP 0137
Let's Ska And Rocksteady	US	1990	VP Records	
No Baptism (& The Tribe)	JA	1991	Crystal	CLP 17
Original Reggae Hit sound	GB	1986	Trojan	
Owner Fe De Yard	US	1994	Heartbeat	
Reggae Power		1969		
Sir J.J. & Friends		1993	Lagoon	
Slave Call	US	1988	Rohit	RRTG 7716
Skaville Princess		2000	Dressed To Kill	
Train To Skaville		1999	Charly	
Train To Skaville: Anthology 1965-75	GB	2002	Trojan	
Tuffer Than Stone		1999	Warriors	
Woman Capture Man	GB	1970	Trojan	TBL 112
World Goes Ska	GB	1992	Trojan	

Owen Gray

Baby It's You		2005	World Sound	
Battle Of The Giants Round 1	GB	1983	Vista Sounds	
Better Days		2002	World Sound	
Cupid		1969		
Derrick Morgan And Owen Gray	GB	1996	Rhino	
Dreams Of Owen Gray	GB	1978	Trojan	TRLS 150
Fire And Bullets	GB	1977	Trojan	TRLS 139
Forward On The Scene	GB	1975	Trojan	
Hit After Hit After Hit	GB	1998	Carib Gems	CGLP 13
Hit After Hit Vol. 2	GB		Carib Gems	
Hit After Hit Vol. 3	GB		Vista Sounds	
*Hit After Hit Vol. 4	GB		Vista Sounds	STLP 1013
Instant Rapport		1989	Bushranger	
Jesus Loves Me		2004	True Gospel	
Let's Make A Deal			World Enterprise	
Little Girl	GB	1984	Vista Sounds	
Living Image		1996	Genesis Gospel Singers	
Mr. Soul Of Jamaica	GB	1990		
Max Romeo Meets Owen Gray At King Tubbi's Studio	JA	1984	Culture Press	
Memory Lane	GB	1992	Pioneer Intern.	
Miss Fire Waist			Jet Star	
Mumbo Jumbo		2005	Revenge	
None Of Jah-Jah's Children Shall Ever Suffer		198x	Imperial	
Oldies But Goodies (split with Delroy Wilson)	GB	1983	Vista Sounds	
On Drive		2000	Jet Star	
Owen Gray Sings		1961	Starlite	
Owen Gray Sings Bob Marley	GB	1984	Sarge	
Out In The Open	US	1997	VP Records	
Prince Buster Memory Lane		1986	Phil Pratt	
Ready Willing And Able		1989	Park Heights	
Room At The Top	US	1986	World Enterprise	WENLP 3028
Shook, Shimmy And Shake: The Anthology		2004	Trojan	
Sly And Robby Presents Owen Gray On Top		1994	Rhino	
Something Good Going On	JA	1990	Weed Beat	WB 171
Stand By Me	GB	1986	Hitbound	
The Gospel Truth Vol 1			Bushranger	
The Gospel Truth Vol 3		1999	Bushranger	
True Vibration		1998	Jet Star	
Turning Point		1977	Venture	
Watch This Sound	GB	1986	Sky Note	

Justin Hinds

Early Recordings	F	1991	Esoldun	
Jezebel	D		Island	ILPS 9416
Justin Hinds	US	1990	Jwyanza	JL 1004
Just In Time	D		Island	200 413
*Travel With Love	US	1984	Nighthawk	309

Derrick Morgan

21 Hits Salute	US	1997	Sonic Sounds Miami	SON 0877
And His Friends	GB	1968	Island	ILP 990
Best Of JA			Beverly's	
Blazing Fire Vol. 1	GB	1990	Unicorn	PHZA 68
Blazing Fire Vol. 2	GB	1990	Unicorn	PHZA 72
Blazing Fire (CD) cont. both	GB	1990	Unicorn	PHZCD 80
Conquerer	GB	1985	Vista Sounds	
Derrick Morgan In London		1969		
Derrick Meets The High Notes		2004		
Derrick Top The Top		2003		
Feel So Good (feat. Hortense Ellis)		1975	Attack	ATLP 1016
Forward March	GB		Island	ILP 903
Greatest Hits	US		D & M	
I Am The Ruler	GB	1992	Trojan	
In The Mood	GB		Magnet	MGT 004
Love City				
Meets The High Notes Live		2003		
Moon Hop		1970		
Moon Hop (Mini-Lp)	GB	1989/90	Unicorn	PHZA 63
Moon Hop: The Best Of The Early Years 1960-69		2003		
Original Reggae Recordings `68-70'		1997	Topbeat Records	
People Decision	GB	1977	Third World	TWLP 203
Ride The I	GB	1990	L.A.I Unicorn	LALP 3
Send A Little Rain	GB		Joe Frazier	
Seven Letters		1969		
Ska Man Classics	US	1995	Heartbeat	HBEA 170
Ska Man Classics		1997		
Still in Love (feat Hortense Ellis)		1977		
Sunset At Moonlight City				
The Legend Of Vol. 1	CDN	1980	Imperial	IC 8014
Time Marches On (CD)	US	1997	Heartbeat	HBEA 153 GB
Tougher Than Tough		1992	Rudie in Court	
Two Knights of Ska, Double LP, with Laurel Aitken	GB	1990	Unicorn	PHZD 61
With Hortense Ellis	GB		Conflict	
You Can't Change Me	GB		JR Productions	

The Skatalites

African Roots	US	1978	United Artists	LA-799-H
Ball Of Fire	JA	1998	Island	
Bashaka		2000	Marston Recording Corporation	
Celebration Time	JA		Studio One	SOLPO 01101
Celebration	JA	2002	Studio One	
Foundation Ska	US	1997	Heartbeat/Pgd	
From Paris With Love		2002	World Village	
I'm In The Mood For Ska	GB	1993	Trojan	
In Orbit Vol 1, Live From Argentina		2005		
In The Mood For Ska	GB	1995	Trojan	
Herb Dub, Collie Dub		2001	Motion	
Hip Hop Ska	US	1994	Shanachie	
Greetings From Skamania	US	1996	Shanachie	
Guns Of Navarone-Best Of		2003		
Hog In Cocoa (& Friends)	F	1991	Esoldun	
Live At Sunsplash	GB		Synergy	
Lucky Seven		2002		
Nukleaus Of Ska		2001	Music Club	
On The Right Track		2007	AIM	
Plus	JA		Treasure Isle	
Rebirth	JA		Studio One	
Return Of The Big Guns	JA	1984	Island	
Scattered Lights	JA	1980	Top Deck	
*Ska Authentic	JA	1964	Studio One	SOL 9006
Ska Authentic Vol. 2	JA	1967	Studio One	
Ska Ba Da	JA		Studio One	
Ska Splash		2002	Moonska	
Ska-ta-shot		2002		
Ska Vovee	US	1993	Shanachie	
Stretching Out	F		Danceteria	
Streching Out Live		1987	ROIR	
The Best Of	JA		Studio One	
The Legendary	JA		Jam Sounds	JLP 555
The Skatalites		1997	Jet Set	
The Skatalites	JA		Treasure Isle	LP 101/8
The Skatalites Plus	JA		Treasure Isle	TI 0005
Tribute To The Skatalites (Featuring ...)	F	1991	Esoldun	
With Sly&Robbie& Taxi Gang		1984	Vista	

FROM ROCKSTEADY TO REGGAE

Compilations

Catch This Beat The Rocksteady Years 66/68	GB		Island	IRSP 7

Come Rock With Me In Jamaica	JA		Treasure Isle	DSK 3507
Club Rocksteady '68	JA	1968	WIRL	
Dance All Night	GB		Trojan	
Duke Reid Golden Hits	JA		Treasure Isle	
*Gems From Treasure Isle				
- Real Cool Rocksteady	GB	1982	Trojan	TRLS 206
Get Ready Rocksteady	JA		Coxsone	CSL 8007
Greatest Jamaican Beat	JA		Treasure Isle	
Groovy Jo Jo	JA		Moodisc Records	TBL 133
Hottest Hits Vol. 1	JA	1968/74	Treasure Isle	
Hottest Hits Vol. 2	JA	s.a.	Treasure Isle	
Hottest Hits Vol. 3	JA	s.a.	Treasure Isle	
It's Rockin' Time	GB		Trojan	
Jumpin' With Mr. Lee	GB		Trojan	
Real Cool Rocksteady	GB	1982	Trojan	TRLS 206
Reggae Movement	JA	1974	Harry J	TBL 144
Rocksteady Beat	JA		WIRL	
Rocksteady Coxsone Style	JA		Coxsone	CSL 8013
Rocksteady Intensified	JA		WIRL	
Rusty Dusties (60's)	JA		Wild Flower	LP 379
Studio One Showcase Vol. 3	JA		Studio One	SOLP 5555

The Abyssinians

Arise	GB	1978	Front Line	FL 1019
Forward On To Zion (Satta)	GB	1977		
(reissued)		1988	Clinch Rec.	CRLP 27888
Live In San Francisco	US	2002		2b1 II
Satta Massagana	GB	1977	Clinch Records	
Satta Massagana	US	2007	Heartbeat	
*The Abyssinians Forward	GB	1982		
(reissued)		1988	Clinch Rec.	CRLP 101148

Ken Boothe

2 Of A Kind (& Tyrone Taylor)	JA	1987	Tuff Gong	
18 Classic Songs	UK	1991	Trojan	
20 Greatest Reggae Hits	JA		Charmers	LP 7
Acclaimed		1997	TP Records	
Ain't That Lovin You		2005	Brook	
A Man And His Hits	JA		Studio One	SOLP 1117
An Introduction To Ken Boothe		2006	Fuel 2000	
Black Gold And Green	GB	1973	Trojan	TRLS 58
Blood Brothers	GB	1978	Trojan	TRLS 148
Boothe Unlimited	JA		Federal	FIRM 135
Call Me	US		Rohit	
Crying Over You (Anthology 63 -78)	US	2001	Trojan	
Disco Reggae				
Don't You Know	JA		Tappa Records	
Everything I Own	GB		Trojan	TRLS 95

Ken Boothe (cont'd)

Title	Country	Year	Label	Catalog
Freedom Street	GB	1971	Trojan	TRLS 120
Gospel Door To Door				
Got To Get Away Showcase	JA		Phil Pratt	PP 01
Groove To The Beat				
I And I And I		2000		
I'm Just A Man	JA	1994	Bunny Lee	BL 009
Ken Boote	JA		Studio One	
Ken Boothe Collection				
Eighteen Classic Songs	GB	1987	Trojan	
Let's Get It On	GB	1974	Trojan	TRLS 83
Live Good	US	1978	Liberty	LT 51163
Live In Paris	F	2006	A La Folie	
Love Is The Ultimate				
Meets B.B. Seaton & The Gaylads	JA	1971	Jaguar	
More Of Ken Boothe	JA		Studio One	SOL 9010
Mr. Boothe	JA		Wild Flower	XYZ 001
*Mr. Rocksteady	JA	1968	Studio One	S03101
Natural Feeling	JA	1995		
Reggae For Lovers	JA	1979	Tuff Gong	
Power Of Love	JA		New Name Muzik	10068
Rock On Love	JA	1995		
Showcase	GB		Justice	
Talk To Me	JA/US	1990	Redman	VPRL 1106
Who Gets Your Love		1978		
You're No Good		2003		

The Clarendonians

Title	Country	Year	Label	Catalog
Can't Keep A Good Man Down	US	1992	King's Music	
*The Best Of	JA	1968	Studio One	
Reggae Psalms	JA	2001	Jamaican Vibes	

Alton Ellis

Title	Country	Year	Label	Catalog
All My Tears (1965-68)		2006	Brook	
Alton Ellis	JA		Studio One	
Alton Ellis Sings-Heptones Harmonise (1978-80)			Jet Star	
Alton & Hortense at Studio 1	US	1990	Heartbeat	
Alton Ellis' 25th Silver Jubilee	GB	1984	Sky Note	LP 46
Arise Black Man (1968-78)			Moll Selekta	
A New Day		1983	Body Music	
Be True To Yourself	GB	2004	Trojan	
Change My Mind		2000	Orchard	
Continuation	GB	1985	All Tone	
Cry Tough (CD)	US	1993	Heartbeat	
Day Dreaming		1983	Silver Camel	
Family Vibes (& Friends)	GB	1992	All Tone	
Get Ready For Rock				

Reggae Steady (1967-74)		1999	Jamaican Gold	
Greatest Hits = Cry Tough	GB	1973	Count Shelly	
Jubilee Vol. 2	GB	1985	Sky Note	SKY LP 53
Live with Aspo:Working On A Grooving Thing		2001	Belville International/Patate	
Love To Share	US		Third World	
Man Of Studio One	JA	1994	All Tone	MSC 305437 ALT 002
Many Moods Of (1978-80)	US	1980	Tele-Tech	T-T LP-001-80
More Alton Ellis		2001	T.P.	
Mr. Skabeana (& Heptones)	GB	1981	Cha Cha	CHALP 009
Mr. Soul Of Jamaica	JA	1967	Treasure Isle	DSK 3509 (013)
My Time Is The Right Time (1966-71)		2000	Westside	
Reggae Valley Of Decision		1996	House Of Reggae	
Showcase	JA	1984	Studio One	
*Sings Rock And Soul	JA	1967	Coxsone	CSL 8008
Slumming	CDN	198x	Abraham	CRLP 001
Still In Love	GB	1977	Trojan/Horse	HRLP 708
Soul Groover	GB	1997	Trojan	
Sunday Coming	JA	1970	Studio One	PSOL 3423
The Best Of	JA	1969	Coxsone	CSL 8019
With Hortense Ellis				

Freddie McGregor

Across The Border	JA	1984	Big Ship	BS 3302
All In The Same Boat	JA	1986	Big Ship	
Anything For You	US	2002	VP Records	
*Big Ship	JA	1982	Thompson Sound	TS 002
Big Ship Classic Dub	US	1992	VP Records	
Bobby Babylon	JA	1979	Studio One	
Carry Go Bring Come	GB	2000	Greensleeves	
Come One Over	US	1983	RAS Records	RAS 3002
Comin' In Tough	US	2005	VP Records	
Don't Want To Be Lonely	JA		Studio One	SOLP 7777
FM	JA	1992	High Times	
Forever My Love	US	2000	RAS	
*Freddie McGregor	GB	1987	Polydor	POL 5214
Hard To Get	GB	1992	Greensleeves	GREL 175
Heart Is Willing		2003	Charm	
I Am Ready	JA	1982	Coxsone	SOLP 1000
Live At The Town & Country Club	US	1990	Gold Disc	
Live In London 1991		1993	Charly	
Love At First Sight	JA	1982	Joe Gibbs	JGM 0019
Lovers Rock Showcase Jamaica Style	GB	1981	Live & Love	LAP 14
Lovers Rock		2003	Prestige	
Masterpiece	US	200x	VP Records	
Mister Eudaric Riddim		2009		

Freddie McGregor (cont'd)

Mr. McGregor	JA	1979	Observer	OBS 1901
Now	JA	1991	Steely + Clevie	MSC 2792
Push On	JA	2002	Big Ship	
Reggae Max		2003	Jet Star	
Reggae Rockers	US	1989	Rohit	RRTG 7714
Rhythms Of My Heart		2004	Nuff	
Rhythm So Nice	JA	1983	Thompson Sound	
Rumours	GB	2000	Greensleeves	
Roots Man Shanking	US		Clocktower	
Showcase	JA	1981	Observer	
Sings Jamaican Classics	JA	1991	Big Ship	BSLP 1
Sings Jamaican Classics Vol. 2	US	1992	VP Records	VP1276
Signature	US	2000	VP Records	
Super Stars Extravaganza	US	2005	VP Records	

Fabulous Five Inc. (see also Soca)

Fabulous Five Inc.	GB		Ashanti	SHAN 104
My Jamaican Girl	GB	1976	Trojan	TRLS 129

Derrick Harriott

14 Chartbusters	US		Crystal	
Acid Rock	JA	1982	Crystal	CLP 1012
Born To Love You	US	1979	Crystal	1007
Chartbusters 70's Style	US		Crystal	
Derrick Harriott & The Revolutionaires		1977	Reggae Chart Busters Seventies Style	
Disco Rockers	GB	1977	Charmers	
Enter The Chariot	US		Crystal	CLP 1010
Float On	GB		Charmers	
Greatest Reggae Hits	GB		Trojan	TRLS 116
More Scrubbing The Dub	JA	1975	Crystal	
Psychedelic Train	GB		Trojan	TBL 141
Reggae Oldies	GB		Charmers	
Rocksteady Party	GB		Island	ILP 955
*Riding The Musical Chariot	US	1990	Heartbeat	HB 58
Ruthless Combinations	JA	1991	Crystal	
Scrub A Dub Reggae	JA	1974/91	Crystal	
Songs For Midnight Lovers	GB	1981	Trojan	TRLS 198
Sings Jamaican Reggae	GB	1969	Crystal/Pama	
Step Softly & Friends (Reggae and Rock steady from 1965-72)	GB	1988	Trojan	TRLS 267
The Best Of	GB	1965	Island	ILP 928
The Best Of Vol 2	GB	1968		
The Best Of (& The Crystallites)	GB		Island	ILP 983
Undertaker (The Crystallites)	GB	1970	Trojan	TBL 114

John Holt

Title	Country	Year	Label	Catalog
1000 Volts Of Holt (Help Me Make It Through The Night) Sings For "I" Vol.2	JA		Sonic Sounds	TRLS 75
20 Golden Love Songs	D	1980	Trojan	204 805
2000 Volts Of Holt	GB	1976	Trojan	TRLS 134
3000 Volts Of Holt	GB	1977	Trojan	TRLS 143
A Love I Can Feel	JA	1970	Studio One	SOLP 9017
Al Disco Showcase		1981	Taurus	
Before Next Tear Drop		1976	Klik	
Children Of The World	US	1990	Gold Disc	
Dusty Roads	JA	1974	Sonic Sounds	CRPJ 002
Everything To Me	GB	1886	Revue/Creole	BGLP 1
Every time	US	1993	IKUS Records	
For Lovers And Dancers	GB	1984	Trojan	
Further You Look	GB		Trojan	
Greatest Hits Collection (With The Wailers & Sly & Robbie)	JA	1972	Studio One	
Gold	D	1983	Creole	6.25 571
Help Me Make... (1000 Volts of Holt)	D		Trojan	6.230 51
Holt	GB		Trojan	TRLS 43
Holt	JA	1971	Jaguar	JAG 5403
Holt Goes Disco	GB	1978	Trojan	TRLS 160
If I Were A Carpenter	GB	1989	Live & Love	
I Can't Get You Off My Mind (Greatest)	US	2006	Heartbeat	
Impressible (The Impr. John Holt)	JA	1978	Harry J	
In Demand	JA	1978	Dynamic	DY 3375
Introspective	JA	1980	Dynamic	
John Holt & Friends (Paragons & Friends)	JA		Studio One	SOLP 0136
John Holt		1997	Rialto	
John Holt Story (2-CD set)		1996	Graylan	
Just A Country Boy	GB		Trojan	TRLS 161
Just The Two Of Us		1982	CSA	
Legendary/Love Songs	CDN		Micron	
Let It Go On	GB	1978	Trojan	TRLS 163
Like A Bolt	JA		Treasure Isle	DSK 3522/TI 016
Live In London		1984	Very Good	
Love I Can Feel	GB	1974/85	Trojan	
Love Songs Vol. 2	GB		Parish	
My Desire	JA	1980	Jackpot	INCLP 102
OK Fred	GB	1972	Melodisc	
Peace In The Sun	JA		Volt Music	DSR 2329
Peace Maker	GB	1993	Clarendon Sound	
Pledging My Love	JA	1972	Striker Lee	TSL 108
Police In Helicopter	GB	1983	Greensleeves/ Arrival	
Reggae Christmas Hits Album	GB	1986	Trojan	

John Holt (cont'd)

Reggae, Hip House		1993	R&B Flavor	
Rock With me Baby	GB	1988	Trojan	
Roots Of Holt	GB	1977	Trojan	TRLS 147
Showcase (& Uniques)	JA		Justice	JUSLP
Showcase New Disco Style	JA	1977	Snapper	SN 001
Since I Fell For You	US		Joe Gibbs	JGML 6031
Sings For "I"/Sings Classics	JA		Sonic Sounds	SSR 087
Spotlight On	JA		Thunder Bolt	
Still In Chains	JA	1971	Dynamic	DY3325
Sugar	US		Clocktower	CTLP 092
Super Star		1978	Weed Beat	
Sweetie Come Brush Me	JA	1982	Sonic Sounds	Vale 001
The Further You Look	JA	1973	Total Sounds	CRPJ 003
The Reggae Christmas Hits	JA	1986	Sonic Sounds	
This Is Reggae				
(Double-LP & Georgie Fame)	D		Phone-Disc	DLP 2-9016
Time Is The Master	GB	1973	Cactus	CTLP 109
Treasure Of Love	JA	1977	World Beat	WB 11
Up Park Camp	JA	1976	Channel One	
*Vibes	JA	1985	Leggo Sounds	LD 001
Why I Care	GB	1989	Greensleeves	
Wild Fire (with Dennis Brown)		1985	Natty Congo/Tad's	
World Of Love	CDN		Micron	MICCAN 006

Byron Lee and The Dragonaires (see also Soca)

And Mighty Sparrow	GB		Dynamic	DYLP 3002
Art Of Mas	GB	1977	Dynamic	DYLP 1002
Byron 1982	JA	1982	Dynamic	DY 3421
Byron Lee & The Dragonaires	US		Jad	JAS 1004
Caribbean Joyride	GB	1964	Dynamic	DYLP 3012
Come Fly With Lee	JA	1962	Dynamic	B/LP 001
Dance The Ska Vol. 3				1A062-
(Soul Ska Original Rock Steady)	NL		IBC	23955
Dance The Ska Vol. 4 (& Blue Busters)	B		EMI / IBC	1A062- 23956
Dancing Is Forever		1974		
Disco Reggae	JA	1975	Dynamic	DY 3357
Disco Reggae	US	1978	Mercury	SRM-1-1063
Each On Teach (& Blues Busters)	JA		Dynamic	DY 3332
First Class With Lee	JA	1967	Dynamic	BLP 008
Goin' Places		1970		
Jamaica's Golden Hits	JA		Dynamic	DY 3380
Jamaica's Golden Hits Vol.1	GB	1977	State	ETMP 16
Jamaica's Golden Hits Vol.2	JA	1983	Dynamic	DY 3433
Jump Up	JA	1967	Atlantic/Dynamic	SD 33-182
Jump And Wave For Jesus		1999		

Byron Lee and The Dragonaires (cont'd)

Original Rock Steady Hits		1984		
Peolple Get Ready, This Is Rock Steady		1967		
Play Dynamite Ska (With The Jamaica All-stars)	GB		Trojan	TBL 110
Reggae Blast Off!	JA	1969	Dynamic	DYNA 3310
Reggae Fever	JA	1974	Dynamic	DY 3340
Reggae Eyes		1969		
Reggae Hits	JA	1978	Dynamic	DY 3383
Reggae Hot And Cool And Easy	JA	1972	Dynamic	DY 3328
Reggae International	JA	1976	Dynamic	DY 3362
Reggae Round The World	GB	1973	Dragon	DRLS 5001
Reggae Splash Down	GB	1971	Trojan	TRLS 28
Reggae With (Reggay)	JA	1968	Trojan	TRLS 18
Reggae International	GB		Dynamic	DYLP 3008
Rock Steady '67	JA	1967	Dynamic	BRA 4P 3101
Roch Steady Beat		1967		
Rock Steady Explosion	JA		Dynamic	BLP 010
Rock Steady Intensified		1968		
Six Million Dollar Man		1976		
Sparrow Meets The Dragon	JA		SpaLee Records	LP 001
Sparrow Dragon: Again	JA	1988	Dynamic	DY 3460
Soft Lee Vol 1	JA	1983	Dynamic	
Soft Lee Vol 3	JA	1988	Dynamic	DY 3460
Soul Ska		1983		
The Midas Touch	JA	1974	Dynamic	DY 3352
*The Sounds Of Jamaica	JA	1963	Dynamic	LP 006
This Is Carnival	GB		Dynamic	DYLP 3006
Tighten Up	JA	1969	Dynamic	DY 3315

The Melodians

Irie Feelings	US	1983	Ras Records	RAS 3003
Pre-Meditation	GB	1986	Sky Note	SKYLP 18
Rivers Of Babylon	GB	1970	Trojan	
Swing And Dine (CD)	US		Heartbeat	
Sweet Sensation	GB	1980	Island	IRSP 13
*The Melodians (Sweet Sensation)	D	1980	Island	203193

The Paragons

And Friends	JA		Studio One	
For You		198x		
Golden Hits	F	1992	Esoldun	
Heaven And Earth		197x		
My Best Girl Wears				
My Crown	GB	1992	Trojan	TRLS 299
Now	GB	1982	Starlight	SDLP 909
On The Beach	JA	1967	Treasure Isle	TI 004
*On The Beach	JA	1967	Treasure Isle	TILP 100/1

The Paragons (cont'd)

Original	GB		Treasure Isle	
Return	JA		Striker/Lee	SKL 1518
Riding High (The Paragons)	US		Mango	MLPS 9631
Sly And Robby Meet The Paragons		1981		
The Paragons (Riding High)	GB		Island	ILPS 9631/ ISL 1611
The Original Paragons	GB		Treasure Isle	TILP 002
With Roslyn Sweet	GB		Treasure Isle	

The Techniques

Best Of Techniques Hits Vol.2	JA		Techniques	
Classics	JA	1982	Techniques	
Classics Vol 2	JA	1982	Techniques	
I'll Never Fall In Love	JA		Techniques	
Little Did You Know	JA	196x	Treasure Isle	LP 201
Queen Majesty	GB	2007	Trojan	
Rock Steady Classics			Rhino	
Run Come Celebrate	US	1993	Heartbeat	
Techniques In Dub		1997	Pressure Sounds	
Unforgettable Days	JA	1981	Techniques	

Delroy Wilson

20 Golden Hits	GB	1978	Third World	
*22 Magnificent Hits	JA	197x	Striker Lee	BLP 017
Best Of	US	1978	Liberty	
Bettah Must Come	GB	1971	Trojan	TBL 44
Captivity		1973	Big Shot	
Cool Operator	GB	1983	Vista Sounds	VSLP 4010
Dance With Me (& Donna Marie)	GB		Top Priority	KPLP 05
Dancing Mood	JA	196x	Studio One	
Delroy Wilson's Greatest Hits	JA		Jaguar	JAG 5406
For I And I	GB	1975	Grounation	GROL 501
Go Away Dream	GB	1969	Black Music	BMLP 803
Good All Over	JA	1969	Studio One	CSL 8014
Gold Busters In Reggae	JA		Top Rank	
Honey Love	GB	1987	Love People Rec.	LP 002 ailers
I Shall Not Remove	JA	1966	Studio One	
Last Thing On My Mind	JA	1977	Harry J	
Living In Footsteps	JA	1980	Joe Gibbs	
Looking For Love	GB	1986	Phil Pratt	Phil LP 1008
Lover's Rock	GB	1978	Burning Sounds	BS 1020
Million Busters In Reggae	JA	198x	Top Rank	
Money	US	1977	Clocktower	CTLP 100
Mr. Cool Operator		1977	EJI	
My Special Lady	US	1989	Justice	JUSLP 006
Nice Time		1983	Vista Sounds	

Delroy Wilson (cont'd)

Now	GB		Real Wax Rec.	RWLP 1034
Original Twelve Hits (The Best..)	JA		Coxsone	CSL 8025
Oldies But Goodies (& Owen Gray)	GB		Pioneer International	
Oldies But Goodies Vol. 1	JA		Studio One	GW 002
Oldies But Goodies Vol. 2	JA		Studio One	GW 003
Original DJ Classics	JA	1980	Rocky One	RGLP 007
Pioneer Hits				
Prophesy		1980		
Reggae Classics	JA	1984	Top Rank	
Reggae Classics Vol. 3	GB	1988	Trojan	TRLS 256
Reggae Golden Classics	JA	1982	Crystal	CLP 1011
Sarge	GB	1976	Charmers	
Scandal	JA	1979	The Original Matador Rec.	
Supermix	GB	198x	Pioneer International	
The Dean Of Reggae	JA	1985	Alister Tipsy/ Sonic Sounds	
True Believer In Love	CDN	197x	Micron	MICCAN 032
Which Way Is Up	GB	1986	Blue Trac	BMLP 015
Who Done It	GB	1979	Third World	TDWD 008
Worth Your Weight In Gold	GB	1976		
		1984	Burning Sounds	BS 1060
Unedited	GB		Different	

THE REGGAE

Compilations

Oldies But Goodies Vol. 1	JA		Studio One	GW 002
Oldies But Goodies Vol. 2	JA		Studio One	GW 003
Reggae Classics Vol. 3	GB	1988	Trojan	TRLS 256
Reggae Golden Classics	JA	1982	Crystal	CLP 1011
Original DJ Classics	JA	1980	Rocky One	RGLP 007
Taxi Production Presents The Sounds Of The 80's	JA		Taxi	
This Is Reggae Music (Double-LP)	D	1977	Island	300329+30
Tighten Up Vol. 1-3 (Box)	GB	1988	Trojan	TALL 300A-F
Time To Remember	JA		High Note	DSK 3516
Scandal	JA	1979	The Original Matador Rec.	
Wiser Dread (u.a. Bunny Wailer)	US	1981	Nighthawk	301

Junior Byles

Beat Down Babylon	GB	1973	Trojan	TRL 52
Beat Down Babylon				
*The Upsetter Years'	GB	1987	Trojan	TRLS 253

Junior Byles (cont'd)

Jordan	US	1988	Heartbeat	HB 45
Rasta No Pickpocket	US	1986	Nighthawk	NHM 7493
When Will Better Come 1972-76	GB	1988	Trojan	TRLS 269

Jimmy Cliff

Another Cycle	GB	1971	Island	ILPS 9159
Black Magic		2004		
Brave Warrior		1975		
Break Out	JA	1991	Cliff Sounds	
Can't Get Enough Of It	US		V-P	VPS 16536
Cliff Hanger	GB	1985	CBS	GB 281
Club Paradise	JA	1986	Oneness	SL 40404
Fantastic Plastic People		2002		
Follow My Mind	D	1975	Reprise	REP 54061
Give People What They Want	JA	1981	Oneness/Sonic Sounds	
Give Thanx	D	1978		WB 56558
Fundamental Reggae	GB	1975/87	See For Miles	
Hanging Fire		1988		
Hard Road To Travel		1968		
Higher And Higher		1998		
House Of Exile	JA	1990	Cliff Sounds	
Humanitarian		1999		
*I Am The Living	D	1980	Wea	K 99089
Images	US	1989	Vision Records	VP 3312
Jimmy Cliff	D	1985	Island	
207147				
King Of Reggae	D	1976	EMI	5C052-05404
Live In Concert	D	1976	Reprise	REP 54086
Many Rivers To Cross	D		Island	200 393
Music Maker	US		WB	MS 2256
Oh Jamaica	GB		EMI	NUT 3
Pop Chronic	D		Island	87577
Pop Gold	D	1975	Island	28642
Save Our Planet Erarth		1990		
Sense Of Direction	US		Sire	7501
Special	GB	1982	CBS	CX 85878
Struggling Man	GB	1973	Island	ILPS 9235
The Best Of	D		Island	800 013
The Harder They Come (Soundtrack)	JA	1972	Island	ILPS 9202
The Power And The Glory		1983		
Unlimited	D	1973	EMI	1C062-05404
Warrior	GB		EMI	EMC 3078
Wonderful World, Beautiful People	D	1970	Island	

Culture

Title	Country	Year	Label	Catalog
17 Chapters Of Culture		1992		
Africa Stand Alone	JA	1978	April	ADI-735x33
Baldhead Bridge	GB	1983	Blue Moon	LASL 7
Born Of You		1996	Conquer The World Rec	
Chanting On (CD)	US	2004	RAS	
Culture	US		Joe Gibbs	JGML 6038
Cultural Livity - Culture Live 98		1998		
Culture At Work	GB	1986	Blue Mountain	BMLP 014
Culture Dub (= Culture In Dub)	JA	1978	High Note	
Culture In Culture	JA	1986	Music Track	
Cumbolo	JA	1979	High Note	
Good Things	US	1989	Ras Records	RAS 3048
Harder Than The Rest	GB		Front Line	FL 1016
Harder Than The Rest	JA	1978	High Note	SP 0028
Humble African		2000		
Innocent Blood = Innocent Blood	US	1981	Joe Gibbs	JGML 6017
*International Herb	GB	1979	Front Line	FL 1047
Lion Rock	US	1982	Heartbeat	HB 12
Live In Africa		2002		
Live In Negril		2003		
More Culture = More Culture	US	1990	Rocky One	JGML 6038
Nuff Crisis	GB	1988	Blue Mountain	BMLP 022
Obeah, Peace and Love				
One Stone	JA		Gorgon Records	TRB 814132 IGOR 0006
Pass The Torch (7 diff. tunes of Joseph, and son Kenyatta)				
Payday		2000		
Rasta	GB		Rasta	RHLP 003
Rare And Unreleased Dub		1989	Revolver Records	
Roots & Culture (& Don Carlos)				
Scientist Dubs Culture Into A Parallel Universe		2000		
Stoned: One Stone In Dub engineered by Fathhead & Jim Fox	US	1997	RAS	
Stronger Than Ever (Sampler)	US	1990	Rocky One	RGLP 003
The Production Somethings, 12 Inch mix Three Sides To My Story	US	1991	Shanachie	
Trust Me		1997		
Two Seven Clash	US	1977/87	Shanachie	
Too Long In Slavery	JA	1989		
Vital Selection	GB	1978/81	Virgin	VX 1001
Wings Of A Dove	US		Shanachie	43097
World Peace		2003	Rounder	

Marcia Griffiths

At Studio One	JA		Studio One	SOL 1126
Carousel	GB	1990	Mango	
Electric Glide	US	1989	Mango	
I Love Music	JA	1986	Mountain Sound	LP 004
Kemar (& Bob Andy)	JA		Harry J	
Melody Life	JA		Studio One	
Marcia	JA	1988	Penthouse Records	
*Naturally	JA		Disc Pressers	
Really Together (& Bob Andy)	GB	1987	I-Anka	
Rock My Soul	US		Pioneer International	PILP 29
Rock My Soul (Tracks diff.)	JA		56 Hope Road	
Steppin'	GB		Sky Note	SKYLP 17
Strugglin' In Babylon				
Sweet Bitter Love	GB	1974	Trojan	TRLS 94

The Heptones

And Friends	GB		Trojan	TBL 183
Better Days	GB	1978	Third World	TDWD 1
20 Golden Hits	JA	1992	Sonic Sounds	
Back On Top		1983		
Big And Free With 20 Massive Hits	GB	1969	Trenchtown	TTLP 0045
Black Is Black	JA	1970	Studio One	
Book Of Rules	JA	1973	Jaywax/Harry J	HJ 112
Changing Times	US	1986	Moving Targets	
Cool Rasta	GB	1976	Trojan	TRLS 128
Deep In The Roots	US	2004	Heartbeat	
Freedom Line	JA	1971	Studio One	SOL 0111
Good Live	GB	1979	Greensleeves	GREL 6
Heptones	JA	1967	Studio One	SOL 9002
In A Dancehall Style	GB	1983	Vista Sounds	
In Love With You	US	1978	UA	LA-805-A
King Of My Town	GB		Jackal	
Legends From Studio One	JA		Trench Town	TTLP 0042
Mr. Skabeana (& Alton Ellis)	GB	1980	Cha Cha	CHALP 009
Mr. T (CD)	F	1991	Esoldun/Lagoon	LG 2 1008
Nightfood	GB	1976	Island	ILPS 9381
Night Food In A Party Time	GB	1977	Trenchtown	
On The Road Again	JA		Trenchtown	TTLP 0047
On The Run	US	1982	Shanachie	
On Top (The Best Of)	JA	1968	Studio One	SOL 0016
One Step Ahead	JA		Sonic Sound	
Party Time	US	1976	Mango	MPLS 9456
Place Called Love	US	1987	Moving Target	
Pressure	JA	1995	Tappa	
Rainbow Valley		1996	Prestige	
Sing Good Vibes	GB		Clarendon Sound	CSLP 005
Street Of Gold	US		Park Heights	PHLP 001

The Heptones (cont'd)

Sweet Talking		196x		
Swing Low		1985		
The Heptones aka Fattie Fattie	JA	1967	Studio One	
The Best Of The Heptones		2001	Music Club	
*The Original Heptones	JA	1976	Trenchtown	TTLP 0041
Ting A Line	JA		Studio One	SOL 2222
Trenchtown Experience	JA		Trenchtown	TTLP 0044

I-Three

*Beginning	GB	1986	EMI	ST17222

Inner Circle

Bad Boys		1994		
*Bad To The Bone	D	1992	Wea	9031-766520-1
Barefoot in Negril		2001		
Barry Biggs & Inner Circle	GB		Trojan	TRLS 142
Big Things		2000		
Blame It On The Sun	D	1979	Trojan	6.23972
Black Roses	US	1990	Ras Records	RAS 3062
Da Bomb		1996		
Dread Reggae Hits				
Everything Is Great	D	1979	Island	200378
Forward Jah-Jah People (Live)		1999		
Heavyweight Dub		1978		
Heavy Reggae				
Identified		1991		
Jah Jah People		2001		
Jamaica Me Creazy		1999		
Killer Dub	JA	1978	Top Ranking	
New Age Music (last with Jacob Miller)	D	1980	Island	202524
Ready For The World	D	1979	EMI	1C038-85210
Reggae Dancer (last with Carlton Coffee)		1994		
Reggae Thing	D	1976	EMI	5C038-85042
Rewind! Pt.2: The Singers		1990		
Rock The Boat	D	1974	Trojan	6.24148
One Way	GB	1987	Ras Records	RAS 3030
Something So Good	D	1982	Carrere	2934146
Speak My Language		1998		
State Of Da world		2008		
This Is Crucial reggae		2004		

Israel Vibration

Best Of	JA		Sonic Sounds	
*Forever	GB	1991	Ras Records	RAS 3080
Israel Vibration IV	US	1993	Ras Records	RAS 3120
On The Rock	US	1995	Ras Records	Ras 3175
Praises	GB	1990	Ras Records	RAS 3054

Israel Vibration (cont'd)

Strength Of My Live	GB	1988	Ras Records	RAS 3037
Thc Bcst Of	JA		Sonic Sound	
The Same Song	JA	1980	Top Ranking	
The Same Song Dub	JA		Top Ranking	
Unconquered Dub				
Unconquered People	JA	1980	Israel Vibes/ Tuff Gong	
Vibes Alive (2 LP)	GB	1992	Ras Records	RAS 3091
Why You So Craven	JA	1990	Arrival	AL 001

Luciano

Alpine Rocket		2003	Perlon	
Amelie On Ice		2002	Mental Groove Records	
Cadenza Contemporary and Cadenza Classics (2CD)		2007	Cadenza	
DJ Face Off		2005	DJ Magazine	
Fabric 25 (Radio Mix)	GB	2005	Fabric	
Fabric 41 (Comp)	GB	2008	Fabric (London)	
Fashionist?-Session 2		2005	Brickhouse Records	
Introducing Light And Sound		2004	Lo Fi Stereo	
Live @ Weetamix	D	2002	Max Ernst	
Listen And Dance Compilation 02		2004	Multicolor Recordings	
Orange Mistake		2003	Cadenza	
Remixes From Moffou	F	2004	Universal Music Jazz	
Sci Fi HiFi 02 (Comp)		2006	Soma Quality Recordings	
Shake It Up Tonight	JA	1996	Big Ship	
Stick Of Joy (2 CD)		2004	Kosmo Records	
The Ride (Comp)		2004	Nova Mute	
Where There Is Life	JA	1995	Xterminator	

Cedella Marley Booker

Awake Zion	F	1991	Danceteria	DANLP 067
Smiling Island Of Song	US	1982	Music for Little People	S42521-2

Bob Marley

All The Hits	US	1991	Rohit	
A Taste Of The Wailers (promo for press and radio)		1975		
African Herbsman	D	1977	Trojan	6.23049
Babylon By Bus	D	1978	Island	300150
Bob, Peter, Bunny and Rita	D	1985	Metronome	827001-1 ME
Bob Marley & The Wailers	B		Surprise	JTU AL 33
Bob Marley & The Wailers Dreams Of freedom-Ambient Translations Of Bob Marley In Dub		1997	Island	

Bob Marley	JA	1988	Urban Trek	UT 3002
Burnin'	D	1973	Island	203202
Catch A Fire	D	1973	Island	203201
Chances Are	D	1981	Wea	K 99183
Cheer Up	D		Bellaphon	23007001
Confrontation	JA	1983	Tuff Gong	205482
Crying For Freedom	S		Babylon	B 80014
Early Music	NL		CBS	31584
Early Music Featuring Peter Tosh	GB/NL	1977	Epic	Epic 82067
Exodus	D	1977	Island	28819 XOT
Featuring Peter Tosh	D		Bellaphon	2207001
Greatest Hits Of Bob Marley	S		Babylon	B 80015
Jah Joys And Rainbow (bootleg)	NL		Ze Anonym Plattenspieler	ZAP 7889
Interviews	JA	1982	Tuff Gong	
In The Beginning	GB	1983	Trojan	TRLS 221
Kaya	D	1978	Island	25821 XOT
Legend		1984	Island	
Live	D	1978	Island	89728-1
Live At Reggae Sunsplash	CH		Ps Record	PS 1002
Live Recording Live In Milano 27.6.80 (bootleg)	JA		Massi	
Magic Marley	D		Bellaphon	220.07.077
Marley Tosh Livingston And Associates-The Wailers	JA		Studio One	FCD 4041
Natty Dread	D	1974	Island	ILPS 9281
Nice Time	F	1991	Esoldun,Lagoon	
Memorial (Double Album)	D		Bellaphon	310.07.001
One Love		1991		
Rasta Revolution	D	1988	Trojan	6.203050
Rastaman Vibration	D	1976	Island	27236 XOT
Rebel Music		1986	Island	
Reflection-Rasta Revolution	D		Fontana	9299967
Reggae Rebel	D		Bellaphon	25007003
Reggae Greats	US	1984	Mango	
Reggae Rebel	F		Disques Esperance	ESP 7505
Reggae Rebel	B		Surprise	JTU AL 88
Reggae Revolution Vol. 1	S		Time Wind	50027
Reggae Revolution Vol. 2	S		Time Wind	50028
Reggae Revolution Vol. 3	S		Time Wind	50029
Reggae Revolution Vol. 4	S		Time Wind	50034
Riding High	D	1982	Bellaphon	305.07.001
Shake Down	F		Disques Esperance	ESP 165513
Shakedown	CDN		Splash	SH-8002
Soul Captives	US		Ala Records	ALA 1986
Soul Almighty: The Formative Years		1995	Anansi, Kuch	
Soul Rebel	F/GB	1981	New Cross	NC 001

Bob Marley (cont'd)

Soul Rebels	GB	1970	Trojan	TBL 126
Soul Revolution	B		Surprise	JTU AL 54
Soul Revolution Featuring Kaya	CDN		Splash	SH-8030
Soul Revolution Part 1	JA	1971	Upsetter	
Soul Revolution Part 2 (instrumental)	JA	1971	Upsetter	
Soul Revolution Part 3	JA		Upsetter	
Survival	JA	1979	Tuff Gong	
Talking Blues	JA	1991	Tuff Gong	TGLLP 12
The Best Of	E		RCA	SNL 1-7854
The Best Of	JA	1970	Beverly's	BLP 001
The Best Of	JA		Studio One	FDC 127
The Best Rarities Of	S		Time Wind	B 50037\
The Best Of The Early Years 1969-73	GB	1992	Music Club	
The Best Of The Early Years 1969-73	GB	1993	Trojan	
The Birth Of A Legend 1240	US	1976	Calla (Double-LP)	2 CAS
The Birth Of A Legend Featuring Peter Tosh	NL	1991	Epic	EPC 8206
The Bob Marley Memorial Album	D		Bellaphon	310.07.001
The Box Set		1982	Island	
The Upsetter Record Shop Pt1\ The Complete Soul Rebel	F	1991	Esoldun, Lagoon	
The Upsetter Record Shop Pt2\Rarities	F	1991	Esoldun, Lagoon	
The Wailers	D	1985	Island	207145
*The Wailing Wailers	JA	1965	Studio One	S 1001
*Trench Town (Disco)	JA	1982	Tuff Gong	
Trench Town Rock	D		Bellaphon	220.07.220
Uprising	D	1980	Island	202462
We Never Give Up (bootleg)				
Wing Of Reggae	S		Time Wind	50083
With Peter Tosh	US		Hallmark/Pickwick	SHM 3048
Songs Of Freedom 4 CD Box-Set	JA	1992	Tuff Gong/Island	TGCBX 1 (512 280-2)

Rita Marley

Harambe	JA	1982	Rita Marley Music	
Harambe	D	1983	Ultraphone	6.25597
We Must Carry On	US		Rita Marley M/Shanachie	43032
*Who Feels It Knows It	D	1980	Strand	6.24532

Jacob Miller

Dread Dread	US	1978	Liberty	LT 51162
Greatest Hits	JA	1987	Top Ranking	TR 79-5
Ital Christmas (& Ray Man I)	JA		Top Ranking	TRS 3

Killer	US	1987	Ras Records	3205
Lives On	US		Joe Gibbs	JGML 6016
*Mixed Up Moods	D	1980	Island	202883
Natty Christmas	JA		Top Ranking	Xmas 1
Reggae Greats	D	1984	Island	207141
Tenement Yard (Dread Dread)	D		Island	20108
The Killer Rides Again	JA	1976/90	Sonic Sounds	VPRL 2029
Wanted	JA		Top Ranking	TRS 2
Who Say No Dread (& Augustus Pablo)	GB	1975/92	Greensleeves	
With The Inner Circle Band (& Augustus Pablo)	F	1992	Esoldun	

Judy Mowatt

Black Woman	JA	1979	Ashandan	
Life	JA		Judy M Records	MSC 305412
*Look At Love	JA	1991	Judy M Records	MSC 2797
Love Is Overdue	GB	1986	Greensleeves	GREL 103
Mellow Mood	JA	1975	Sonic Sounds/ Ashandan	
Mr. Dee-J	JA		Sonic Sounds/ Ashandan	
Only A Woman	US	1982	Shanachie	43007
Working Wonders	JA	1985	Ashandan	43028

Lee Perry

Africa's Blood	GB	1973	Trojan	TBL 166
Alien Starman		2003		
Alive More Than Ever		2006		
Battle Axe	GB		Trojan	TBL 167
Battle Of Armageddon	GB	1986	Trojan	
Best Of Clint Eastwood				
Black Ark Experryments (with Mad Professor)		1995		
Black Ark In Dub	GB		Starlight/Black Ark	BALP 400
Blackboard Jungle Dub	US	1973	Clocktower	LPCT 0115
Chicken Scratch	US	1989	Heartbeat	
Clint Eastwood		1970		
Cloak And Dagger	GB	1973	Rhino	SRNO 8002
D.I.P. Presents The Upsetters	GB	1975	D.I.P.	DLP 5026
Double Seven	GB	1974	Trojan	TRLS 70
Dub Fire		1998		
Dub Take Woodoo Out Of Reggae		1996		
Earthman Skanking		2003		
Eastwood Rides Again	GB	1970	Trojan	TBL 125
Encore		2003		
End Of An American Dream		2007		
Excaliburman	GB	1992	Seven Leaves	
Experryments Of The Grassroots of Dub		1995		

Lee Perry (cont'd)

From the Secret Laboratory		1990		
Give Me Power (& Friends)	GB	1988	Trojan	
Heart Of The Dragon		1975		
Heart Of The Ark	GB		Seven Leaves	SLLP 1
*History, Mystery, Prophesy	JA	1984	Lion Of Judah	LP 001
In Satan's Dub	F		Danceteria	
Jamaican E.T.		2002		
Judgment In Babylon (Maxi)	JA		Lion Of Judah	LPD 001
Kung Fu Meets The Dragon	GB		D.I.P.	DLP 6006
Lord God Muzick	D	1991	Zensor	
Magnetic Mirror Master Mix	GB	1989	Anachron	
Meet Mafia & Fluxy In Jamaica	F	1992	Esoldun	
Many Moods of the Upsetter		1970		
Megaton Dub	GB	1979	Seven Leaves	
Megaton Dub 2	GB	1979	Seven Leaves	
Message From The Yard		1988		
Musical Bones (& Rico)	GB	1975	D.I.P.	DLP 6000
Mystic Miracle Star (with Majestics)		1982		
Mystic Warrior (& Mad Professor)	GB	1989	Ariwa	
Mystic Warrior In Dub (& Mad Professor)	GB	1989	Ariwa	
News Flash	F	1991	Esoldun	
On The Wire		1988		
Open The Gate (& Friends)	GB	1989	Trojan	
Out Of Many, The Upsetter	GB	1991	Trojan	
Panic In Babylon		2004		
Public Jestering (& Friends)	GB	1990	Attack	
Prisoner	GB		Trojan	TBL 127
Reggae Greats: Lee Perry	D	1985	Island	IRG 12
Reminah Dub (The Upsetters & Sly & The Revolutionaries	GB		Original Music	
Repetance		2008	Narrack Records	
Return Of Django	GB	19	Trojan	TRL 19
Return Of Pipecock Jackson	NL		Black Star Liner	BSLP 9002
Return Of The Super Ape	JA	1978	Lion Of Judah	
Return Of Wax	GB	1975	D.I.P.	DLP 6001
Revolution Dub	GB	1975	Creole/Cactus	CTLP 112
Rhythm Shower	GB	1973/74	Trojan	
Satans Dub		1990		
Satan Kicked The Bucket		1988		
Scratch & Company Chapter 1 - The Upsetters	US		Clocktower	
Scratch Came Scratch Saw Scratch Conquered		2008		
Scratch On The Wire	D		Island	200 881
Scratch The Upsetter Again	GB	1970	Trojan	TTL 28
Sensi Dub Vol. 2 (& The Upsetters/King				

Tubby & & Sly & The Revolutionaries)	GB	1989	Original Music	
Shocks Of Mighty (& Friends)	GB	1988	Attack	
Some Of The Best (Feat...)	US	1985	Heartbeat	
Son Of Thunder		2000		
Songs To Bring Back The Ark		2000		
Sounds From The Hotline		1991		
Spiritual Healing	CH	1990	Black Cat	
Super Ape	GB	1976	Island	ILPS 9417
Super Ape Inna Jungle		1995		
The Best Of	GB		Jet Star	PTLP 1023
The Best Of Vol. 2	GB		Pama	PTPLP 1026
The Good The Bad And The Upsetter	GB	1970	Trojan	TBL 119
The Mighty Upsetter		2008		
The Original Super Ape		1998		
The Return of Pipecock Jackxon		1980		
The Upsetter		1969		
The Upsetter Collection	GB	1981	Trojan	TRLS 195
The Upsetter Presents Roast Fish Collie Weed & Corn Bread	JA	1978	Black Ark	
Time Boom X De Devil Dead		1987		
Val Bennet & The Upsetters	US		Carl's	CR 1010
Who Put The Woodoo Pon Reggae (with Mad Professor)		1996		

Max Romeo

A Dream By Max Romeo	GB	1970	Pama	PMLP 11
Cross Or The Gun	JA	1995	Tappa Zukie	
Far I - Captain Of My Ship	GB	1992	Jah Shaka	
Holding Out My Love To You	US	1981	Shanachie	43002
I Love My Music	GB	1979	Solid Groove	SGL 106
In This Time		2001	3D	
Let The Power Fall	JA	1972	Dynamic	DY 3313
Love Message		1999	Warriors	
Meets Owen Gray	GB	1984	Culture Press	VSLP 5004
Open The Iron Gate (Revelation Time)	US	1978	Liberty	LT 51165
Perilous Times		2001	Mediacom	
Pocomania Songs		2007	Ariwa Sounds	
Reconstruction	JA	1977	Dynamic	DY 3378
Revelation Time		1975	Black World	
Rhondos	GB	1980	King Kong	KANT 1
Something Is Wrong		1999	Warriors	
Selassie I Forever	JA	1998	Chamax Music	
Transition	US	1989	Rohit	
*War In A Babylon	GB	1976	Island	ILPS 9392

Sly and Robbie

*A Dub Experience	D	1984	Island	207134
Black Ash Dub (Sly&The Revolutionaires)	GB	1978	Trojan	

Sly and Robbie (cont'd)

Crucial Reggae	US	1981	Island Mango	
Disco Dub	JA		Taxi	
DJ Riot		1990	Island	
Drum & Bass Strip\				
To The Bones By Howie B		1999	nyc music	
Dubs For Tubs	US	1990	Rohit	
Dub Rockers Delight		1991	Magnum Music Corp	
Gamblers Choice	JA		Taxi	
Friends		1999	Island	
Funkcronomicon		1995	Axiom	
Hard Core Dub (& The Revolutionaries)	GB		Original Music	
Hits 1978-1990	US	1990	Sonic Sounds	
Kings Of Reggae		1983	Keystone	
King's Dub	JA		Manzie	
Language Barrier	GB	1985	Island	
Many Moods Of	US	1994	Sonic Sounds	
Master Of Ceremony	CDN		Imperial	IC 8018
Meet King Tubby	F	1991	Esoldun	
Present Taxi		1981	Island	
Present Gregory Isaacs	US	1988	RAS	
Present Mykal Rose	JA	1995	Taxi	
Present Taxi Christmas	US	1998	RAS	
Ragga On Top		1993	Pow Wow	
Rebel Soldier	JA	1982	Taxi	
Remember Precious times		1992	RAS, Taxi	
Rhythm Killers		1987	Island	
Silent Assassin	JA	1989	Taxi	
Simply Slyman		1978	Virgin Frontline	
Sixties Seventies and Eighties	US	1991	Mango	
Sly, Wicked And Slick	JA	1979	Taxi	
Sly And Robbie		1999	Rhino	
Sly-Go-Ville		1982	Island	
Sound Of Sound		1993	Pow Wow	
Sounds Of Taxi	JA	1984	Taxi	
Sound Of Taxi Vol. 2	JA	1986	Taxi	LP 005
Sound Of Taxi Vol. 3	JA	1987	Taxi	LP 009
Summit	US	1988	Ras	
Taxi	JA	1981	Island/Taxi	ILPS 9662
Taxi Connection Live In London		1987	Island	
Taxi Fare	US	1986	Heartbeat	
Taxi Gang	JA		Taxi	
Tax Wax	JA		Taxi	
Two Rhythms Clash	US	1988	RAS	
The 60's, 70's Into The 80's	JA		Taxi	ILPS 9668
The Punishers		1997	Island	
The Sting		1986	Island	

| The Summit | GB | 1988 | Greensleeves | |
| Version Born (prod. Bill Laswell) | | 2004 | Palm Pictures | |

The Meditations

For The Good Of Man	GB	1988	Greensleeves	GREL 114
*Greatest Hits	US	1984	Shanachie	43015
Guidance	JA	1979	Gorgon	101 578
I Love Jah (rec. 1982)	US	2002	Wackies	
Message From The Meditations	US	1978	Liberty	LT 51164
No More Friend	GB	1983	Greensleeves	GREL 52
Rasta Must Conquer	JA		Disc Pressers	
Reggae Crazy	US	2007	Meditations Music	
Stand In Love	US	2004	Meditations Music	
The Return Of The Meditations	US	1993	Heartbeat	
Wake Up	JA	1978	Sonic Sounds	TWS 929

The Mighty Diamonds

4000 Years	D		Virgin	300 593
Backstage	JA	1983	Music Works	MWRT 11986
Back To The Roots		1979		
Bust Out		1993		
Changes	GB	1981	Music Works	111 981
Changes Dubwise				
Deeper Roots	GB	1979	Front Line	FLD 6001
Dubwise (Dubwise Kouchie Wise)	JA	1981	Music Works	
Get Ready	JA	1988	Music Works	
Go Seek Your Rights		1990		
Heads Of Government		198x		
Ice On Fire	D	1977	Virgin	800 329
If You Looking For Trouble	GB	1986	Live & Learn	LLLP 22
I Need A Roof		1976		
Indestructible	US	1981	Alligator	Al 8303
Inna De Yard		2008		
Jam Session	GB	1991	Live & Learn	LLLP 032
Kouchie Vibes	GB	1984	Burning Sounds	BS 1061
Leaders Of Black Country	JA	1983	Tappa	
Live In Europe	GB	1989	Greensleeves	
Moment Of Truth		1992		
Never Get Weary	GB	1988	Live & Learn	LLPP 29
Paint It Red		1992		
Pass The Kouchie		1986		
Planet Earth	D		Virgin	800 344
Planet Mars Dub - The Icebreakers With The Diamonds	D	1978	Front Line	800 242
Ready For The World	US	1989	Shamar	
Reggae Street	US	1981	Shanachie	43004
Right Time	US	1983	Shanachie	43014
Rise		2001		

The Mighty Diamonds (cont'd)

Stand Up To Your Judgment	JA	1992	Channel One	
Struggling	JA	1986	Live & Learn	LLLP 013
The Best Of		1978		
Tell Me What's Wrong	JA	1992	Channel One	
The Moment Of Truth	GB	1992	Mango/Island	MLPS 1098
*The Real Enemy	GB	1987	Greensleeves	GREL 102
The Roots Is There	US	1982	Shanachie	43009
Thugs In The Street		2006		
Trinity Meet				
The Mighty Diamonds	JA		Gorgon/Sonic Sounds	
Vital Selection	D		Virgin	802 205

Third World

96 Degrees In The Shade	JA		Jah's Music	Island/25504
All The Way Strong	JA	1983	Jah's Music	
Arise In Harmony	D		Island	202 108
Committed	US	1992	Mercury	
You've Got The Power	NL	1982	CBS	
You've Got The Power	JA		Jah's Music	
*Journey To Addis	GB	1978	Blue Mountain	005
Live It Up	JA	1995	Third World Prod.	MSC 305428 TWP 01
Prisoner In The Street Live	D		Island	201055
Rock The World	JA		Jah's Music	
Sense Of Purpose	JA	1985	Jah's Music	
Serious Business	US	1989	Mercury	836952-1
Street Fighting	JA		Federal	
The Story's Been Told	JA	1979	Jah's Music	
Third World, Reggae Greats	D	1985	Island	207139
Third World	JA		Jah's Music	

Toots and The Maytals

20 Massive Hits		2000		
54-46 Was My Number: Anthology 1968-2000 2-CD set		2001		
An Hour Live (Toots Hibbert)		1988		
Bla Bla Bla		1993		
Broadway Jungle: The Best Of 1968-73		2001		
Dance The Ska Vol. 2 - The Sensational Maytals (Sensational)	JA		Dynamic	
Don't Trouble (Reggae Best)		1995		
Do The Reggae 1966-1970	GB	1988	Attack	ATLP 103
Experience		1995		
Fever		2001		
From The Roots	GB	1970	Trojan	TRLS 65
From The Roots (remastered)		2003		

Title	Country	Year	Label	Catalog
*Funky Kingston	GB	1976	Island	ILPS 9186
Funky Kingston/In The Dark: De Luxe Pack		2003		
Hallelujah	JA	1966	Jamaica Recording Studios	
In The Dark	GB	1974	Trojan	TRLS 202
Jamaican Monkey Man 2CD set		1999		
Just Like That	D	1980	Island	201852
Knock Out	D	1981	Island	204 179
Life Could Be A Dream	JA	1989	Studio One	SOLP 1958
Live at Reggae Sunsplash		1983		
Live at the Hammersmith Palace		1980		
Live In London 2CD set		1999		
Light Your Light		2007	Concord	
Monkey Man	GB	1970	Trojan	TBL 107
Monkey Man (with 13 bonus tracks)		2003		
Monkey Man From The Roots		1999		
Never Grow Old	JA	1964	Coxsone	JBL 1113
Original Golden Oldies Vol. 3	JA	1974	Prince Buster	PB 11
Pass The Pipe	D	1979	Island	200471
Pressure Drop (Best Of)		1979		
Pressure Drop (The Definitive Collection) 2CD set		2005		
Reggae Got Soul	JA	1976	Dynamic	DY 3356
Reggae Collection		2002		
Reggae Greats		1984	Island, Mango	
Recoup		1995		
Rhythm Kings		2005		
Roots Reggae		1974		
Roots Reggae six CD set (the early Jamaican albums)		2005	Trojan	
Sensational (Dance The Ska Vol. 2 - The Sensational Maytals)	JA	1965	Dynamic	
Slatjam Stoot	JA	1972	Dynamic	
Ska To Reggae		1999		
The Best Of	GB	1984	Trojan	TRLS 171
The Maytals		2001		
The Millennium Collection		2001		
The Very Best Of		1997		
The Very Best Of		2000		
Ska Father		1998		
Sweet And Dandy	JA	1968	Beverly's	
Sweet And Dandy		2003		
Toots In Memphis	D	1988	Island	259 534
Time Tough: The Anthology 2-CD set		1996		
That's My Number		1998		
The Maytals Greatest Hits		1971		

Toots and The Maytals (cont'd)

The Originals		1999		
Toots And The Maytals, Reggae Greats	D	1985	Island	207131
Toots Presents The Maytals	GB	1977	State	ETAT 16
Toots Live	D	1980	Island	203087
Toots Live (remastered)		2004		
True Love (duets with friends)		2004		
Workd Is Turning		2003		

Peter Tosh

20th Century Masters-The Millenium Collection: The Best Of Peter Tosh Black Dignity: Early Works Of The Stepping Razor

Bush Doctor 1C064-61708	D	1978	Rolling Stones Rec.	
Buk-In-Ham Palace (Maxi)	D	1979	EMI	
Captured Live	D	1984	EMI	
Can't Blame The Youth				
Complete Captured L:ive		2004		
Don't Look Back (Maxi) & Mick Jagger	D	1979	EMI	
Equal Rights	NL	1977	CBS	81937
I Am That I Am		2001		
Island Zorro (bootleg)	US		Excitable Record Works	4503.1
Johnny B. Good (Maxi)	D	1983	EMI	
*Legalize It	NL	1976	CBS	81556
Live At The One Love Peace Concert		2000		
Live&Dangerous: Boston 1976		2001		
Live At The Jamaica World Music Festival 1982		2002		
Mama Africa	D	1983	EMI	
Mystic Man	D	1979	Rolling Stones Rec.	1C064-62914
Negril		1975		
No Nuclear War	D	1987	EMI	
Talking Revolution				
The Essential Peter Tosh: The Columbia Years	D	1981	Rolling Stones Rec.	C064-64378

Bunny Wailer

Back To School (Maxi)	GB	1982	Solomonic	BWD 014
Blackheart Man	GB	1976	Island	ILPS 9415
Blackheart Man (diff arranged)	JA	1976	Solomonic	
Communication	JA	2000	Solomonic,Tuff Gong	
Conqueror/Version (Maxi)	JA	1981	Solomonic	
Crucial Roots Classics		2003	Sanctuary Records	
*Dance Massive	JA	1992	Solomonic	SOL 2546
Dub disco Vol. 1	JA	1978	Solomonic	SP 007-34
Dub disco Vol. 2	JA	1980	Solomonic	

Electro Rap/Soul Rocking Party (Maxi)	GB		Solomonic	SM 12 021
Gumption	JA	1990	Solomonic	SMLP 014
Hall Of Fame: A Tribute To Bob Marley	US	1996	RAS	
Hook Line & Sinker	JA	1982	Solomonic	
In I Father's House	JA	1978/79	Solomonic	005
Just Be Nice	JA	1990	Solomonic	SMLP 013
Liberation	JA	1988	Solomonic	
Live	JA	1983	Solomonic	009
Market Place	JA	1986	Solomonic	010
Peace Talks/Rockers (Maxi)	US	1984	Shanachie	5009
Protest	GB	1977	Island	ILPS 9512
Protest (different arrangement)	JA		Solomonic	
Resistance (not released)	JA		Solomonic	
Retroprospective		2003	Sanctuary Records	
Rock'n Groove	JA	1981	Solomonic	
Roots man Skanking	JA	1987	Solomonic	
Roots, Radicks, Rockers, Reggae	US	1983	Shanachie	43013
Rule Dancehall	JA	1986	Solomonic	
Rule Dancehall	US	2002	Shanachie	
Sings The Wailers	D	1981	Island	203380
Struggle	JA	1977/78	Solomonic	009\
The Never Ending Wailers		1991		
The Wailers Legacy(with The Wailers)		2006	Solomonic	
Time Will Tell				
(2 tracks more than Tribute)	US	1990	Shanachie	43072
Tribute	JA	1982	Solomonic	
World Peace	JA	2003	Solomonic	

The Wailers

I.D.		1989		
Marley Tosh Livingston				
And Associates - The Wailers	JA		Studio One	FCD 4041
Majestic Warriors	GB	1991	Tabu	
My Friends		1995		
The Wailers	D	1985	Island	207145
*The Wailing Wailers	JA		Studio One	S 1001
Tribute To Carly Barrett	GB	1987	Atra	

THE REGGAE AFTER BOB MARLEY

Dr. Alimantado

Best Dressed Chicken In Town	GB	1978	Greensleeves	GREL 1
Born For A Purpose (CD)	GB	1987	Greensleeves	GRELCD 22
In The Mix	GB	1985	Keyman	
In The Mix Part 2	GB	1987	Keyman	

Dr. Alimantado (cont'd)

In The Mix Part 3	GB	1988	Keyman	
In The Mix Part 4	GB	1989	Keyman	
In The Mix Part 5	GB	1989	Keyman	
Kings Bread	JA	1979	Ital Sounds	ISDA 5000
Kings Bread Dub	JA	1979	Ital Sounds	
Love Is	GB	1983	Keyman	
Privileged Few	GB	1989	Keyman	
Reggae Review Pt. 1	GB	1985	Keyman	KM 002
Songs Of Thunder	GB	1981	Greensleeves	GREL 22
Wonderful Time	GB	1988	Keyman	

Aswad

25 Live: 25th Anniversary		2001		
Aswad	GB	1976	Island	ILPS 9399
Aswad Crucial Tracks		1989		
Beauty is Only Skin Deep	US	1989	Mango	
Big Up	US	1997	Atlantic Records	
Bubbling		1985	Simba	
Cool Summer Reggae		2002		
Crucial Tracks	JA		Mango/Island	
Distant Thunder	GB	1988	Island	ILPS 9895
Dread Broadcasting Corp: Rebel Radio (2CD)	GB	2004	Trojan	
Dub: The Next Frontier		1995	Mesa	
Firesticks		1993	Alex	
Hulet	US	1979	Mango	MLPS 9611
Jah Shaka Meets Aswad in Addis Ababa Studio	JA	1985	Jah Shaka Music	LP 850
Live & Direct	GB	1983	Mini LP	205 912
New Chapter	GB	1981	CBS	32473
New Chapter Of Dub	GB	1982	Island	ILPS 9711
Next To You		1990	Alex	
*Not Satisfied	GB	1982	CBS	85666
On & On (Maxi)	GB	1989	Mango	12MNG 708
On The Top		1986	Simba	
Renaissance	GB	1988	Stylus Music	
Rebel Souls	US	1984	Mango	
Rise And Shine	JA	93/94	Rhino Entertainment	
Rise And Shine Again		1995	Mesa	
Roots Revival		1999	Ark 21	
Rough Trade Shops: Counter Culture 1976		2007	V2 Records	
Showcase	D	1981	Island	203 624
Smile	US	1980	Mango	
To The Top	GB	1986/87	Mango	
Too Wicked	GB	1990	Mango	MLPS 1054

Aswad (cont'd)

Warrior Charge-Dub Charge	GB	1980	Island Records	
Ways Of The Lord	GB	1982	CBS	
The BBC Sessions	GB	1997		

Big Youth

A Luta Continua (The Struggle Continue)	US	1986	Heartbeat	HB 28
Chanting Dread Inna Fine Style	US	1982	Heartbeat	HB 08
Chi Chi Run (just three songs)	GB	1972	Melodisc/Fab	MS 8
Cool Breeze-Ride Like Lightning - The Best of Big Youth		1972-76		
Dread Locks Dread	D	1978/83	Virgin	800 002
Everyday Skank	GB	1977/80	Trojan	TRLS 189
Get Up Stand Up (Hit The Road Jack)	D	1976	Teldec	6.22958
Hit The Road Jack	GB	1976	Trojan	
Higher Grounds – JR	US	1995	VP Records	
Isaiah - The First Prophet Of Old	D	1978	Virgin	800 245
Jamming The House Of Dread F		1991	Danceteria	
Live At Reggae Sunsplash	GB	1982	Trojan	
Live At Reggae Sunsplash		1983	Genes	
Manifestation	US	1988	Heartbeat	
Musicology	JA	2006	Tuff Gong	
Natty Cultural Dread	GB	1976/80	Trojan	TRLS 123
Natty Universal Dread		2000	Blood & Fire	
Progress	JA	1979	Negusa Nagast	
Reggae Gi Dem Dub	JA	1978	Negusa Nagast	
Reggae Phenomenon	JA	1977/90	Negusa Nagast	
Rock Holy	JA	1980	Negusa Nagast	
Screaming Target	GB	1973	Trojan	TRLS 61
Save The Children		1995	Declic	
Some Great Big Youth	US	1981	Heartbeat	HB 03

Black Uhuru

Anthem	JA	1983	Island	ILPS 9769
Black Sounds Of Freedom (re-release of Love Crisis)	GB	1977	Greensleeves	GREL 23
*Black Uhuru	D	1980	Virgin	202 513
Black Uhuru	GB	1980	Island	IRG 13
Brutal	GB	1986	Ras Records	
Brutal Dub	GB	1986	Ras Records	
Chill Out	D	1982	Island	204 698
Dub Factor	JA	1983	Island	
Dubbin It (summer 2001 at Paleo Festival)		2001		
Dynasty		2001		
Guess Who Is Coming To Dinner (CD)	US	1991	Heartbeat	TEC P 25854
In Dub (& Prince Jammy)		2001		
Iron Storm	GB	1991	Mesa	

Black Uhuru (cont'd)

Iron Storm Dub		1992		
Live In New York City	US	1988	Rohit	
Live 1984		2000		
Love Crisis	GB	1977	Third World	TWS 925
Love Dub (Uhuru In Dub re-edition)		1990		
Mystical Truth	GB	1993	Mesa	
Mystical Truth Dub		1993		
Now	JA/US	1990	Mesa	
Now Dub	US	1990	Mesa	
Positive	GB	1987	Ras Records	
Positive Dub	GB	1987	Ras Records	
Red	D	1981	Island	203 775
Reggae Greats (Comp)		1985		
Showcase	JA	1979	Taxi	
Sinsemilla		1980		
(Stalk Of Sinsemilla)	D		Island	202 525
Strongg		1994		
Strongg Dub				
Tear It Up - Live (and Video)	D	1982	Island	204 367
The Dub Factor		1983		
The Dub Factor (4 CD set)		2004	Hip-O-Select	
The Positive Dub		1987		
Uhuru In Dub		1982		
Unification		1998		

Dennis Brown

Africa (Westbound Train)	F		Celluloid	LTM 1028
Beautiful Morning	GB	1992	World Records	
Blazing	GB	1992	Greensleeves	
Brown Sugar	JA	1986	Taxi	LP 004
Classic Gold	JA	1978	Rocky One	RGLP 006
Cosmic	GB		Observer	Nine 01
Cosmic Force (CD)	US	1993	Heartbeat	HB 135
Could It Be	US	1996	VP Records	VPRL 1478
Death Before Dishonour	JA	1989	Tappa	
Deep Down (So Long Rastafari)	JA		Observer	
Dennis Brown & Horace Andy (Reggae Superstars Meet)	JA		Striker Lee	BLP 4
Foul Play	US	1981	A & M	SP 4850
Friends For Live	JA	1992	Black Scorpio	
Give Praises	JA	1994	Tappa Zukie	LP TZ-012
Good Vibrations	GB	1989	Yvonne's Special	
Greatest Hits	US		Rohit	
Hold Tight	JA	1986	Live & Learn	LL-LP-021
How Can I Love Someone	US	1993	IKUS Records	
I Don't Know	CDN		Abraham	AALP 1600

Title	Country	Year	Label	Catalog
If I Follow My Heart	JA		Studio One	SOL 1119
In Concert	JA	1987	A Yeola Records	AYLLP 003
*Inseparable	JA	1987	J & W Records	WKLP 7
Joseph's Coat Of Many Colours	D	1980	Wea	ATL 58111
Joseph's Coat Of Many...	JA	1980	Leggo Records	
Judge Not (& Gregory Isaacs)	GB	1984	Greensleeves	
Just Dennis	GB	1975	Trojan	TRLS 107
Light My Fire	JA	93/94		
Limited Edition	JA	1993	Artistic/VP	VPRL 1277
Live At Montreux	D	1979/84	Wea	ATL 50654
Love Has Found Its Way	US	1982	A & M	SP 4886
Love's Gotta Hold On Me	GB	1986	Blue Moon	BMLP 033
Meets Harry Hippie	GB		Pioneer	PIONLP 2
Money In My Pocket	GB	1981	Trojan	TRLS 197
More Of	JA		Dynamic Sounds	
My Time	US		Rohit	
No Contest (& Gregory)	JA	1989	Music Works	VPRL 1064
No Man Is An Island	JA		Studio One	SOL 0112
Nothing Like This	GB	1994	Greensleeves	GREL 199
Overproof	US	1991	Two Friends Records	
Reggae Giants (& Freddy McGregor)	US	1990	Rocky One	
Revolution	CDN		Yvonne's Special	YSLP 4
Rare Grooves Reggae R 'N' B				
Vol. 1	JA	1992	Yvonne's Special	IVO 002
Vol. 2	JA	1992	Yvonne's Special	IVO 003
Sarge	GB	1990	CPL	
Satisfaction Feeling	CDN		Yvonne's Special	YSLP 0011
Slave Driver (Maxi)	GB	1984	Blue Moon	BMS 1002
Slow Down	JA	1985	Jammy Records	
Smile Like An Angel	GB		Blue Moon	BMLP 034
Some Like It Hot	JA	1993	Observer	
Songs Of Emanuel	JA	1995	Yvonne's Special	YVO 004/ TRB 814134
Spellbound	GB	1985	Blue Moon	BMLP 026
Stage Coach Showcase	CDN		Yvonne's Special	YS 001
Super Reggae & Soul Hits	GB	1972	Trojan	TRLS 57
Superstar	CDN		Micron	MICCAN 003
Temperature Rising	US	1995	VP Records	VPRL 1382
The Best Of Part 1	US		Joe Gibbs	JGML 6048
The Best Of Part 2	US	1982	Joe Gibbs	JGML 6054
The Exit (Exit)	JA	1986	Jammys Records	
The Facts Of Life	JA	1994	Diamond Rush	DIA LP 0002
The Prophet Rides Again	JA	1983	Rocky One	JGML 8099
Unchallenged	JA	1988	Music Works	VPRL 1115
Wake Up	JA	1985	Natty Congo	NC 004 LP
Wolf & Leopards	JA	1977	Weed Beat	MOLP 01
Words Of Wisdom	GB	1979		
		1982	Blue Moon	BMLP 002

Dennis Brown (cont'd)

Title	Country	Year	Label	Catalog
Victory Is Mine	JA	1992	Leggo Records	LGB 004
Visions	GB	1985	Blue Moon	BMLP 21
Yesterday, Today And Tomorrow	US	1982	Joe Gibbs	6057

Burning Spear

Title	Country	Year	Label	Catalog
100th Anniversary (double)	US	1987	Mango/Island	Mango 9377
(A)Live In Concert	JA	1998	Burning Music Productions	
Appointment With His Majesty	JA	1997	Burning Music Productions	
Best Of Burning Spear	JA	1995	Burning Music Productions	
Best Of The Fittest	GB	2001	EMI	
Burning Spear	JA		Studio One	SOLP 0150
Burning Spear		2001	Pressure Sounds	
Burning Spear, Reggae Greats	D	1985	Island	207 135
Calling Rastafari	JA	1999	Burning Music Productions	
Chant Down Babylon: The Island Anthology	JA	1996	Island	
Creation Rebel	US	2004	Heartbeat	
Dry & Heavy	D	1977	Island	800 593
Farover	GB	1982	EMI	
Forever	US		Heartbeat	HB 11
Free Man	JA	2003	Burning Music Productions	
Garvey's Ghost	D	1976	Island	800 621
Gold		2005	Island	
Hail H.I.M.	GB	1980	Burning Spear	RDC 2003
Harder Than The Best 1975-78	D	1979	Island	200827
*Jah Kingdom	JA/US	1991	Mango	
Jah No Dead		2003	Island	
Live '77	JA	1977	Burning Spear/ Tuff Gong	
Live At Montreaux	JA	2001	Burning Music Productions	
Live In Paris Zenith '88	GB	1988	Greensleeves	GREL 120
Live In South Africa 2000	JA	2004	Burning Music Productions	
Living Dub Vol. 1 (Social Living)	JA	2003	Burning Spear	
Living Dub Vol. 2 (Hail H.I.M.)	JA	2003	Burning Spear	
Living Dub Vol. 3 (Rasta Business)	JA	1996	Burning Music Productions	
Living Dub Vol. 4 (Appointment With His Majesty)	JA	1999	Burning Music Productions	

Burning Spear (cont'd)

Living Dub Vol. 5 (Calling Rastafari)	JA	2005	Burning Music Productions	
Living Dub Vol. 6 (Free Man)	JA	2004	Burning Music Productions	
Never Club Mix	JA	2006	Burning Music Productions	
Love & Peace Burning Spear Live!	JA	1994	Burning Music Productions	
Man In The Hills	GB	1976	Island	ILPS 9412
Marcus Garvey	GB	1975	Island	ILPS 9377
Marcus Garvey (as Island but no "Resting Place")	JA		Tuff Gong	
Marcus' Children (Social Living)	JA	1978	Burning Spear	WRLP 102
Mek We Dweet	JA/US	1990	Mango/Tuff Gong	
Mistress Music	JA	1986	Burning Spear	
Our Music (with DVD)	JA	2005	Burning Music Productions	
People Of The World	JA	1986	Burning Spear	
Rare And Unreleased	SA	2001	Revolver Records	
Rasta Business	JA	1995	Burning Music Productions	
Reggae Greats	US	1984	Mango/Island	
Resistance	US	1986	Heartbeat	HB 33
Rocking Time	JA	1974	Studio One	SOLP 1123
Sounds from The Burning Spear		2004	Soul Jazz Records	
Studio One Presents Burning Spear	JA	1973	Studio One	
The Best Of Burning Spear		2001	Island Def Jam	
The Burning Spear Experience	JA	2007	Burning Music Productions	
The Fittest Selection	GB	1987	EMI	
The Fittest Of The Fittest	JA	1983	EMI/Tuff Gong	RDC 1077681
The Original	US	1992	Sonic Sounds	
The World Should Know	US	1993	Heartbeat	HB 119
The World Should Know (with DVD)	JA	2005	Burning Music Productions	
Ultimate Collection		2001	Hip-O	

Chalice

Augmented		2003		
Best Of Reggae Sunsplash (Comp)		1982		
Blasted	JA	1981	Pipe Music	
Calm That Was A Storm		2007		
Catch It	US	1989	Rohit	RRTG 7737
Chameleonation				
Chronicles Of Chalice		2006		
Crossfire	JA	1986	CTS	
Digital Boulevard		2000		
Funny Kinda Reggae, Maxi	D	1984	Ariola	601 166

Chalice (cont'd)

Good To Be There	D	1984	Ariola	206 099
Illusion To The Tempor		2006		
Live at Reggae Sunsplash		1983		
Ras Reggae (Comp)	US	2004	RAS Records	
*Si Me Ya	JA	1990	Peace Pipe	
Stand Up!	GB	1985	CSA	
Up Till Now	US	1987	Ras Records	

Carlene Davis

15 Classics		1991		
At The Right Time	GB		Carib Gems	CGLP 10
Author And Finisher		2004		
Carlene	GB	1992	Gee Street/Island /PLG/Eko	314-512-767-1
Christmas Reggae		1992		
Echoes Of Love	JA	1995	Eko Music	
I Remember				
Jesus Is Only A Prayer Away (Gospel Reggae)	JA	1989	Eko Music	LP 001
No Bias	JA	1990	Eko Music	
*Paradise	JA	1984	Orange Records	OLP 002
Passion Of Pain		1995		
Reggae Song Bird	US	1988	Rohit	RRTG 7703
Redeemed		2000		
Rock Me Jesus		2005		
Taking Control	JA	1987	Nicole	VPRL 1040
Vessel	JA	1998	Big Ship	
Yesterday, Today, Forever	JA	1986	Nicole	VPRL 1030

Dillinger

3 Piece Suit		1993	Culture Press	
Answer My Questions	GB	1979	Third World	TWS 928
At King Tubbys	GB	2006	Attack	
Babylon Fever	US		UA	LA-795-R
Badder Than Them	GB	1981	A & M	AMLH 68528
Best Of Live	GB	1988	Trojan	
Bionic Dread	D	1976	Island	25467
CB 200	D	1978	Island	25249
Clash (& Trinity)	GB	1977	Burning Sounds	BS 1003
Cocaine In My Brain	JA	1984	Sonic Sounds	SSR 005
Cornbread	D	1978	Bellaphon	BBS 2598
Cup Of Tea	D	1980	Bellaphon	2607001
Dillinger	B		Surprise	JTU AL 65
Dub Organizer		197x	Scandal Bag	
*Funky Punk Rock to My Music	D	1979	Bellaphon	BBS 2578
Jamaica Sound				
Jamaican Dollars	F		Celluloid	LTM 1032

Title	Country	Year	Label	Catalog
Join The Queue		1983	Oak Sounds	
Killer Man Jaro	F		Esoldun	
King Pharaoh		1984	Blue Moon	
Live At London	GB	1981	Echo/Valdence	JSPL 0020
(& Clint Eastwood)				
Live At The Music Machine	D	1979	Bellaphon	BBS 2576
Marijuana In My Brain	GB	1979	Jamaica Sound	JSLP 002
Non Stop Disco Style	US	1978	Clocktower	
Ranking Dillinger - Non-stop				
Disco Style & Dubwise	F		Amo	
Ranking Dillinger Superstar	JA		Weed Beat	WB 10
Ready Natty Dreadie	JA	1975	Studio One	SOL 1125
Say No To Drugs	F	1991	Esoldun	
Superstar	JA	1977	Weed Beat	
Talking Blues	D	1977	Bellaphon	BBS 2577
Ten To One		2007	Dream Catcher	
Top Ranking	GB	1977	Third World	TWS 919
Tribal War		1986	New Cross	
Youthman Veteran		2001	Jah Warrior	

Beres Hammond

Title	Country	Year	Label	Catalog
A Day In The Life	US	1998	VP Records	VPRL 1534
A Moment In Time	US	2008	VP Records	
A Love Affair	GB		Penthouse Rec.	PHLP 14
Beres Hammond	JA	1986	WKS Rec.	WKS LP 005
Beres Hammond And Friends				
Coming At You	JA	1988	WKS Rec	
Expressions				
From My Heart With Love				
(+ Dennis Brown)	US	1994	Rocky One	RGLP 026
Full Attention	GB	1993	Charm	CRLP 17
Forever Yours				
Have A Nice Weekend	JA		WKS Rec.	VPRL 108
In Control	JA	1994	Harmony House	
Just A Man	US		Joe Gibbs	JGML 6000
Just A Vibes (& Derrick Lara)	JA	1991	Star Trail	
Let's Make A Song	JA		Brotherhood Music	
Live & Learn Presents				
(& Barrington Levy)	US	1990	Live & Learn	LLLP 031
Love Has No Boundaries				
Love From A Distance				
Music Is Live				
Putting Up Resistance	JA	1989	Tappa	
Red Light (Comin' at You)	GB	1988		
		1992	Charm	
*Soul Reggae	JA	1976	Kly Water	Arco LP 003
Sweetness	US	1993	VP Records	VPRL 1330

Gregory Isaacs

Title	Country	Year	Label	Catalog
All I Have Is Love	GB	1976	Trojan	TRLS 121
All I Have Is Love, Love, Love	JA	1986	TAD's	TRDLP 15586
At The Mixing Lab	GB		Mixing Lab	
Brand New Me	JA	2008	African Museum	
*Boom Shot	JA	1991	Black Scorpio/ Shanachie	
Call Me Collect	GB	1990	Ras Records	
Can't Stay Away	JA	1992	X-Terminator	5464-51239-1
Come Along	JA		Jammys	
Cool Ruler	JA	1978	African Museum	FL 1020
CooYah!	US	1990	New Name Muzik	
Crucial Cuts	GB	1983	Virgin	
Dancing Floor	US	1990	Munich Records	MR 148
Dancehall Don (and Friends)	JA	93/94		
Dapper Slapper	US	1999	Ras Records	
Double Dose (with Sugar Minott)		1986	Blue Track	
Dreaming	US	1995	Heartbeat	
Early Records	GB		Trojan	
Easy	JA	1985	TAD's	TRD 31984
Enough Is Enough	JA		Mixing Lab	
Extra Classic	GB	1983	Vista Sounds	STLP 1003
For Everyone	GB		Success	SRLLP 012
Future Attraction	US	2000	VP Records	
Gilbert	US	1988	Firehouse	
Give It All Up	US	2004	Heartbeat	
Gregory In Red	JA	1988	Tappa	TZ 20
Guilty For Loving You	GB		Jammys	
Hardcore	JA	1992	Top Ranking	
Hardcore Hits		1997	Ikus	
Heartache Avenue	GB	1994	World Records	WRLP 009
Heartbreaker	JA	1990	Jammys	
Hold Tight	US	1997	Heartbeat	
Hold Tight		2008	Mafia & Fluxie	
I.O.U.	JA	1989	Music Works	
In Person	JA	1975	GG's Records	004
Judge Not (& Dennis Brown)	JA	1984	Music Works	MWRT11988/ GRL 72
Kingston 14 Denham Town	JA	1988	Jamaican Vibes	
Let Off Supm!..Gregory/ Dennis Brown (Maxi)	GB	1985	Greensleeves	GRED 181
Let's Go Dancing	JA	1989	Jammys	
Live	D	1985	Island	207132
Live's Lonely Road		2004		
Lonely Lover	JA	1980	Pre	
Looking Back	US	1996	Ras Records	

Title	Country	Year	Label	Catalog
Love Me With Feeling (Maxi)	GB	1983	Island (Pre-Release)	IPR 2066
Lovers Rock (Double)	GB	1980	PRE	PRED 10
Masterclass	GB	2004	Greensleeves	
Maximum Respect		1996	House Of Reggae	
Meets Ronnie Davis	US	1979	Joe Gibbs	JGML 6030
Meets Them All	GB		Sting	
Midnight Confidenial	GB	1994	Greensleeves	
More Gregory	JA	1981	African Museum	PRE X 9
Mr. Cool	US	1996	VP Records	
Mr. Isaacs	US	1982	Shanachie	43006
Mr. Number One	US	1990	Heartbeat	
Negrea Love Dub (Slum In Dub)	GB		Burning Sounds	BS 1051
New Dance	GB	1999	BG Records	
Night Nurse	D	1982	Island	
No Contest (& Dennis Brown)	GB	1989	Greensleeves	
No Intention	US	1990	Gold Disc	
No Luck	F	1992	Esoldun	
No Surrender	JA/US	1992	The Punisher/ Grapevine	GVLP 2020
Not A One Man Thing	US	1995	RAS	
On The Dancefloor	US	1990	Heartbeat	
Over The Bridge	JA	1992	Dee Jay	
Out Deh!	JA	1983	African Museum	ILPS 9/48
Pardon Me	F	1992	Declic	
Past & Future	JA	1991	Techniques	WRLP 25
Private Beach Party	JA	1985	Music Works	MWRT 11989
Private Beach Party	GB	1985	Greensleeves	GRED 185
Private Lesson	US	1996	Heartbeat	
Rasta Business		1999	Exworks Records	
Rat Patrol	JA	2004	African Museum	
Red Rose For Gregory	GB	1988	Greensleeves	GREL 1118
Reggae Is Fresh	US	1988	TAD's	
Reserved For Gregory	GB		Exodus	EXLP 1
Revenge		2005	P.O.T.	
Rudie Boo		1992	Star Trail	
Set Me Free	US	1991	VP Records	VP 1174
Showcase	JA	1980	Taxi	1001
Silent Assassin	US	1989	Island	
Slum In Dub (Negrea Love Dub)	GB	1978	Burning Sounds	BS 1051
Sly & Robbie Present G.I.	US	1988	Ras Records	RAS 3206
Soon Forward	GB	1979	Front Line/Virgin	FL 1044
So Much Love		2000	Joe Gibbs Music	
State Of Shock	JA	1991	Leggo Records	L.G.B 007
Substance Free		2005	Vizion Sounds	
Talk Don't Bother Me	US	1987	Skengdon	SKDLP 007
The Best Of	GB	1977	GG Records	GG 030
The Best Of Vol. 2	GB	1981	GG Records	GG 025
The Early Years	GB		Trojan	TRLS 196

Gregory Isaacs (cont'd)

The House Of The Rising Sun	JA	1993		
The Lonely Lover	GB	1980	PRE	PRE X 1
The Sensational Gregory Isaacs	GB	1982	Vista Sounds	VSLP 4001
Turn Down The Lights		1999	Artists Only	
Two Bad Superstars (& Dennis Brown)	GB	1978/84	Burning Sounds	
Unattended		1993	PowWow	
Unforgettable	US		Rohit	
Unlocked	JA	1993	Artistic Records	
Victim	GB	1986	C & E	CSLP 102
Warning	GB		Serious Business	
Watchman Of The City	US	1988	Rohit	
Who's Gonna Take You Home (With Dean Frazer)	US		Rohit	

Linton Kwesi Johnson

Bass Culture	D	1981	Island	202 211
Dread Beat An' Blood	D	1978	Front Line	800 858
Dub Poetry (Comp)	US	1985	Mango	
Forces Of Victory	D	1979	Island	200 459
Independent Intavenshan (Comp)	GB	1998	Island	
*Linton Kwesi Johnson	D	1985	Island	207 136
Live in Paris (also on DVD)		2004	Wrasse	
LKJ A Capella Live	GB	1996	LKJ Records	
LKJ Live In Concert With The Dub Band	GB	1985	LKJ Records	
LKJ Presents	GB	1996	LKJ Records	
LKJ In Dub	D	1980	Island	203 181
LKJ In Dub Vol.2	GB	1992	LKJ Records	
LKJ In Dub Vol.3	GB	2002	LKJ Records	
Reggae Greats	US	1984	Mango	
Making History	D	1984	Island	
More Time	GB	1999	LKJ Records	
Straight To Inglan's Head		2003	Universal	
The Best Of LKJ (Comp) NL		1980	Epic	
Tings An' Times	GB	1991	Sterns	

June C. Lodge

I Believe In You	GB	1987	Greensleeves	GREL 104
Reggae Dance	D	1992	Arcade	
Reggae Nights	NL	1983	K-Tel International	
*Revealed	JA	1984	WKS Records	WKS 002
Selfish Lover	JA	1990	Works Records	VPRL 1156
Someone Loves You Honey	D	1982	Ariola	204 858
Someone Loves You Honey	US		Rocky One	JGML 6053
Tropic Of Love	JA	1991	Tommy Boy	TB 1032
Tropical Super Hits	NL	1984	K-Tel International	

Sugar Minott

African Girl	GB	1981	Black Roots	BRLP 3000 E
African Soldier	US	1988	Heartbeat	
A Touch Of Class	JA	1991	Jammys	
Bitter Sweet (Give The People)	GB	1979	Warrior	WARLP 2001
Black Roots	JA	1979	Thunderbolt	
Breaking Free	US	1994	RAS	
Buy Off The Bar	JA	1988	Powerhouse	
Dancehall Showcase	GB	1983	Black Roots	
Easy Sqeeze		1999	World	
Ghetto Child	US	1989	Heartbeat	
Ghetto - Ologie	GB	1979	Trojan	TRLS 173
Ghetto Youth Dem Rising	US	1988	Heartbeat	
Good Thing Going	US	1983	Heartbeat	HB 13
Happy Together	US	1991	Heartbeat	
Herbman Hustling	GB	1984	Black Roots	
Hit Man	JA	1992	Black Roots	
Inna Reggae Dancehall	US	1986	Heartbeat	
International	US	1996	RAS	
Jamming In The Streets	US	1987	Wackies	
Leader Of The Pack	US	1985	Striker Lee	
Live Loving	JA	1978	Studio One	
Lover's Revival	JA	1991	Black Roots	
Lovers Rock Inna Dancehall	GB	1988	Youth Promotion	
Meet The People In A Lovers Dubber's Style (& Black Roots Players)	GB		Black Roots	BRLP 007
More Sugar	JA	1982	Studio One	
Musical Murder	US	1997	VP Records	
Riddim	JA	1985	Powerhouse	
Rockers Award Winners (& Leroy Smart)	GB	1985	Greensleeves	
Roots Lovers	GB	1980	Black Roots	BRLP 001
Run Things	US	1993	VP Records	
Showcase	JA	1979	Studio One	
Showdown Vol. 2 (& Frankie Paul)	JA	1983	Enterprise	JJ 160
Slice Of The Cake	US	1984	Heartbeat	
Smile	US	1989	L & M	
Sufferers Choice	US	1983	Heartbeat	HB21
Sugar & Spice	US	1986	RAS Records	
Sugar Minott And The Youth Promotion		1988	NEC	
Sweeter Than Sugar	JA		Sonic Sounds	
The Best Of Vol. 1	GB		Black Roots	LMLP 20283
The Boss Is Back	US	1989	RAS	
Time Longer Than Rope	GB	1985	Greensleeves	
Wicked Ago Feel It	US	1984	Wackie's	
With Lots Of Extra		1983	Hitbound	

Mutabaruka

Any Which Way...Freedom	GB	1988	Greensleeves	GREL 131
Dub Poets Dub	US	1983	Heartbeat	
Blakk Wi Blakk	US	1992	Shanachie/Koch	
*Check It	US	1983	Alligator	AL 8306
Check It	US	2008	Aligator	
Gathering Of The Spirits	US	1998	Shanachie	
Life Squared	US	2002	Heartbeat	
Live At Reggae Sunsplash		1982	Sunsplash	
Melanin Man	US	1994	Shanachie	
Muta In Dub	US	1998	Blackheart	
Mutabaruka	US	1990	Rounder	
Outcry	US	1984	Shanachie	43023
Sister Breeze	US	1982	Heartbeat	HB 12001
The Mystery Unfolds	US	1986	Shanachie	43037

Frankie Paul

Alesha	JA		Powerhouse	
At His Best	GB		Techniques	
At Studio One	JA	1992	Studio One	SOLP 1961
Best In Me	US	1991	Gold Disc	
Casanova	JA		Jammys	
Classic	JA		Tappa	
Close To You	JA	1990	Jammys	
Detrimental	US		Rohit	
Double Trouble (& Michael Palmer)	GB	1985	Greensleeves	
Every Nigger Is A Star	GB	1991	Greensleeves	
Frankie Paul & Friends	US		Super Power	
Frankie Paul The Greatest	GB	1992	Fashion	
Freedom Blues	US	1992	Moodies	
Give Me That Feeling	US		Moodies	
Give The Youth A Chance	JA	1992	High Times	
Heartical Don	JA	1990	Jammys	
Jammin'	US	1991	VP	
Live & Love	US		Jammys	
Love Affair	GB		Techniques	
Love Line	GB		Glory Gold	
Money Talk	GB	1991	Jammys	
Over The Wall	US	1985	Crystal	
Pass The Tu Sheng Peng	GB	1984	Greensleeves	GREL 75
Reaching Out	GB	1988	Blue Mountain	
Rich & Poor	GB		Classic	
Ripe Mango	JA		Thunderbolt	
Rub-A-Dub Market	GB	1987	Mango	
Sarah	GB	1987	Live & Love	LALP 17
Slow Down	JA	1988	Redman Int./ Tuff Gong	
Start Of Romance	JA	1991	Black Scorpio	

Title	Country	Year	Label	Catalogue
Still Alive	JA		Jammys	
Strictly Reggae Music	JA		Top Rank	LP 005
The Champions Clash (& Leroy Sibbles)	GB	1985	Kingdom	KVL 9024
*Tidal Wave	JA	1985	Powerhouse	
Timeless	US	1992	Tan-Yah	
Tomorrow	JA	1991	Jammys	
True	US	1987	Black Scorpio	
Turbo Change (& Pinchers)	GB	1988	Super Supreme	
Warning	GB	1987	Ras Records	

Steel Pulse

Title	Country	Year	Label	Catalogue
African Holocaust		2004		
Babylon the Bandit	GB	1985	Elektra	EKT 30
Caught You (Reggae Fever)	D	1980	Island	202 200
Earth Crisis	JA	1984	Elektra	603 15-1
Handsworth Revolution	US	1978	Mango	MLPS 9502
Living Legacy		1998		
Living Legend		2002		
Rastafari Centennial	US	1992	MCA	
Rage And Fury		1997		
Tribute to The Martyrs	GB	1979	Island	ILPS 9568
*True Democracy	JA	1982	Dynamic Sounds	E1-60113
Steel Pulse	D	1985	Island	207 133
State Of Emergency	GB	1988	MCA	255 620-1
Victims	US	1991	MCA	101 72

Junior Reid

Title	Country	Year	Label	Catalogue
Boom Shack-A-Lack (CD)	GB	1985	Greensleeves	GRELCD 78
Firehouse Clash (& Don Carlos)	GB	1986	Live & Learn	
Listen To The Voices	JA	1994	JR Productions	
One Blood	JA	1989	JR Productions	
Progress	GB	1991	Big Life	BLR LP 6
Progress (different tracks)	JA	1992	JR Productions	
Two Of A Kind (& Teezy)	GB		Tamoki Wambesi	
Visa	JA		JR Productions	JRP 001

Tapper Zukie

Title	Country	Year	Label	Catalogue
Black Man	JA	1978	Tappa	
Earth Running		1979		
Deep Roots				
Dub Master (Escape From Hell)	JA	1977	Stars / Tappa	TZ 007
In Dub	GB		Front Line	FL 1029
International	JA		Tappa	
Living in The Ghetto	JA	1976-78	Stars/Tappa	WF 543
Man Ah Warrior	JA	1973	Mer	MER 101
*MPLA	GB	1976	Front Line	FL 1006
Peace In The Ghetto	GB	1978	Front Line	FL 1009
Raggy Joe Boy	JA	1982	Stars	

Tapper Zukie (cont'd)

Tapper Roots		1978		
Tapper Zukie	GB		Front Line	FL 1032
Tapper Zukie In Dub		1976		
Tapper Zukie International		1978		
The Man From Bosrah	JA	1978	Stars	

UB 40

Baggariddim	GB	1985	Virgin	
Cover Up		2001		
Dub Sessions				
(at concerts and for downloads)		2007		
Geffery Morgan		1984		
Guns In The Ghetto		1997		
Homegrown		20		
*Labour Of Love	D	1983	DEP International	205 716
Labour Of Love II		1989		
Labour Of Love III				
Labour Of Love IV		2009		
Live At Montreux		2002		
Love Songs		20029		
Move UB40 Music		1983		
Present Arms	NL	1981	Epic	85126 DEP
Present Arms In Dub	NL	1981	Epic	85390 DEP
Present The Fathers Of Reggae		2002		
Promises And Lies		1993		
Rat In The Kitchen		1986		
Signing Off (incl. Maxi)	GB	1980	Graduate/Ariston	
The Best Of UB40 Vol 1		1987		
The Best Of UB40 Vol2		1995		
The Best Of Vol1 & 2		2005		
The Singles Album	GB	1982	Graduate	GRADLSP 3
The UB40 File		1985		
Twentyfourseven		2008		
UB40 CCCP-Live in Moskow				
UB 40		1988		
UB40 Live		1983		
UB40 Present The Dancehall Album		1998		
UB44 / UB40	D	1982	DEP International	205 039
Who You Fighting For		2005		

U-Roy O.D.

Dread In A Babylon	GB	1975	Virgin	V 2048
Dreadlocks In Jamaica		1977		
Crucial Cuts	GB	1983	Virgin	VX 1013
Jah Son Of Africa	D	1978	Virgin	800 259
Line Up And Come		1987		
Love Gamble	US		State Line/TR	TR 506

Music Addict	GB	1987	RAS	RAS 3024
Natty Rebel	D	1976	Virgin	800 320
Original DJ	US	1976	Caroline	CAR 7506
Originator	US	1990	Justice	
Rasta Ambassador	D	1977	Virgin	800 338
Rock With I	US	1992	RAS Records	RAS 3219
Serious Matter		2000		
Smile A While	GB	1993	Ariwa	ARI 85
Small Axe	GB	1977	Virgin	VS 18712
Super Boss	F	1992	Esoldun	
True Born African	GB	1991	Ariwa	ARI 71
The Best Of (African Roots)	GB		Live & Love	LALP 008
The Lost Album-Right Time Rockers		1999		SS001
The Originator (& NU - Roy)	GB		Carib Gems	CGLP 107
*U - Roy (With Words Of Wisdom)	GB	1974	Attack	ATLP 1006
With A Flick Of My Musical Wrist	GB	1988	Trojan	TRLS 268
With Words Of Wisdom	US	1979	Front Line	FLX 4004
Version Galore	JA	1973	Treasure Isle Rec.	
Version Of Wisdom (reissue)	US	1990	Caroline	CAR 1679
Version Galore & Words Of Wisdom	JA	1972	Treasure Isle Rec.	TI 345
Your Ace From Space	GB	1995	Trojan	TR 359

Yellow Man

Bad Boy Shanking (& Fathead)	GB	1982	Greensleeves	
Blueberry Hill	GB	1987	Greensleeves	
Don't Burn It Down	GB	1987	Greensleeves	
Duppy Or Gunman	JA		Jah Guidance	VPRLP 1009
Galong Galong Galong	GB	1985	Greensleeves	
Girls Them Pet	JA		Taxi	
Going To The Chapel	GB	1986	Greensleeves	
In Bed With Yellowman (Mellow Yellow)	GB	1993	Greensleeves	
Just Cool				
King Of The Dancehall	US		Rohit	
Live At Aces (& Fathead)				
Live In London	JA		Thunderbolt	
Live Stage Show At R.W.E.C. (Sassafrass/Peter Metro)	JA	1983	Roots Rockers	
Meets Charlie Chaplin	JA		Powerhouse	
Mr. Yellowman	GB	1982	Greensleeves	GREL 35
Negril Chill (& Charlie Chaplin)	F		Danceteria	
Nobody Move Nobody Get Hurt	GB	1984	Greensleeves	
One In A Million	US	1989	Shanachie	
One Yellowman (& Fathead)	GB		Hit Bound	JJ-067
Operation Eradication (10)	GB		Pama	PMLP 3215
Party	US	1991	Ras Records	
Reggae Calypso Encounter (& General Trees)	US	1988	Rohit	
Reggae On The Move	F	1992	Declic	

Yellow Man (cont'd)

Title	Country	Year	Label	Catalog
Showdown Vol. 5 (Purpleman)	US	1984	Empire	
Sings The Blues	US		Rohit	
Them A Mad Over Me	US		J & L	LPJJ-060
Total Recall Vol. 3	US	1992	VP	
Two Giants Clash(Josey Wales)	GB	1984	Greensleeves	
Under My Fat Thing	JA		Arrival	
Walking Jewel Store	JA	1985	Powerhouse	
Yellow Like Cheese	GB	1987	Ras Records	
Yellowman Rides Again	GB	1988	Ras Records	
ZungguZungguguZungguzeng	GB	1983	Greensleeves	

Ziggy Marley and The Melody Makers

Title	Country	Year	Label	Catalog
Conscious Party	US	1988	Rita Marley Music	ST 17234
Dragonfly		2003	Private Music	
Falle Is Babylon	GB	1997	Electra	
Family Time	JA	2009	Tuff Gong	
Free Like We Want 2 B	JA	1995	Ghetto Youth	
Hey World	US	1986	Rita Marley Music	ST 1017
Jahmeyka	JA	1991	Ghetto Youth	
Joy And Blues	JA	1993	Ghetto Youth	
Joy And Blues	GB	1993	Virgin	CVDUK 65
Love Is My religion	JA	2006	Disleased	
One Bright Day	D	1989	Virgin	210054
Play The Game Right	JA	1985	Ghetto Youth	ABL 110070
Reggae Is Now	GB	1998	EMI	
Spirit Of Music	GB	1999	Electra	
Time Has Come (Best Of)	GB	1988	EMI-Fame	
What A Plot (Maxi)	US	1985	Shanachie	5006
Ziggy Marley & The Melody Makers Live Vol.1	GB	2000	Electra	

THE SOCA

Compilations

Title	Country	Year	Label	Catalog
Carnival Fever	JA		Studio One	SOL 3192
Party Time In Jamaica	JA		Studio One	SOL 9009
This Is Soca Music	GB	1984	Oval Records	OVLP 512
This Is Soca (Double LP)	GB	1987	London	43

Arrow

Title	Country	Year	Label	Catalog
Arrow Strikes Again		1973		
Beat De Drum		200		
Deadly	JA	1985	Arrow Music	025
Double Trouble	JA	1982		
Classics Plus	JA	1994	Arrow Music	042

Heat	JA	1982	Dynamic	DY 3434
Heavy Energy	F	1987	Blue Moon	BM 113
Hot Hot Hot	JA	1982	Dynamic	DY 3424
Instant Knock Out	JA	1980	Romey's	CR 017
Keep On Jamming		1975		
Knock Dem Dead		1987		
Massive	GB	1988	Arrow Music	031
Model De Bam Bam	JA	1992	Arrow Music	039
No Rules		202		
O'La Soca	GB	1989	Mango	210043
On Target	JA	1974		
Outrageous	JA	1993	Arrow Music	040
Phat		1995		
Ride De Riddem		1996		
Soca Dance Party	JA	1990	Arrow Music	032
Soca Savage	JA	1984	Dynamic	DY 3447
The Mighty Arrow On Target		1971		
Turbulence		1988		
Zombie Remixes		1991		
Zombie Soca	JA	1991	Arrow Music	035

Fabulous Five Inc (see also From Rocksteady To Reggae)

A Jamaican Christmas Gift	JA	2002	Stage	
All Night Party	JA	1989	Stage	012
Best Of Fab 5		1991	KK	
Back To Back 1 (Yu Save & All Night Party)		2002		
Don't Wear None	JA	1993	Stage	016
Dugu Dugu	JA	2000	Stage	
Fab 5 Inc		1971	New Dimensions	
Fab 5 Greatest Hits	JA	2002	Stage	
Fab 5 Ska Time	JA	2002	Stage	
Fab 5 Live – The Stage Ultimate Jamaican Vintage Party Mix, Part 1		1988	Stage	
Fab 5 Live – The Stage Ultimate Jamaican Vintage Party Mix, Part 2		2002	Stage	
Fab 5 Live – The Stage Ultimate Jamaican Vintage Party Mix, Part 3		2004	Stage	
Fab 5 Live – The Stage Ultimate Jamaican Vintage Party Mix, Part 4		2007	Stage	
FFI		1976	Tit For Tat	
Good Buddy	JA	1995	Stage	
Jamaica Soca	JA	2002	Stage	
Jamaican Woman	JA	1987	Stage	007
Miles And Miles Of Music	JA	1985	Stage	
*Mini	JA	1990	Stage	013
My Jamaican Girl	JA	1973	Harry J	
Shape	JA	1999	Stage	
Yu Safe	JA	1986	Stage	

Byron Lee and The Dragonaires (see also From Rocksteady To Reggae)

Byron 1982	JA	1982	Dynamic	DY 3421
Carnival In Trinidad		1974		
Carnival 75		1975		
Carnival 81		1981		
Carnival City 83		1983		
*Carnival Fever	JA	1991	Dynamic	DY 3467
Carnival Experience	JA	1979	Dynamic	DY 3391
Dancehall Soca	JA	1993	Dynamic	DY 3487
De Music Hot Mama	JA	1988	Dynamic	DY 3459
Heat In De Place	JA	1984	Dynamic	DY 3442
Jamaica Carnival '90	JA	1990	Dynamic	DY 3462
More Carnival	GB	1978	Dynamic	DYLP 3012
Socarobicas	JA	1997	Dynamic	
Soca Bacchanal	JA	1989	Dynamic	DY 3461
Soca Butterfly	JA	1994	Dynamic	DY 3490
Soca Carnival (incl. Disco 45)	JA	1980	Dynamic	DY 3401
Soca Engine	JA	1996	Dynamic	DY 3493
Soca Inna Jamdown Stylee	JA	1999	Dynamic	
Soca Frenzy	JA	1998	Dynamic	
Soca Girl	JA	1986	Dynamic	DY 3450
Soca Greatest Hits	JA	1997	Dynamic	
Soca Tattie	JA	1995	Dynamic	DY 3491
Soca Thunder	JA	1987	Dynamic	DY 3457
Soca Thriller	JA	2000	Dynamic	
Soca Tremor	JA	1999	Dynamic	
This Is Carnival	GB	1976	Dynamic	DYLP 3006
Trinidad Tobago Carnival City		1997		
Wine Down	JA	1992	Dynamic	DY 3479
Wine Miss Tiny	JA	1985	Dynamic	DY 3449

THE NINETIES

Compilations

Bam Bam (Beres Hammond, Tony Rebel, Gregory Isaacs)	JA	1992	Star Trail	STLP 006

Anthony B

Black Star	GB	2005	Greensleeves
Confused Times		2005	Penitenary
Judgment Time		2003	2B1 Records
Gather And Come		2006	Penitenary
Higher Meditation	GB	2007	Greensleeves
Justice Fight		2004	Nocturne
Life Over Dead		2008	Trendsetter

Live On The Battlefield		2002	Jahmin Records	
More Love		2001	AO Records	
My Hope		2005	Altafaan	
Powers Of Creation		2004	Nocturne	
Predator And Prey		1996	Alpha Enterprise	
Reggae Max		2002	Jet Star	
Rise Up		2009		
So Many Things	JA	1996	Star Trail	VP 1482
Seven Seals	US	1999	VP Records	
Smoke Free		2003	Bogalusa Records	
Street Knowledge	US	2003	VP Records	
Suffering Man	JA	2006	Tad's Records	
That's Live	US	2001	VP Records	
True Rastaman		2008	Penitenary	
Universal Struggle	US	1997	VP Records	
Untouchable		2004	Togetherness records	
Voice Of Jamaica Vol 2		2003	Nocturne	
Wise Man Chant		2004	Black Scorpio	

Beenie Man

All The Best	JA	1995	Inspired Corporation
Art and Life	US	2000	Virgin Records
Back To Basics	US	2004	Virgin Records
Beenie Man Meets Mad Cobra	US	1995	VP/Universal
Beenie Man Vol. 2 Reggae Max	US	1999	Jet Star
Best Of Beenie Man:			
Collectors Edition (2-CDs)	US	2000	VP/Universal
Black Liberty		2001	
Blessed	JA	1995	Island Records
Concept Of Life	JA	2006	
Cool Cool Rider	JA	1991	Penthouse
Dancehall Queen (with Chevelle Franklyn)	US	1997	Polygram Records
Defend It	US	1994	VP/Universal
Dis Unu Fe Hear	US	1994	Hightone Records
Doctor	US	1999	VP/Universal
Dude Pt. 2 (CD Single)	US	2004	Virgin Records
Dude (CD Single)	US	1994	Virgin Records
Feel It Boy	GB	2003	EMI
From Kingston To King:			
Greatest Hits So Far, CD/DVD	US	2005	Virgin Records
Girls (CD Single)	GB	2006	
Girls Dem Sugar	GB	2001	EMI
Gold	US	2000	Jet Star
Greatest Hits So Far		2005	
Haters and Fools/Analyze This (CD Single)	US	1999	Virgin Records
Heavyweight Dancehall Clash		2002	
Hundred Dollar Bag	US	2005	Movie Play Gold
Jet Star Reggae Max		1997	Musicrama

Beenie Man (cont'd)

King Of The Dancehall	JA	2004		
Live In San Francisco		2004		
Love Me Now (CD Single)	GB	2000	EMI	
Many Moods Of Moses	US	1994	VP/Universal	
Miss Angela	US	2006	Movie Play Gold	
Monsters Of Dancehall		2007		
Ruff 'N' Tuff		1999	Varese Sarabande	
Street Life (CD Single)	GB	2003	EMI	
Tell Me (with Angie Martinez)	US	1998	VP/Universal	
Ten Year Wonder	JA	1984	Bunny Lee	
The Best Of Two Bad DJs (with Spragga Benz)	US	1997	VP/Universal	
The Invincible Beenie Man The Doctor		1999		
The Legend Returns		2009		
The Maestro	JA	1996	Island Records	
The Magnificent Beenie Man	US	2004	Cleopatra	
Tropical Storm	US	2002	Virgin Records	
Undisputed	US	2006	Virgin Records	
Who Am I (CD Single)	US	1998	VP/Universal	
Y2K	JA	1999	Artists Only Records	
Youth Quake	JA	2001	Artists Only Records	

Bounty Killer

5th Element	US	1999	VP Records	
Down In The Ghetto	GB	1994	Greensleeves	
Face To Face	US	1994	VP Records	
Ghetto Dictionary-The Art Of War	US	2002	VP Records	VP 1641
Ghetto Dictionary-The Mystery	US	2002	VP Records	VP 1641
Ghetto Gramma	GB	1997	Greensleeves	
Guns Out	GB	1994	Greensleeves	
Jamaica's Most Wanted	GB	1994	Greensleeves	
My Xperience	US	1996	VP/TVT Records	
Nah No Mercy-The Warlord Scrolls	US	2006	VP Records	
Next Millennium	US	1998	VP/TVT Records	
No Argument	GB	1995	Greensleeves	
Roots, Reality & Culture	GB	1994	Greensleeves	

Buju Banton

20th Century Masters	CDN	2006	Universal	
Banton Affair (& Friends)	GB	1993	Sriker Lee	
Best Of Buju Banton		2002	Hip-O Records	
Buju and Friends	US	2004	VP Records	
Dubbing With Buju Banton		2000		
Early Years (90-95)	US	2001	VP Records	
Friends For Life	US	2003	VP Records	
Friends For Life	JAP	2003	JVC Victor	

Guns Out	GB	1997	Greensleeves	
Inna Heights	US	1997	VP Records	
It's All Over	JAP		Phono	
Love Me Browning	JA	1992		
Mr. Mention	GB	1992	Penthouse	
Rasta Got Soul		2009		
Rude Boys Inna Ghetto	JA	2000	Jamaican Vibes	
Rude Boys Inna Ghetto	NL	2000	Jamai	
Stamina Daddy	GB	1992	Techniques	
Til Siloh	US	1996	Umvd/Mercury	
Too Bad	US	2006	Gargamel Music	
Toppa Di Top	US	2006	Big Cat Records	
Ultimate Collection		2001	Hip-O Records	
Unchained Spirit	US	2000	Anti	
Voice Of Jamaica	US	1993	Mercury	
Want It	US	2002	NYC Music	

Ninja Man

Anything Dead Test, Reggae Anthology 2 CD	US	2001	VP/Universal	
Artical Don		1994		
Bounty Hunter	US	1991	VP/Universal	
Booyakka Booyakka		1994		
De Man Good (Picture Disc)	US	1991	Act III	
Hardcore Killing		1993		
Hollow Point Bad Boy		1994		
Jungle Move (Remarc Remix)		1995		
Kill Then And Done	US	1990	Wackie's	
My Weapon	US	1990	Mr. Dodd Music	
Ninjaman vs. Johnny P (with Johnny P)	GB		Pick Out	
Ninjaman Megamix		2000		
Original Front Teeth Gold Teeth Pon Teeth Don Gorgon!		1993		
Out Pon Ball	JA	1990	Exterminator	
Run Come Test		1993		
Sunsplash	JA	1990	Pickout	
Target Practice	US	1991	VP	VP 1187
Ting A Ling A School	GB	1992	Greensleeves	
*The Return	JA	1992	Junio & Volcano	
When It Done/Mad Again		2004		

Shabba Ranks

A Me Shabba		1995		
Raw As Ever	US	1991	Sony/Epic	
Best Baby Father	JA	1989	Digital – B/ Dynamic Sounds	
Caan Dun	US	1995	VP Records	
Get Up Stand Up		1998		

Shabba Ranks (cont'd)

Golden Touch	GB	1990	Greensleeves	
Greatest Hits	US	2001	Epic	
Just Reality	US	1990	Digital - B	
Love Punany Bad	F	1993	Jammys	
Loverman	US	1999	Sony Music	
Mr. Maximum	GB	1992	Greensleeves	
Rappin' With The Ladies	GB	1990	Greensleeves	
Rough & Ready Vol. 1	US	1992	Epic / Sony	E 52 443
Rough & Ready Vol. 2	US	1993	Epic / Sony	
Shabba & Friends (Comp)	US	1999	Epic	
Star Of The 90's	GB		Jammys	
X - Tra Naked	JA	1992	Shang	

Tony Rebel

20 Man Dead (with Cutty Ranks)		1991	Charm	
Connection		2004	Next Music	
Die Hard	JA	1991	Penthouse Records	
I Rebel	JA	2007	Flames	
If Jah	US	1997	VP/Universal	
Jah Is By My Side	US	1997	VP Records	
Realms Of Rebel	US	2001	RAS Records	
Real Rough (& Capleton & Ninjaman)	US	1991	V P	
Rebellious'	US	1992	RAS Records	
Rebel With A Cause	JA	1992	Penthouse Records	
Rebellion	US	1992	RAS Records	
Tony Rebel Meets Garnet Silk In A Dancehall Conference	US	1994	Heartbeat HB 152	
Tony Rebel Vol. 1		1999	Germaine	
Tony Rebel Vol. 2		1999	Germaine	
Vibes Of A Time	US	1993	Sony	

Garnet Silk

100 % Silk	US	1993	VP Records	VPRL 1326
Buju Banton Meets Garnet Silk And Tony Rebel In A Dancehall Conference		1993	Rhino	
Collectors Series	US	1999	Heartbeat	
Gold	GB	1993	Charm	CRLP 20
*It's Growing	JA	1992	Digital-B	
Journey	US	1996	VP Records	
Kilimanjaro Remembers		1999	Jamdown	
Legends Of Reggae Vol. 5		2001	Artists Only	
Live At Reggae Sunsplash 1994		1999	Tabou	
Lord Watch Over Our Shoulders	GB	1994	Greensleeves	
Love Is The Answer	JA/GB	1993	Steely & Clevie	SCLP 3
Meets The Conquering Lion		2000	Earthman	
Nothing Can Divide Us	US	1995	VP Records	VPRL 1401
Reggae Anthology: Music Is The Rod		1994	VP Records	

Reggae Max Part 1		1996	Jet Star
Rule Dem	GB	2006	Trojan
Silky Mood	US	1993	VP Records
The Very Best Of Garnet Silk-Gold		2002	Jet Star
The Definitive Collection	US	2000	Atlantic
The Definitive Collection (2 CD)	US	2001	Atlantic
This Sound Leads The Way (& The Dis)		2001	Rhino

OUTSTANDING ARTISTES IN THE NEW MILLENNIUM

Baby Cham

2 Bad Riddims '99	US	1999	Platinum
Ghetto Story	US	2006	Atlantic/Wea
Wow… The Story	US	2000	Artist Only Records
Vitamin S	US	2004	Atlantic/Wea

Shaggy

Angel	US	2001	MCA
Boombastic Hits	US	2004	Virgin
Boombastic	US	1995	Virgin
Boombastic/In The Summertime	US	1995	Virgin
Church Heathen	US	2007	
Clothes Drop	US	2005	Geffen Records
Dance & Shout	US	2000	
Essential Shaggy	US	2003	
F.T.F.O.	US	2006	Explicit Lyrics
Friends United: The 90's	US	2003	
Fuck Off (EP)	US	2003	
Hey Sexy Lady (CD Single)	US	2001	MCA
Hey Sexy Lady 2 (CD Single)	US	2002	MCA
Hope (CD Single)	US	2003	
Hot Shot	US	2000	MCA
Hot Shot Ultramix	US	2002	MCA
I Got You Babe (Bainbridge/Shaggy)	US	2004	
It Wasn't Me (CD Single)	US	2001	MCA
Lucky Day	US	2002	MCA
Luv Me Luv Me	US	2002	
Me Julie (with Ali G)	US	2002	
Midnite Lover	US	1997	Virgin
Mr.Lover Lover: The Best of Shaggy	US	2002	Virgin
Nice & Lovely	US	1994	
Oh Carolina	US	1993	
Original Doberman	US	1994	
Original Shaggy in Dub	US		

Shaggy (cont'd)

Title	Country	Year	Label
Piece Of My Heart	US	1997	
Pure Pleasure	US	1993	
Ready Fi Di Ride/Sexy Gyal Whind	US	2001	
Something Different	US	1995	
Strength Of A Woman	US	2003	
The Best Of Shaggy Part One	US	2002	
The Essential Shaggy	US	2003	EMI
Ultimatum	US	2006	
Unauthorized Souvenir: The Story Of Shaggy	US	2001	
Why You Treat Me So Bad	US	1996	
Wild Tonite	US	2005	
Wild Tonite Pt. 2	US	2005	

Sean Paul

Title	Country	Year	Label
(When You Gonna) Give It Up To Me		2006	
Baby Boy	D	2003	Wea/Atlantic
Dutty Rock	US	2002	VP Records/Wea
Dutty Rock (Clean)	US	2002	VP Records/Wea
Ever Blazin	D	2005	
Ever Blazin & Rare Tracks	D	2006	Wea International
Ever Blazin Pt. 2	D	2005	Wea/Atlantic
Get Busy	D	2003	Wea International
Gimme The Light	D	2002	Wea/Atlantic
Hood Items		2006	
Hot Gal Today		2000	Big Daddy Distribution
I'm Still In Love With You	D	2004	Wea/Atlantic
Imperial Blaze	US	2009	Atlantic
I'm Still In Love With You Girl (CD Single)	D	2004	Wea/Atlantic
I'm Still in Love With You/ Top of the Game (CD Single)	D	2003	Wea/Atlantic
Like Glue	D	2003	
Maximum Sean Paul	US	2003	Chorme Dreams
Maximum Sean Paul: The Unauthorized Biography	US	2003	Chorme Dreams
Never Gonna Be The Same	D	2006	Wea International
Stage One	US	2000	VP/Universal
Temperature (CD Single)	D	2006	Wea/Atlantic
Temperature Pt. 2 (CD Single)	D	2006	Wea/Atlantic
The Trinity	US	2005	VP Records/Wea
Trinity New Edition	US	2006	VP Records/Wea
We Be Burnin'	D	2005	Wea International
We Be Burnin' Pt. 2	D	2005	Wea International

Damian Marley

Title	Country	Year	Label
All Night	JA	2006	Universal

Beautiful Pt. 1 (CD Single)	JA	2005	Umvd Labels	
Beautiful Pt. 2 (CD Single)	JA	2005	Umvd Labels	
Half Way Tree	JA	2001	Motown	
King And A Prince	JA	2006		
Me Name Jr. Gong (CD Single)	JA	1998	Lightyear	
Mr. Marley	JA	1996	Umvd Labels	
Searching (So Much Bubble)	JA	1996	Lightyear	
Still Searchin'	JA	2001	Lightyear	
Welcome To Jamrock	JA	2005	Lightyear	
Welcome To Jamrock Pt. 2	JA	2005	Lightyear	
Welcome To Jamrock/Lyrical. 44	JA	2005	Lightyear	
Where Is The Love	JA	2001		

CHRISTMAS REGGAE

Compilations

A Reggae Christmas	US	1984	Ras Records	
Blue Mountain Christmas Party	GB	1989	Blue Mountain	
Caribbean Christmas Cheer	JA		TSOJ	
Christmas In Jamaica	JA		Studio One	SOL 7946
*Christmas In The Tropics	JA	1973	Dynamic	DY 3341
Christmas Seasons	JA	1991	Sir Tommy's	
Christmas Stylee	JA		Studio One	
Christmas Time	JA		Studio One	
Dancehall Christmas	US	1988	Wackies	2746
Have A Rockin' Christmas	JA	1990	Rocky One	RGLP 009
Merry Christmas From Black Roots	JA		Black Roots	
Merry Xmas (Enterprise Family)	JA		World Enterprise	
Reggae Christmas	US	1988	Wackies'	2745
Reggae Christmas	US	1992	Pow Wow	
Reggae Christmas From Studio One	JA	1985	Tuff Gong	
Reggae Disco Mix Vol. 17 Christmas Song Book	JA	1979	Crystal	2016
Sir Coxsone's Family Album				
Selektra Christmas	JA	1989	Selektra	
Wackies Reggae Christmas	US		Wackies	LP 2200
Yard Style Christmas	JA	1981	MC Productions	

Carlene Davis

Christmas Reggae Rock	JA	1988	Nicole	

Dobby Dobson

Sweet Christmas	JA		Top Ranking	

Hortense Ellis & Trinity

African Christmas	JA		Top Ranking	

Byron Lee and The Dragonaires

Christmas Party Time	JA	1966	Dynamic/Soul Rec. BLP 012	

John Holt

The Reggae Christmas Hits Album	JA	1986	Sonic Sounds	

Lovindeer

Bright Christmas	JA	1987	TSOJ	

Jacob Miller

Ital Christmas (& Ray Man I)	JA		Top Ranking	TRS 3
Natty Christmas	JA		Top Ranking	Xmas 1

Sugar Minott & The Crew

Christmas Jamboree	GB	1989	Youth Promotion	

FILM AND REGGAE (SOUNDTRACKS)

* The Harder They Come	D	1972	Island	36381
* Club Paradise	JA	1986	Oneness	SL 40404
* Countryman	JA	1982	Fifty Six	ISTDA 1
* Rockers	US	1979	Mango	MLPS 9587

THE STEEL BANDS

*Classics To Calypso, Melodisc, MLP 12-195

MUSIC VIDEOS

Bob Marley Live At Santa Barbara County Bowl
Bob Marley And The Wailers
60 min   US   1981   Thorn EMI   TXE 9007074
including "Exodus", "Get Up Stand Up", "Ambush In The Night".

Bob Marley One Love Peace Concert (1978)
90 min   GB   1981   Hendring   HEN 2014 D
Bob Marley, Peter Tosh, Dennis Brown, Jacob Miller and more.

Bob Marley: Time Will Tell
90 min   GB   1991   Island/Polygram Video Int.
Up to the 10th Anniversary of the death of Bob Marley; the life history with interviews and live recordings from rehearsals and concerts.

Legend: The Best Of Bob Marley And The Wailers
40 min   GB   Island   BMVB 100
including "I Shot The Sheriff", "Buffalo Soldier", "No Woman No Cry", "One Love"
etc. from the LP of the same name.

Eddy Grant Live At Notting Hill Carnival
Eddy Grant
30 min   GB   1981   VCL Comm.   2752-40
including "Walking On Sunshine", "Living On The Front Line".

Reggae Sunsplash '90 Vintage Night
60 min   GB   1990   Charley Records Ltd   VID JAM 37
Chalice, Alton Ellis, Inner Circle, Hopeton Lewis, Pat Kelly, Leroy Sibbles. Eric
Donaldson and   more.

Reggae Sunsplash '90 Variety Night
60 min   GB   1990   Charley Records Ltd   VID JAM 34
Bunny Wailer, Lasana Bandele, Judy Mowatt, deejays U-Roy, Admiral Bailey,
Peter Metro, Shinehead, Aswad, Skatalites.

Splashin' The Palace '84
59 min   GB   1984   Hendring   HEN 4015 Z
From the concert at the Crystal Palace Football Stadium; Aswad, Black Uhuru,
Dennis Brown, Leroy Sibbles, Skatalites and more.

The Cool Ruler
Gregory Isaacs Live At The Academy
60 min   GB   1984   Palace Video   PVC 3012 M
including "Number One", "Go Deh", "Too Young", "Love Is Overdue", "Night
Nurse" and more.

The Best Of Reggae Sunsplash Vol. 1
80 min   US   1988   Synergy Production   PAL 002
Live from Reggae Sunsplash X, 1987, and XI, 1988; Wadada, Dennis Brown,
John Holt, Chalice, Bunny Wailer, Gregory Isaacs and more.

The Mighty Digger (Musical)/Runaway To Ocho Rios
50/10 min   JA   Harvey Film Prod.   NTSC 525
The musical tells in song and dance the old story of a village – dweller going into
the city to make his fortune, only to discover that all that glitters is not gold.
Village life goes on in his absence – work and play – and as in villages, the world
over – quarreling. The music was taken from the African musical "Ipi N Tambia"
and is arranged to reflect the Jamaican's Caribbean heritage and African roots.
Additionally, the film contains 10 minutes of documentation about Ocho Rios on
the Jamaican north coast titled "Run Away To Ocho Rios".

This Is Ska
38 min mono   GB   1989   Island   IVA 038
Jimmy Cliff, Prince Buster, The Maytals and more - with Byron Lee And The Dragonaires

Carnival Fever
Byron Lee and The Dragonaires
90 min   JA   1991   Dynamic/Lee Enterprise   DV 44291
Scenes from the annual "Carnival" in Kingston. The songs played by Byron Lee And The Dragonaires can be heard on the LP of the same name.

Wine Down
Byron Lee and The Dragonaires
90 min   JA   1992   Dynamic/Lee Enterprise   DV 44291
Scenes from the 1992 "Carnival" in Kingston.

SOURCES

USED SOURCES AND LITERATURE

APA Guide, Nelles Verlag München.

Bob Clarke, of IRIE FM, Ocho Rios, Jamaica - Interviews

Trevor "Boots" Harris, responsible journalist at the *X-News*, Kingston - Interview

Movies

The Daily Gleaner and *Sunday Gleaner* 1983 - 1997, Kingston, Jamaica

Brian Jahn and Tom Weber. *Reggae Island: Jamaican in the Digital Age. (*Kingston Publishers Limited: Kingston, Jamaica), 1992.

Own record collection - information from the record covers and booklets

Reggae Magazine (USA), Publisher/ Editor, Peggy Quattro

German Reggae Magazine, Publisher/Editor Jörg Wortmann

Star Trail Records, Jamaica

Udo Vieth, Michael Zimmermann. *Reggae Musiker-Rastas-und Jamaika.* (Fischer Taschenbuch Verlag GmbH, Frankfurt am Main), 1981.

For the update of this English version: the internet and watching the Jamaican TV station *TVJ*

SUGGESTED READING

Breitwieser, Thomas and Hermann Moter. *Made in Kingston, Jamaica*. 1981.

Henzell, Perry. *Reggae, Rastas, Rum*. 1987.

Michels, Peter M. *Rastafari*. Trikont. 1980.

Morris, Dennis. *Bob Marley: Rebel With A Cause*. A Photographic Recording of the Visions and The Message of the King of Reggae from *Natty Dread* to *Exodus*. 1986.

Moter, Hermann. *Reggae Discography*. Minotaurus Projekt (Pfungstadt). 1983.

Mutabaruka. *The First Poems/The Next Poems*. Paul Issa Publications. 2005.

Thelwell, Michael. *The Harder They Come*. The X Press. 1996.

White, Timothy. *Bob Marley, Reggae, Rastafari: A Short Fast Life*. 1984.

White, Timothy. *Catch A Fire: The Life of Bob Marley*. Holt Paperbacks. 1998.